The

Punctual Actual Weekly

An emotional memoir
of the Hawkeye Theatre
at 2019 Blake Street in Berkeley

by

Michael Lyons

HiT MoteL Press
www.hitmotel.com

Copyright 2007 by Michael Lyons
All rights reserved.
First Edition

Library of Congress Cataloging in Publication Data

Lyons, Michael
       The Punctual Actual Weekly
I. Title

ISBN: 0-9655842-8-3

Published by HiT MoteL Press

Designed by Michael Lyons

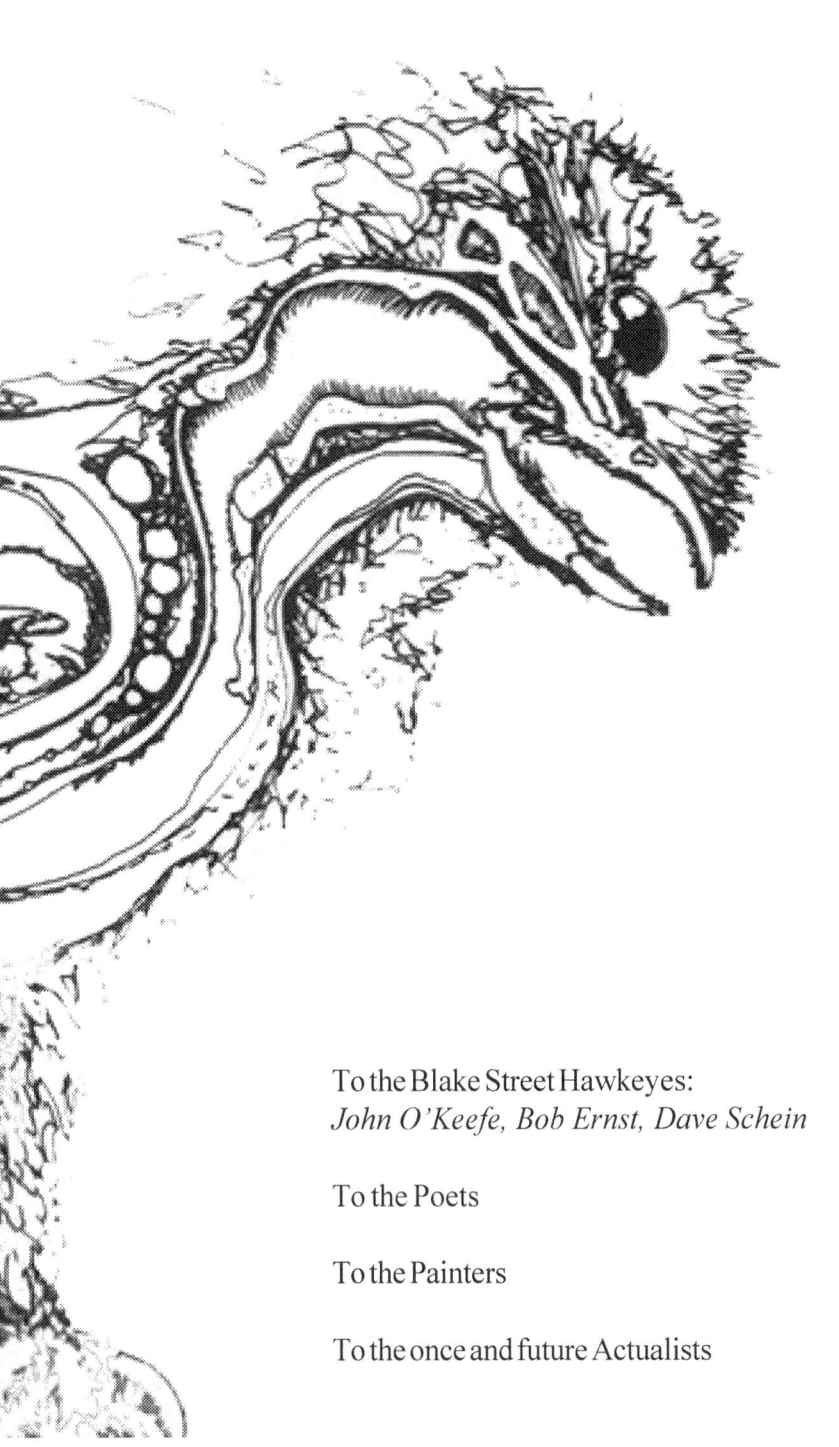

To the Blake Street Hawkeyes:
John O'Keefe, Bob Ernst, Dave Schein

To the Poets

To the Painters

To the once and future Actualists

> It is a dream clear as day
> feeling your way as you go—
> remote as a rose below a diminishing star
> we earn our keep by being what we are.
>
> —Darrell Gray
>
> from
> *The Sadness of First Principles*

Table of Contents

1. The Punctual Actual Weekly 1
2. The Warehouse as the Edge of the World 4
3. Apotheosis Extract 8
4. Ah, Berkeley 12
5. Shadowoman, Pythia of the Amphictyon 15
6. Figurative Abstraction 19
7. Bay Bridge Mandala 27
8. Princess Rain 32
9. A New Zine on the Scene 50
10. What is Actualism 58
11. Dog !? 70
12. Boley Shuman & Dwan Kumm 77
13. Krishna Glass & Phillipe Mignon at Dejeuner 93
14. Taxi Unlimited: The Trainee 101
15. General Semantics Rides Again 108
16. In the Theatre of the Body 112
17. *from* A Notebook of Darrell Gray 121
18. Some Art Business 155
19. Hogs Tale 162
20. The Divine Plant 167
21. A Many Worlds Interpenetration 175
22. Dropouts 180
23. Prismatic Fountains Flow Forth 191
24. Rug Man and The Terrible Thing 197
25. Moving in the Syntax of Poetry 207
26. The Subliminal Kid 217
27. The Journal of Pre-Verbal Behavior 229

Appendix

A1. The Bell Tower 232
A2. Episodic Imprint & the Liquidity of Consciousness . 263
A3. *from* The Transcendental Poetics of Actualism ... 301
A4. Further Attributions 339
A5. Epilogue 339

The Punctual Actual Weekly

Editor's Note:
Welcome to this Punctual Actual Weekly special edition. Fate let me do a residency at the Hawkeye theatre in Berkeley during a very exciting time when they were forging something I'll just call for now, the California Zen Aesthetic. Maybe just Flow would be a better term. The work done and the discoveries made in that experimental theatre became legendary throughout the theatre community. They pretty much invented solo theatre. All kinds of artists thrived in the vigor and the rigor and the generosity of the experimental atmosphere. I was privileged to publish some of the writing and art in the humblest of zines. Because of all the letters we've received asking about how we got started and for reprints of these ephemera, we want to dedicate this issue to that story of where we come from. It's pretty cool so here goes. Enjoy.

The Punctual Actual Weekly, was a mimeograph zine put out by a few friends centered around the exploits and artistic adventures of the actors, artist and writers working out of a warehouse/theatre in the Berkeley of 1975-76. These people were the Blake Street Hawkeyes—the founders John O'Keefe, Bob Ernst and David Schein—and George Coates, and the artists of the warehouse—Doug Wilson, Russ Conlin, and the other actors and actualists. A lot of inspiring artists and thinkers and writers came through that place over the years; some went on to become celebrities. But mainly this is about the poet Darrell Gray, the painter Peter Loschan and me; oh, I'm Michael Lyons aka Krishna Glass.

I called myself Krishna Glass as in the Glass family, created by J.D. Salinger. There was Seymour Glass who met an untimely end; there were Franny and Zooie; and others. It was mainly Seymour that I looked up to. Especially those letters that he wrote to the librarian. For me the letter was the finest example of literary behavior there was; it was intimate and informal and loose and funny and spontaneous, and like I say, it took chances with the writer revealing him / her self.

This is pretty much a true account of life around what we called "the Warehouse" at 2019 Blake Street in Berkeley. It was a magical time fomented around the theatre there, what Doug once called 'The Amphictyonic Theatre.' For me the Warehouse was sacred space, a place to slow down and in the company of others also insisting on living the life of the imagination, come to sense, for whole moments, the self. It was such a hotbed of creative influences that the zine was, for me at least, a place to experiment, to try on lots of different personae, and styles. The linguistical crystallization from the constant interaction with the creative agents of the warehouse into some kind of writing or art was a way to embody a dynamic and altering quest for vision and sense of the self manifesting. The aesthetic was of not being coerced by the consensus reality but to look behind phenomenology to the whole systems from which it was a projection. There was love there, too, or at least tolerance and camaraderie of the common struggle.

I think I was a bit confused about my identity back then. There were a number of entities, sub personalities, pseudonyms, autonomies, alter-egos, ulterior motives—these agential operatives might be heteronyms but really they are what you might call mimeological homeomorphisms — they were embodiments of great aesthetic and archetypal energies I saw in the people around the theatre. In addition to Krishna Glass there were: Iearto Webster, Zoon Phonata, Blind Blues Hawker Blake, Lorelei Lovelum, Ed Note, Ganja Ganef, Ray Beausolei and others. But I am getting ahead of myself. We'll go into their work and biographies in due time.

So one aspect of Punctual Actual Weekly (the zine was never punctual, and we might have achieved weekly once) is an essay on the aesthetic of the warehouse. I am just a humble student, trying to *see* through the forms of art given us by visual artists: action painting, expressionism, realism, dada, surrealism; in the theatre arts: physical theatre, Grotowski, poor theatre, the beginning of performance art; in poetry: the influences of incantation, surrealism, WCW, Frank O'Hara, Berrigan, sound poetry, minimalist poetry. It was an honor to be part of the Amphictyonic Theatre. After every one is gone, I'll still be there — an old monk at the temple, sweeping up.

The Pit at the Edge of the World

March 20, 1975. I got off the bus in front of the Durant Hotel in Berkeley. I hoisted my yellow back pack with its external frame and attached sleeping bag onto my shoulders and walked through the strident street scene of Telegraph Avenue until I found Blake St. Then I headed down toward the bay, strolling among the wood and wisteria bedecked old houses, looking for the address-- — 2019. It was a clear day in the spring of 1975. I was scheduled to read at an Actualist Convention being held at a theatre run by Bob Ernst and Dave Schein. I had met them in Montreal and hung out with them in Vermont. They were two traveling writer / actors who seemed to lead the coolest life possible. They looked like wild Tibetan monks with their colorful Quebec knits and mufflers and Vermont macks and vests made by loving hippie girl hands. Bob had a thin moustache and long hair and an earring. They were traveling mystics on cross-country tour doing their solo theatre pieces in odd off of off off off Broadway venues and converted warehouse spaces and universities.

In Berkeley I didn't know what to expect. I had come all the way across America for a poem. Bob Ernst exposed me to the poem in the forests of Vermont that last fall, as we sat cross legged like monks in the warm shifting air. He showed me how to do some poetry they called Sound Cadas. These were (mainly unvoiced) breathing measures of open vowel sounds, the eeeehhh and the ahhhh, sometimes articulated with various stops and fricatives attacking the open vowel streams. And it was such an experience to be breathing and chanting and making sound in that glorious Vermont autumn light. In the green forest fuse shot through with rivulets of bright orange, yellow, and rived with the reds of fall foliage, with the sound we were making glowing in my heart, I fell into a rapture brought on by the breathing. Something in the warm shifting air pressed and released its force on us.

I became entranced by the bright but hushed sound energy of the unvoiced vowels, became touched by the physicality of the mechanism of articulation, became high on the breath control and above all by the terrific melding of sound poetry with spiritual practice. I was filled with a rapture I had only experienced with drugs and thus had not been able to really experience at all. Doing the Sound Cadas I had became transported both away from and more deeply into this world. The level of poetry expressed showed a love and trust and sophistication for my generation that was beyond anything I had ever seen. My mind began to expand, and I got a sense of myself as belonging in the world and content to belong in the world; it was my right, I really belonged here.

How long we sat there lost in the masterpiece of choral chanting, I have no idea. I got it in my head: Oh . . . this is what rhapsody is. What the old poets knew going back to brave blind Homer. I thought, wow, this goes directly for the feelings. Whoever came up with this poetry has got to be one of the most creative and amazing writers of our time. I have got to some how go and study with this guy. When we finally got to our feet and headed back to the house, I knew I had to follow this California Zen aesthetic into the future. They told me it was written by one of the founders of their theatre, John O'Keefe.

While in Montreal, I videotaped Bob performing his solo theatre piece called *Trunk 15*. He did it for the CGEP, a kind of artistic college in Montreal. I was very moved by this solo theatre piece especially a moment where he realizes his father is really deceased, when he takes the man's pack of cigarettes off the dashboard of his truck. What a completely human and candid divulgence. I also got it that the play had a lot of visual still moments like you were looking at a painting; he did a lot of things with his face, that suggested familial trait absorption. I was able to use the zoom to good effect on this, I think. I had never seen anything like this kind of intimate theatre.

After Montreal, I got stranded in Texas for a while, nursing a broken heart, and wrote several letters to Bob and Dave. Dave liked one with an essay about *The Tesseract Theatre*. And then one day I received in the mail a program for the 4th Actualist Convention with my name on it! And a time slot for me to read. They had made the decision to invite me — this unknown from Texas — to read at the Actualist Convention. This was an offer I couldn't refuse.

It was like a dream. I still couldn't believe how I had hitched all the way to California to read at a poetry reading. It was to be my first, on the vernal equinox.

I found 2019 Blake Street address and stepped into what looked like a busy industrial warehouse. It was bustling with fabrication activity, table saws whining and mallets hammering metal topped tables, and workers coming and going. I asked somebody where the theatre was, and was directed to the back of the warehouse building, down the long wide hallway with the brick-colored floor. Sky lights in the roof let glorious shafts of bright sunshine burst onto blond-colored untreated wooden plank doors breaking up the white sheet-rock walls. With all the announcements for plays and yoga classes and martial arts classes and theatre classes festooned among the many theatre posters, the place seemed to be some kind of ad-hoc community center. At the back of the warehouse I found the theatre doors closed with a sign that said: Rehearsal in Progress, Do not Disturb. I paused for a moment. I could hear shouting and singing going on behind the closed double doors of the theatre.

I poked my head into the room across the hall; it was a large open artist's studio where Dave lived. I introduced myself to the artist who shared the studio with him, Russ Conlin. He had a great big joyous smile and a wild head of hair. He said he was a friend of Bob and Dave and this was his studio. There was something very boyish yet businesslike in his artful seriousness. One liked him immediately. He had a kindness and sweetness that was endearing right from the get-go. One of his main artistic influences was Sam Francis, though I wouldn't have known it at the time. Russ was definitely post-60s. He had the coolness of jazz improvisation in color and movement gesture in his bright chaotic canvas. It had the power of a Jackson Pollock but was more joyous. This made a strong emotional presentation yet was also understated and minimalist. It was not academic though it was a hydromorphic rendering for grounding the projections of *Dasein*; we could recognize it was from us, for us. From the moment I entered the Hawkeye warehouse, my life had changed forever.

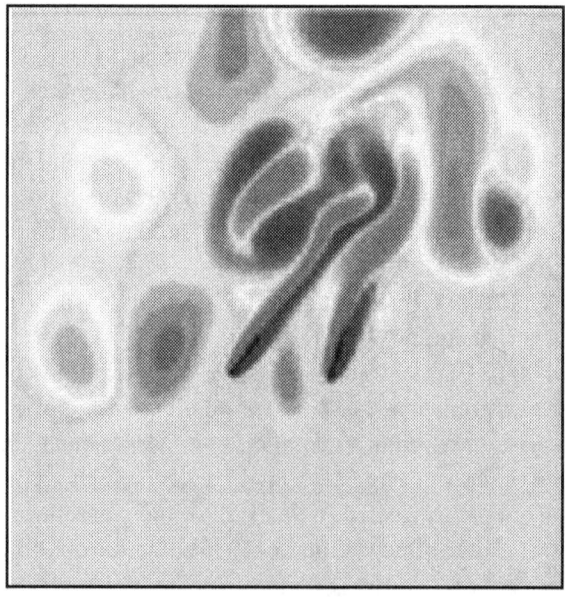

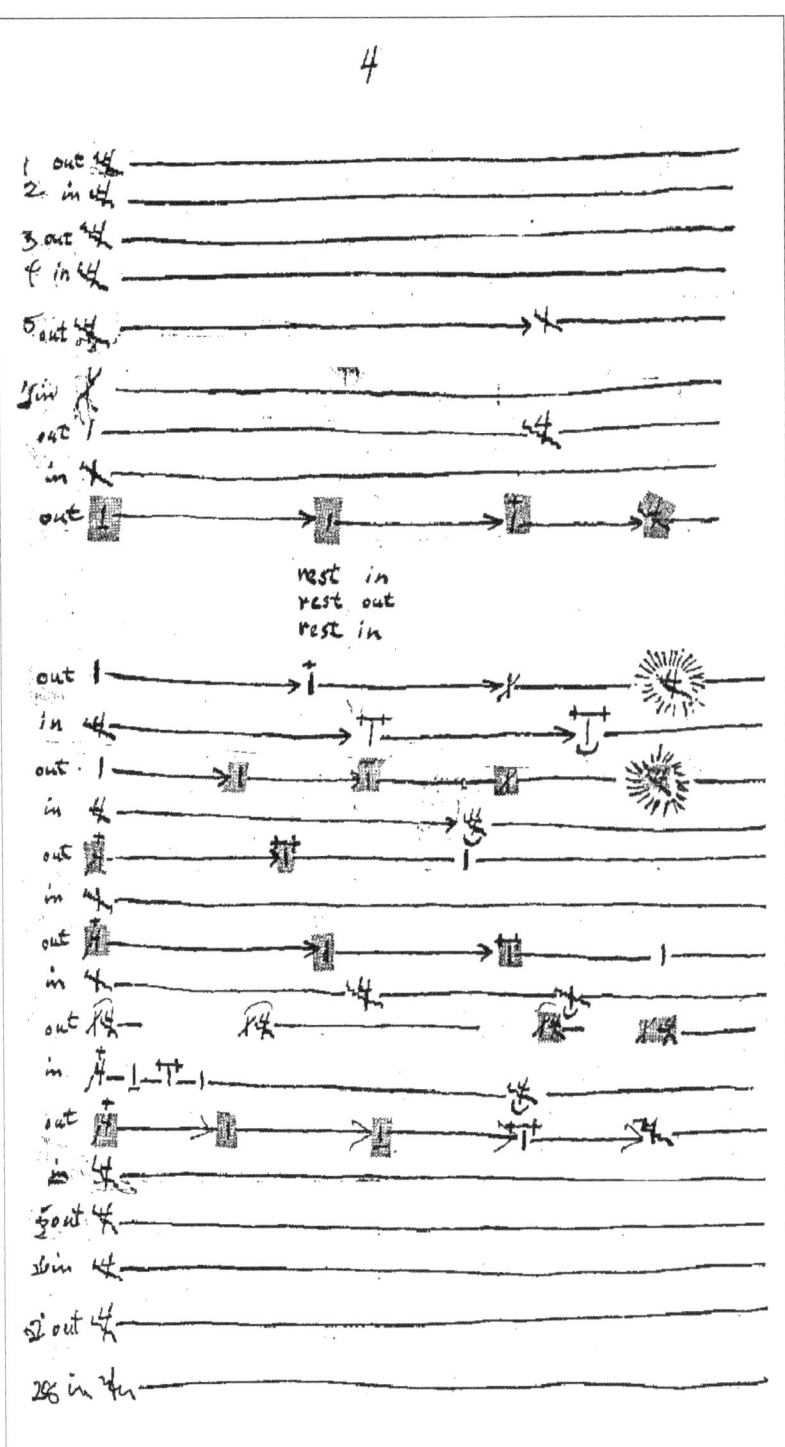

Cada of 4 by John O'Keefe (in the Number Sound Notation of Jonathan Albert)

Apotheosis Extract

Russ had a hot plate in his studio and made us some instant coffee. Dave ducked in and we got reacquainted. After a while everybody got busy working to get set up for the event. Many theatre acts and poets were coming to read in the three day convention. Doug Wilson, another artist had a sound proof room in the warehouse. He generously let me roll out my bag on the floor to get a little sleep.

Before, when I lived in Austin, Paul Spragens, one of the mavens of the Church of the Coincidental Metaphor group, had given me a couple of pens to bring out to the convention. He had them made. The were long ball-point pens with the legend *Apotheosis Extract* written in gold leaf along the shaft. It was my intention to honor the writer of the Cadas with one of these, and give one to some other stellar writer.

The Convention itself was wild. I had not actually read in public. I had done some radio plays with the Church of the Coincidental Metaphor back in Texas, and had done some reading with close friends, but not in front of an audience of strangers.

The convention was a wonderful serge of energy. Jim Nisbet, a very handsome, smiling, affable guy carried on an easy conversation between jumping up and down doing the sound recording. He had set up a reel-to- reel across the hall from the main theatre room in the artist studio of Russ Conlin, with lines going back into the microphones set up for great stereo separation. All kinds of poets came through. I was told in Texas to be on the lookout for one Andrea Codrescu, a Transsylvanian poet. Tom Clark read. And Anselm Hollo. And others from the Iowa school.

I got to read to a large audience. I could see them milling and not paying attention, so I started singing, "Doesn't it make you absolutely mad when people don't take you seriously. Don't you go absolutely Wild when people don't take you SERIOUS-LY." Holding the pitch high at the end. And that got everybody to shut up. And I launched into my story, titled *The Institute for the Advancement of Absurdist Thought*. It was a fictionalized brag on the crew I ran-with back in Austin. The audience was laughing, so I guess it was good.

When I was finished, Bob Ernst motioned for me to follow him, climbing up the ivory covered burglar bars at the back of the theatre over the ramparts onto the roof. It was like being on the roof of the Potala at Lasha in the heart of the world, looking at the sun setting over the distant Golden Gate. We smoked and had a pow-wow and he was very welcoming.

I got to meet O'Keefe when he put in a cameo appearance. He was a ruddy mick, wiry and quick, with piercing intelligent blue eyes, set in a crafty happy face beneath normal hair. He was slightly older and had that jubilant, devil-may-care hero of the playground ebullience about him. I gave him a pen. He graciously accepted my gift and accolades. Somehow the conversation got onto electronic music, and I had experience in that. Back at UT, an artful don had split our electronic music class into musicians and technicians; I had to go with the technicians and work on equipment all the time. O'Keefe astounded me by making the sound of a ring modulator with his mouth. And as if that wasn't enough, he made a chant. Of the name of the Egyptian god of creation, *O Sirius*, going through an envelope generator and filter of a Moog or an Arp Synthesizer. He soon gave me to realize that the founder of the theatre did not have a whole lot of patience for the great unwashed influx of self-promoting poets descending like mongol hoards on his scene. I was supposed to give the other pen to Andre Codrescu but he breezed through in his leather jacket with long white silk scarf trailing in his wake, two beautiful girls on his arm and then just as quick breezed out after he read.

I met a fabulous poet named Darrell Gray. A big affable moon-face fellow, he had an air of being above the chaos and of totally belonging. His eyes lit up with interest as the conversation drifted into Korzybski and General Semantics. When I was waxing enthusiastic about the Count's classification of entities, matter being energy binding, plants being space binding and animals being time binding, Darrell Gray said, "Time rents me."

I thought that was all right. The thing I liked the most about the convention was staying up late at night with Darrell and a few other poets — a young Tom Clark with short cropped hair and a world-weary attitude; a big, wild Rasputin-looking guy David Lerner; an older, white-bearded G. P. Skratz — after everyone had gone, and reading poetry while sitting cross-legged like monks on the floor in that theatre. Giving good attention. Being supportive. Letting people bring out their riskier stuff.

There was a Word List upon which people were writing their favorite words and quotes and I wrote one word: *abphiety*. Just contemplating this word that I had invented made me shudder with joy. It was a concept like absurdity: holding the mystery and terror that the Pythagoreans felt when they realized the fields in which they kept the whole number animals of their flocks had an irrational number on its diagonal and they had to face the maturing invention of making the first field extension. Also, it expressed the serious humor that Duchamp and Tzara brought into the world during WWI with their program of absurdity. For me abphiety was a spiritual mathematic based on the transcendental number phi; ϕ was the secret mystery at the heart of the universe, it was the perfect ratio, golden mean, the transcendental shift; it was the design of nature's phyllotaxy of all living forms. For me this sacred geometry that nature used to construct the world and keep all its parts in a kind of phase shifting dance of implicative synchronized harmonies was the enactment of the basic idea that parallel processes could convolve in a mutually beneficial exercise of self-fulfillment. It was synchronicity. It was how things could communicate on sub-fields, and tune in to capture phase shifting information. It was in the spiral face of flowers and trees, in the disposition of facial features, in the proportion of the hand, it was the design of beauty, it was the enactment of symmetry. I hoped to write a book about it someday. I was so jazzed to be in this creative milieu that I wrote some poetry on the door of the theatre. It was a refrain of "When you ride on the bus / you get a view of humanity." Mine went:

> "When I fly
>   in an airplane
> I get   the feeling
> of being
> well-educated."

As I was doing it, Jim Nisbet looked at me, shocked and said, "Are you coming off with a poem?" But for me it felt OK; it was the first time I could share these feelings in public with strangers: the rush of seeing connections making meaning forming images in the mind.

Darrell Gray read a poem called *The Catastrophic Unrush of Beauty* and it just blew me away. I was in awe of it. I gave him the other pen.

THE CATASTROPHIC UNRUSH OF BEAUTY

Ideas
we are that
spread out!
Flesh of the centrifuge that went berserk,
pool of numerals, centuries
dissolving' like chocolates
left out in the sun . . .

Don't tell me that truth
lies parallel to the laundry,
that by driving new cars
-the sex of a starfish is altered
or even improved.
Who cares whether the chicken
comes before or after the egg?

The catastrophic unrush of beauty
astounds us. Our poems grow horny
and literal, like monks
on speed.

Oh paranoia of judges, fireworks, and bars
Backbone of the record stuck in its groove!

Calculations.
Glances
Explosions fill the air like a difficult prose
Embryonic gods & goddesses, under so many stars!
Transfigurations flutter ~~~
rudimentary
as the conceptual flower of the soul.
Or like the first windowpane hit by the rising dawn.

DARRELL GRAY

blue wind press july 4972 iowa city iowa number

Broadside of poem by Darrell Gray

Ah, Berkeley

The warehouse was about a quarter acre and it sat on about another acre of parking lot, this all surrounded by a row of fine Victorian houses on Dwight Way across from the Herrick Hospital. And more industrial buildings on the other side of the lot, and doctors offices beyond that. And beyond that there were several automobile dealerships in the area, that's why they called it auto row. Most of the neighborhood belonged to the kindly old landlord, a Mr. Mafley who I guess had been married to the Herrick daughter. With his relaxed air of authority, his stately white mustache and sense of probity, he looked like the dapper man in tails and top hat from the Monopoly Game.

Wow. There are all these cafes in Berkeley, and people coming and going, and the bookstores! Moe's and Shambala and Shakespeares not to mention the biggest book store I had ever seen: Cody's

In Berkeley, there was a feeling of the cooperative in the air. The Viet Nam war had just ended, the world had not. The Hippie Aesthetic was still hanging on, there were Free Boxes on every street. Though it was long since the Summer of Love and there was definitely a sense of hard core filth and drug addicted helplessness waiting if you continued too far down that path —"Shoeless oblivion," Jim Nesbit called it— people here were still hoping to find their way without giving up their freedom.

There was a kind of freedom in the air. Down on Shattuck Ave. and Dwight a porn movie house showing Deep Throat. And there are all these cream of the crop co-eds. The best and the brightest come here.

There were definitely a lot of free-wheeling people on the streets, and a sense of sticking up for each other against 'the Man." The scene with knights-of-the-road roving scholar poets mixed with college students was right out of the Graduate. UC Berkeley honored my UT stack pass and gave me the run of all the libraries. I felt at home in the musty stacks, tracking down associations. At the Warehouse I wrote the first poems that don't embarrass me now. One went:

It was on a stroll down Shattuck Ave. in Berkeley,
that I encountered a very large spade dude
addressing the passersby from under the shade of a tree,
 — it was one of those tiny "parks" with benches
they have in the wide sidewalk of the boulevard. He said:
"They are causing the computer to switch
off black and white against each other."
 —He is a street preacher in cut-offs and a sweat shirt;
he stretches out an arm in an expansive gesture, a sower
casting pearls before swine, doing the Lord's work,
bearing witness: "They have put narcotics in everything.
You can get high on every blade of grass here in Berkeley."
 —People were passing by, going around him
like he was a rock in the flow of the river.
The preacher looks at his moving flock, following
a woman with his intense gaze. "Any woman you meet,
they are either a radical feminist lesbian or
they want a dark-skinned man."
He looked at me straight and said: "Now is that
natural to you? It's because
these dark skinned men
have white brains! They done had
the brain-transplant done on 'em."
He paused for a moment
then pounded his hand
  with his fist. "The lesbian
is against nature. Cause it says so in the bible.
And the bible   is the word of god!
Woman is put here to be 'an help to man'."

The scene on and around the Berkeley campus was a technicolor parade like something out of Fellini movie. At Sproul Hall, lined with these strange knobby baobab tree, you had all kinds of street preachers, Swami X, and others practicing oratory. I jammed with the conga drum players and felt the tribal unity. On the streets you had seedy looking Bohemian intellectuals. I had studied out of the Berkeley Physics series. It was really gorgeous. I shall never forget the pages of space time diagrams as they derived special relativity from the generation of a magnetic field due to motion of an electron. Some of that imagery found its way into this poem invoking the spirit of Bishop Berkeley the arch-Idealist.

Wild flung out kind of diagram, sheets of space time,
like the Nude Descending the Staircase.
Duchamp was the champ. Except for *the* Champ,
the once and future all time champ Muhammad Ali.
Very colorful place.
Bishop Berkeley might take his stiff church collar off,
might even remove his frock on a warm autumn day. Looking a bit
like the healthy thee and thou talking freeman, stepped right off the
cylindrical box of Quaker oats.
Stroll around the Drag with his leggings and
his Presbyterian waistcoat and ascot and wooden clogs.
Would the Bishop eat the fabulous burritos at Mario's,
or go across the street to the cavernous restaurant
with the famous People's Park mural on it,
and get a real bargain.
He might even be up at the Quarter meal in the basement of the old
Presbyterian church doing works of charity.
I might see him smoking a pipe reading a book in the sun under the
awning at the Bongo Burger.
Their home fried potatoes are, indeed, divine.
He used to tell us, that since the secondary aspects of the objects,
"color, for example" are in the mind (did he know about rods and
cones?) We might as well expect the primary attributes, "like
extension of the object in space," for example, are also "ideas".
We have come to be suspicious of ideas in our time, the ego too.
But we'll get into that.
He loved Descartes and often talked about him as though they were
passionate proponents in philosophical debate via belles lettres.
Making "sense" of it all.
He looked into the faces of the people on the street.
He went into the Hydra Head Shop,
but they didn't have much of a clue.
Idealism was afoot.
The fundamental question of metaphysics is
does the human brain produce consciousness
or does it "merely" serve as a vehicle for consciousness.
It is the mind body problem.
Are all phenomena epiphenomena?
Esse se percipi:
To be is to be perceived.
Yeah, I could do with a little of that.

Shadowoman, the Amphictyon

The theatre had its own padded cell, built by another citizen of the warehouse one Doug Wilson, a fabulous artist with a completely different take than Russ. Doug was a photo-realist painter. He had big glasses and sharp eyes that did not miss a thing. Whereas Russ was young and flamboyant and joyous — into the chance element of art, Doug was more serious, literary and precise. He is the architect who designed and built himself the sound proof room. It had double thick walls and a window with double thick glass panes that opened out onto a hidden part at the back of the warehouse. It was a beautiful room about 8x8, completely empty, all covered in carpet with a sky light above. He used this room to study Primal Scream therapy. Primal Scream Therapy, based on the ideas in a book by Janov, incorporating the somatic Reichian quest for bioenergy liberation, was all the rage then. If one screamed loud and long, it freed up the tension that the body constantly carried itself in. It was supposed to open up circuits that had been closed since birth trauma, and perhaps before, so that one was able to get a tremendous release of freed-up energy, making you feel like an enriched human being. Doug called it Sound Travel. Artaud would have been proud.

Doug was a sweet intelligent guy, a stalwart steward of the warehouse that he called 'the Pit." He told me that it was an Amphictyonic Theatre. I liked that, it sounded like a kind of amped fiction.

"What is that?" I asked

"Well that is what they called the Oracle at Delphi back in ancient Greece. The Amphictyonic Theatre was the focal point of a region. There were several of them around Greece, but the one at Delphi became the most famous."

He continued. "They had a woman who worked there, she was called the Pythia of the Aphictyon. And she is the one who would pronounce the oracular sayings. They wrote them down. Apparently they used to have the Pythia suspended on a kind of swing above some vapors and fumes that came out of an opening in the earth. And this would produce some kind of hallucination."

"Oh, yeah!" I said. "Now I remember. I read about that in

Masters and Houston. *The Varieties of Psychedelic Experience*."

He said, "Anyway, the pythia made her oracular pronouncements from within a trance. There were all kinds of misunderstandings having to do with fate for her sayings were very dense and hard to interpret."

"Oh, that's where the word pithy must come from!"

"*Right* . . ."

A couple of days later I got to see the real thing in action in the warehouse theatre. Debbie Gwyn was premiering her new solo theatre piece titled *Shadow Woman*. I had never seen any kind of theatre like that. It was like she was the Oracle on this the Path with Heart and heart was the Sorcerer's Swing.

She is a good looking older woman in her 30's, with a great skittish vulnerability. She looks at everyone in the audience with big, unblinking, open, excited, eyes. As though she can read the questions they bring to her. With that she was the Pythia, the priestess at the altar of tribal spectacle, looking out with ever clear eyes. She says directly to them: "My heart is warm and my thoughts are cool."

Shadow Woman starts walking around the room in some convenient path. She plays the floor like a drum with her step. She began to recite the words of a trance inducing mantra-like ritual, as she beat out the rhythm with her feet. "I like," (step step). . . "the rhythm " (beat beat) of-my heart (step step) because it suits (beat beat) my mood."

She pauses, listens. The silence is strong when the drum walk stops. We can hear an after beat, just by suggestion of anticipated syncopation. She listens closely to its beating; cueing us too. Now she began to fit the steps of her feet on the floor into the beat of her heart — lub-dubbing, pumping. She is fluid; it began to play the heartstrings of our mind. The feet stepping out a slow rhythm. "I like the rhythm (boom boom) of my heart (step step) because it suits (boom boom) my mood."

Now it changed into an embellishment around the heart. She kept moving around stomping it out: "I like the rhythm (boom boom) of my heart because it suits my mood."

She double-timed the beats of the feet her heart made "I likes the rhythm (boom boom) of my heart boom, because it suits my . . ."

She had entered an aerobic trance as her breathing kept pace. In fact she was using her drum beat feet to make little embellishments all around the line of words which was being said at the original pace.

"I like the rhythm (step step) of my heart (boom boom) because it suits (step step) my mood."

The actors of this Amphictyonic Theatre at 2019 Blake Street used the floor as a drum and jammed with their heart beats. Then the heart gets beating faster to maintain this, but you just get into it as a back beat and start to riff off it. The wild movement had Shadow Woman working now, here hair wet, sticks in passionate spit-curls beside one ear. She is, by physical theatre, going into an ecstatic state, as though she were nearing orgasm or right after, when she was lying entwined with her love.

You could see it in the line of her theatre. Words are now the fundamental for which the movement, breathing and heart beat are overtones of that fundamental. Thus the word was made flesh. In physical theatre the playing back and forth, becomes actually resonating because of the biofeedback bridge built up between the drummer and his heart. Between the dancer and the dance.

Later I had a realization: The *plot* of this theatre is a projection drawn from the chaotic physical activity like a pen attached to some machine running in a higher dimension. For this is Amphictyonic Theatre — the word made flesh. This 'making flesh' is what one does to create Amphictyonic Theatre: Do these warm up exercises, and —thinking of Bob Ernst in the parking lot doing the long boxing exercises — do these often, and as much as you can and in a short space of time you will feel a lightness, followed by a warmth. And in action, context of story will surround you like a aura of now ritual sacrament.

Trying to understand the belief system that might trigger the states achieved at 2019 Blake, I had some gigantic fantasy: I imagined, 'This is what some call the Astral Body of the Self. It is what your body would feel like anywhere in the universe without the gravity of this specific planet. Thus you will get in touch with the self actuating, inward, mnemonic theatre of the body and the poetry of mantras, or the mantras of poetry.'

Then more and more, visions and imaginings will come to you. Learning how to attach the right words to these visions, is like attaching a code that will enable you to reproduce them.

It was all the more astounding because she was out there without any net, no props, no scenery, no other actors, no nothing. Just herself in a space with the story to perform.

Another woman denizen of the Pit, an actress who had developed and performed a solo theatre piece — it was about how getting married was like falling from the 8,000 foot level —took me to bed. I thought that was all right. It was so nice to get off the road and get into something with a girl. I even entertained courtship notions. But the next day she gave me the cold shoulder. Silly me. Hippie walking the streets of Berkeley grinning in my British bus driver's coat with all the red piping and gold buttons. Turned out she did that with all the boys. Now thanks to her, we were all *brothers of the flesh*. It was just the liberated woman of 1975, exercising her empowered right to allow herself to feel herself in sex, if they want.

I might not have been at my best. I was a bit freaked out at what possibilities of future might hold. But things in California were looking up. At least a guy could get laid here. Unlike in Texas where they are just deeply suspicious of any man who is literate or intelligent and not a cowboy.

I went from crashing on the floor of the sound room to a couch in Russell's studio, then a bed in the loft above the door in Russell's studio. It was nice sleeping in a loft, up a ladder, over the door. Russell had painted the walls of his studio all white. The better to see his wild paintings that adorn the walls; one of crisscrossed lines of paint, like heavy 3D rope going serpentine across the canvas. He uses those large squeezable bottles, ketchup bottles, to write his designs on canvas so that they sink in and stain the canvas. It is a nice wet effect.

He had a gigantic table made from four sheets of plywood butted together to make a vast working surface over drawers of materials.

He has three new paintings on his wall side by side, made by soaking white canvas in some kind of chemical, so that when he put them out in the wind, the canvasses hardened and captured the shape of the wind distorting them.

Figurative Abstraction

Darrell Gray lived in a basement flat on Milvia, a couple of blocks away from the Warehouse, around the corner behind Herrick Hospital. We could come over there toward evening and stooping down on the sidewalk, tap on his window. It was good to see him throw open the curtains and motion for you to circulate around and come in the side entrance through the gate in the tall whitewashed clapboard fence. To get to his room you went through the basement, past a huge laundry sink across from the washer and dryer, then you had to duck under a furnace duct 'till you came to his door, that always had a large green bottle of Gallo wine and stacks of books beside it. You could maybe squeeze about three people in that room.

Darrell Gray had a wide open expansive face, with big sensitive eyes. He was a big fellow, and could have been called lumbering, for he might have been a bit out of touch with his body. He was often slightly tipsy. He had a marvelous sway, when he was three sheets to the wind. His moon face was trustworthy. He let you be yourself, and hid his greatness except when he did readings, then the words of his poetry were so sweetly humorous you knew you were encountering a great mind at play in the fields of percipience. He had a sweet sense of humor, but there was an only-child loneliness about him too. There was a genius vulnerability about him that you wanted to protect. At least that's the way I felt about him, for I was always — even though younger — the Big Brother type, the ACA caretaker type.

Over to his place we'd get into some high speed gabfest. I had read Korzybski and most of the structuralists, Levi Strauss, Roland Barthes, and he liked to talk to somebody about that. I said I really liked Barthes, because it is a scathing and sarcastically witty critique of culture. A great Communists perspective. Barthes said that most artists are manipulating the signifiers of their art in order to communicate to readers that what they are consuming is, indeed, literature. Where's the creativity in that? Darrell liked Barthes too. I was really trying to understand signifier and signified and all that, and he understood it.

I said, " But Korzybski, the way he talked about the nervous system with that Structural Differential — wasn't that just the most unruly mishmash of nodes and strings?" Darrell Gray, laughed and said something about 'Noumenal Ingression into the nervous system.' Darrell Gray was modest and would always read somebody else's poetry, he was friends with Berrigan, Creely, Duncan, Jack Marshal, Anselm Hollo — had their poetry books around, open, face-down, with copious marginalia in them. He would sometimes read their poems aloud.

He began to take my most ignorant self into the poets education. I was born in Montreal, baptized Catholic before I left the hospital; it is actually the same thing as a birth certificate there, so I was aware of the possibility of being condemned to the eternal torment in hell. I grew up in San Antonio where it *is* like hell. Graduated from the University of Texas in Physics, though they still called it Natural Philosophy back then. Before university I had hitchhiked back and forth across the country many times, still did. Tried to move back to Canada; finally got to California. And here began my quick introduction to modern literature. My aesthetic at that point might have been only something I thought Kerouac was about, get stoned and groove out on jazz-worded feelings.

It was both inspiring and intimidating to be seeing Darrell Gray, a real, full-time, working poet at his typewriter. And yet, through conversation and at the typewriter, he would invite you into a collaboration in the creation of poems. We'd get to drinking. He'd roll a sheet of paper into his Smith-Corona electric and by typing a couple of lines of poetry, start the Exquisite Corpse rolling in its grave: we were off on a new collaboration.

He had given me a little book of sonnets that he had written in collaboration with Allan Kornblum, another alumnus (along with everybody at the warehouse) of the Iowa Writers School. He showed me journals in which his poems had been published. I realized he wrote his wildly popular Ode to Gibberish, with its first stanza: *I live in a jungle, / pull open the curtains, / and write what comes to me,* while sitting at that little table made out of a door and a stack of cinder blocks, and looking out that window to the Berkeley sidewalk.

I knew I loved poetry, thought T.S. Elliot and Ez Pound were awesome, couldn't get into WC. Williams, Wallace Stevens, or Creely — I had, or course, read some their works, *The Man with the Blue Guitar, Thirteen ways of looking at a blackbird, So much depends (on the little red wheelbarrow*) and admired some of it, but I was such a barbarian. I think I kind of hurt Darrell's feelings and certainly betrayed my ignorance when I blurted out that these guys are doctors and lawyers and insurance salesmen and such. They can't be relevant in poetry! Artists must be vomited forth from the lower class (though, I liked Borges.) I probably knew more about my great master / hero Joyce than any ten graduate students. I had not yet heard of Bukowski.

It was Peter Loschan who introduced me to Bukowski. My introduction was someone had scrawled "All Great Poets Die in Steaming Pots of Shit" on the bathroom wall of the warehouse and I was tasked with finding out who because the theatre management thought that was not appropriate for the theatre-going audience to see.

Peter was another character I met at the warehouse. I introduced Peter to Darrell Gray and the three of us started hanging out more. Peter liked to bring cans of Olympian tall-boys over to Darrell's little apartment. Peter was an insistent and intense German, with the wildest head of unkempt hair I have ever seen. It was a hopeless snarl of knots and mats radiating straight out and up. And he had a hawk like nose, to go with his sharp and aggressive demeanor; it was perhaps frightening until you got past his rué ruse and saw his great artistic sincerity. He wore his pants tucked inside his laced up hiking boots. He spoke with heavy rasping guttural accent, and was out for all the dope and beer he could consume. But he did it from a sincere European philosophical argumentative stance, dare I say imperious, that always questioned what was being received as the truth.

Peter brought me over to his pad one day. He had finished a painting. And he wanted me to see it close up with him. He had a cool cave of an apartment above a garage behind a house on Dwight Way. It was across Grove just a couple of blocks from the Pit. It was a lovely white stucco building for a studio, you squeezed through an exterior door and up the stairs but he had it just totally trashed inside. He drew and painted all the time. Some days he did dozen of drawings, he was an action painter and they were piles of drawings and tubes of paint and easels all over the place. He had just a pallet to crash in on the floor.

The painting was about four by six feet, spray painted on canvas, it was like the action sketches he made in his drawings. It was savage. To me it looked like some kind of horrendous spill had taken place on the canvas. I didn't know what to say.

I knew he was an Action painter. I had heard of his favorite

Drawing of Darrell Gray by Peter Loschan

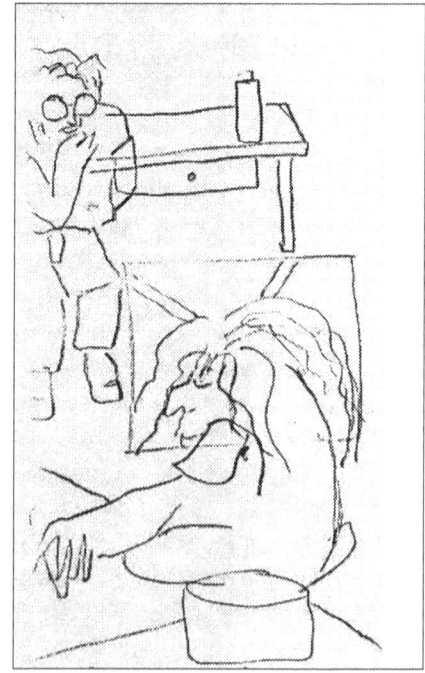

Sketch of Peter Loschan and Michael Lyons by Darrell Gray

painter deKooning but those paintings, did not naturally speak to me. I know these artists used the technique of hallucination by painting to engage the unconscious. I could see deKooning's famous painting *Women,* I guess. I didn't know what to say. Peter had this way of looking at the painting with great intensity, sometimes he held his eye between his fingers; he might even have been squeezing the eye. Presumably this gave him a better vision into the place the action painters called the energetic atemporal. We looked at it for a while. Finally I said, "Wow, that's really wild, man."

"Do you see the figure in it?" he asked.

I always try to be supportive of any creative effort and I said something about how I thought it was a wild mix of colors. Not understanding at all what I was saying.

He looked at me like I was from another planet and said, "But do you see the figure?" And he began gesturing; with his hands. He lifted his right hand in a gesture like someone finger painting or laying on paint with a trawl; he made a *fffhruit* sound blowing air over his lower lip in a kind of unvoiced exhalation of air over an overbite. And then he would quick, gesture like he was molding a muscle — a leg or the roundness of a shoulder.

"Ahhh, uh. . . no. I don't quite see it."

"You've got to squint your eyes," he said, "and make the figure emerge from the background. It is like a gestalt. . . . That's the great beauty of modern art. It is demo-Kratic, it speaks uncompromisingly on its own terms . . . to anyone who will listen. Directly, without the necessity of interpretation, about the primary energies of the universe!"

I made some kind of ameliorating gesture like I was a blind man trying to feel in the dark with my hands.

He stepped up close to the painting, and starting from the bottom right corner, his hands followed the slanting vertical upsweep, halting in the center to bend and make his arms horizontal parallels, which he broke away, and then his hands continued to the angular rise to the left-hand corner.

He looked at the painting with that intense needful way he had. It was a look of expectation, the need to be understood. His head was cocked looking at me sideways. Regarding me as the foreigner I am here. He said, "This painting is an example of Figurative Abstraction. Haven't you heard of that?"

"Ah, not really," I said, shrugging in belittled supplication.

I stepped to the canvas and squinted my eyes, and by golly I began to see this face.

"Don't you get it?"

"Yes! I think I am beginning to see it."

It made me a little stoned, reeling, with my perception trying to make vision emerge from that chaos, seeing. Seeing what he wanted me to, making me question my perception, made me unsure of myself. I held out my hand out, as though holding it, weighing it.

Wallace Stevens came up again at Darrell's place. Blackbirds.

I asked him, "What is the meaning of the blackbird? It is a symbol, right?"

Darrell Gray looks cryptic, closed his eyes into a faraway squint. Looks inscrutable as Fu Manchu. Says, as though in a trace seeing through some kind of all-seeing vision, " 'Among the 20 snowy mountains / nothing moved / but the eye of the black bird.' Yeah, that's how it starts, I think."

"Yeah, I think you are right." I thought about a Canadian landscape. "Man that is beautiful, have you ever been in a snowy landscape where nothing was moving, no one was around and it is completely quiet."

"Oh yeah, lot of snow when I was living on a farm in Iowa."

"Yeah a black and white world."

"It's like a haiku," I said. "I remember trying to write concatenated haiku under the influence of that poem."

"Yeah, haiku-like, and epigrammatic," he added.

Darrell Gray said, "The thing about haiku is that they kind of lead you into sensations. Which is kind of amazing when you think of it, to be able to generate sensations and perceptions in another with just words."

"Yeah it is."

"Can't get over it." I remembered a line: "'A man and a woman are one. A man and a woman and a black bird are one."

He immediately rose and went over to his shelf saying, "I got to look that up." While scanning his finger over the shelf he called out to the book: "Wally. Where's Wally." Like he knew him personally. I thought at the moment that he probably did. He pulled a paperback off the shelf; flashed us the cover: *Poems of Wallace Stevens*. He opened the book to the poem: "Here it is. 'The Blackbird whirled in the autumn winds. / It was a small part of the pantomime.' He has that wonderful word the 'pantomime'."

Darrell read a little more.

I asked again, "So, what is the blackbird a symbol of?"

And he said. "It is like this is some kind of jewel we are looking at. We are looking at it in thirteen ways and each angle of refraction redefines the blackbird as each moment shifts the image. It is a symbol of being, the ever-shifting diamond of existence projecting its presence into the world. And withdrawing it."

He pointed to his typewriter, a black one, sitting on his narrow desk, a desk that was really a door placed atop a stack of blue milk crates, and stacked cinder blocks. "My typewriter could be a blackbird." He paused and talked to the object as though he were calling it, chanting its name. "Typewriter typewriter black bird blackbird." He said this musing.

Then he read, 'I do not know which to prefer, / The beauty of inflections / Or the beauty of innuendoes, / The blackbird whistling / Or just after.'

He paused and thought for a moment: "Blackbirds are like misspelled words. Sometimes they are puns that lead directly into the Freudian unconscious.

"Like look what he does in the second way of looking: ' I was of three minds, / Like a tree / In which there are three blackbirds.' He starts of with the "three" of 'three minds,' and takes out the "h" and that leaves "tree". Then he gives us the unified image of three blackbirds in a tree. Whenever I think of tree now I think of Chomsky and parsing sentences!

"And then he has that wonderful telescoping of time here. 'It was evening all afternoon / It was snowing / And it was going to snow.'"

I laughed.

He said, "I like that. It's like: what is a fence? It's the edge of a field. How does a field know to stop being a field? When it comes to the fence."

He pointed at his typewriter and started reciting. "A blackbirds is sitting / on my typewriter. The sky outside is / full of dark clouds. I began to wonder . . ."

Bay Bridge Mandala

John O'Keefe

    Work was pretty scarce. The first job I got was mowing lawns for the black people in south Berkeley and north Oakland who were kind enough to hire me. I started studying with John O'Keefe and Jonathan Albert as soon as I could. O'Keefe was working at the Exploratorium, an interactive science museum in San Francisco. Frank Openheimer, brother of the famous Manhattan Project physicist Robert, was the curator. O'Keefe was teaching an excellent course in making vocal sound. He took groups into this sweet little soundproof room, it was a little octahedronal room, a many-faceted jewel of carpentry work, right out there on the floor of the cavernous museum, made out of varnished hardwood and glass, that could fit maybe 6 people crowded together, with double pane glass walls, so that when you closed the doors the great clanking and whirring and barrel bonging sound of the Exploratorium vanished.

    O'Keefe, who was already an accomplished theatre director, relished being a wildly enthusiastic choirmaster, ardently leading these innocent museum-goers into a fascinating class of making modern aleatory-jazz, be-bop vocal sound. It was Stockhausen meets Sun Ra, or John Cage meets Pharo Sanders. He'd get us to take apart words and use just some of the syllables as our instrument to blow like jazzers piping in on cue with our phoneme. We'd repeat and repeat a word like a mantra blending and harmonizing, introjecting or trailing.

    I'd ride over to San Francisco on the bus, or hitchhike onto the bridge, then take a bus out into the Avenues. The Exploratorium was in the marina, a gorgeous part of town, with yacht clubs and fine houses like villas from Spain. And I'd catch a ride with O'Keefe back to Berkeley. All the way back we'd be all flushed and high from his sound class at the Exploratorium where he led us on experiments in sound synthesis. We sang electronic music! — by shaping the pure voiced and unvoiced vowel color energy in words with diacriticals of attack, sustain and release. By removing the meaning from articulation this way, you were left with just pure joyous mimetic sound: a meditative practice, a repetitive activity done just for the devotion of it. Long enunciated repetition of the word made it become like a mantra, freezing the word in sound-space and striping the word of its sense. When words loose their sense like that and are held pinned down in the moment, they burst into pieces, and decompose: what were once signs were now pure fundamental vowel energy being shaped into meaningful vehicles by their consonants — their diacritical attacks, sustains, and releases. This releases the spectral energy in the word and it floats out into the world to act like a chaos attractor — a seed syllable penetrating the mind and the body and the world — drawing like energies to it, pushing untoward energies away.

One day, while riding back to Berkeley with O'Keefe, the Bay Bridge mandala happened. I am moving in a car across the San Francisco Bay Bridge. The sun setting behind us is splashing the Oakland cityscape in front of us, glinting of the girders and glancing of the cars racing headlong on the great, wide, double-decker roadway arching across the sky. Vast expanse of Bay below. The East Bay sprawl we are headed into is a shimmering of mirror surfaces, the glass skyscrapers like facets of one large gem. We are in O'Keefe's blue Volkswagen bug convertible, running headlong toward the complexity in a pack, everybody running neck and neck in a race, their cars swarming all around us on the wide road bed. From this height, spanning over the great bay, the ocean-going vessels and ferry boats below look like toys in a bathtub.

Somewhere along the arch between San Francisco and Berkeley, in the monotony of the miles and the rhythmic thump of the tires bumping over the sections of the bridge, I notice we appear to be standing still. Something was wrong with the time. All the cars were proceeding at the same speed in phased lock-step, exactly uniform so that there was no perceptible relative motion — at all. I sat bolt upright in my bucket seat and felt an embracing attention take hold of me, a serotonin cascade in the frontal lobes, a rush of penetrating feeling from somewhere way down inside where the world intrudes like a neuronal dendrite into the subcortical substrate, and fans out to meet the complex geometry of the soul. I think my head actually snapped back, like I was in some kind of premonition — an accident maybe?! I blinked a few times, looked around to check my surroundings to see if we had actually all stopped on this superhuman span of steel. Though we were being carried along in a forceful flow, a river of momentum, it felt like shadows flashing past. We were falling. Falling into the vanishing point. I said: "My god! Look at that. We are all moving in synch! All going at the same speed! No one is moving faster or slower. Like we are standing still. And we are falling into the scene."

Can you imagine? Bits of color on the cars moving beside: red, blue, green — relative flashing motion of color roll together blue red yellow black into the East Bay sprawl, glinting in the sun, flashes of light off the down town buildings — Oakland of endless little roads snaking, antsy-dancing up the far hills. It was like I could see the whole Bay area at a glance, like it was some kind of vast cloud-chamber evidencing the ghostly vapor trails of so much movement strobed into existence with pulses of annihilation and creation. There were islands in the bay, boat waves in the water, contrails in the sky, curved freeway clover-leafs governing the particle trajectories; there were great avenues plowing a wide swath through neighborhoods. These elegant curves left by particle tracks in the cloud chamber show the tracery of primary energies surging into and out of existence. This tracery of forces in the toroidal-ring vacuum of an atom-smashing, particle-accelerator are the mandalas of my time. Berkeley is the home of the cloud chamber, it was invented here. Some how this view from on top of the bridge got super-ordinated into a shift in perspective. It was indeed an avalanche, a serotonin cascade—some damn thing inside me broke. Something was oscillating in and out of gestalt. It was a paradigm shift, a profound shift in perspective. The View into scale. When the space ceases to be merely something you are moving through, and you have driven into a pause, you enter into an expanded moment, and the space bursts into subspaces, niches of free energy that the creatures have adapted to, you have a view into scale. I slipped into a zoom, for the catenary curves of the bridge cables are logarithmic. I saw the scale with man about the middle between the astronomical and the subatomic as my imagination zoomed in powers of 10,

$$10^{-4} \quad 10^{-3} \quad 10^{-2} \quad 10^{-1} \quad (\circ) \quad 10^{1} \quad 10^{2} \quad 10^{3} \quad 10^{4}$$
$$1$$
$$.0001 \quad .01 \quad .01 \quad .1 \quad < \backslash \quad 10 \quad 100 \quad 1000 \quad 10{,}000$$

with man the 1, the point at the center between the microcosm and the macrocosm. I let my spirit go and it flew out from there over the bay, zoomed up to see the hills way off, got higher to see beyond the horizon to see the valley and out to sea. Logarithmic scale space: for every second zoom back out a power of 10 — 1 meter above where you are, see the swirl in your hair; 10 meters above, it is like looking at yourself from a high diving board; at 100 meters, you are seeing yourself from on top of a large high rise, above the towers of this bridge. Next I start to see the two shores — bay and ocean. At 1000 meters it is like looking from an airplane: if it is not cloudy you start to see the two shores at once and way down the whole bay. I looked toward the naval base at Alameda, looked down the far reaches of the bay — way, way to the south where the Bay's water leaks out of the horopter into the horizon. Or zoom the other way, down into my hand, the hairs on the hand, into the pores of the skin, life slipping in and out of holes into capillaries into the blood cells, into the individual cell, down into the mitochondria see the great golden spiral staircase of DNA going down into mass slipping in and out of "holes in space-time" — wells of potential attraction. While passing Treasure Island, looking at the great machines of the Oakland port; I almost lost it, a kind of vertigo was settling in, a kind of existential nausea you get in realization of your own being. The giant container-unloading cranes stationed along the shore stood like invading alien machines — striders walking along the land. Alien-dazzle tractor-beams are moving ALL of us to the secret desires of the heart. All things are in motion, in progression, in change. Even space and time itself. The view! From up there as we traverse the air on this solid and immobile steel. We too are trusses stretched-out, spanning the gap. High up there, I felt a part of the machinery, felt a part of all that was, and all that ever was, the fuel that feeds the fire, part of the history of the earth. I reveled that even molecules of air breathed in by Caesar and exhaled by Jesus and breathed in again by Hitler are still around for all. They could have dispersed and percolated across time through so many mouths into my breath. We are flying in our cars and I thought about you 50 years hence: Will you be flying across the bay in your cars. Just as you 50 years hence will have the same thoughts and feelings I have, will breath the same air that I once breathed, just as you are stuck in a traffic jam so was I once one of the many in this hedgy flow that makes the light through which clarity is transmitted. In my time — the first generation after Einstein, itself a generation after Kant — the debate about space continues: is it absolute and immovable or not. I scramble trying to think about what it meant. If motion is space passed through in time. . . I had slipped, been velocitized, phased, into the tunnel perspective of motion. And I let my imagination go for a minute into creating the mandala, with its central point and its rhythmic isoclines of structure — temples and intricate courtyards were states in a unified presentation of the self as city. I saw Oakland like some golden city of the future set in the Bay Bridge Mandala. Here the whole East Bay backdrop — Oakland with its fearful spots full of wrathful deities and demons, and its wealthy uplands, full of hungry ghosts, its endless struggle between the flatlanders and the mountain people, between the black and the whites, the rich and the exploited class, the student and the teachers. I had fallen head long into a kind of swoon. I almost wanted to rear back in my bucket seat and put my feet on the dash board to brace myself for sliding down the roadway like I was on the upended Titanic — sliding down beneath the sea into a mandala scene. I almost raised some kind of alarm but sweated out the fever myself. The spirals are forming the complex quasi-closed space-time-matter lattice. The whole Universe appears to be alive. There was so much flowing into me that I felt sweaty and saturated — the ego is being flooded out with id. It's the Golden Dream for the future that the immigrants had. I'm an alien here myself. Never been here before. There used to be no bridge here, everyone took the ferry: the women wearing white gloves to the city, men in their fine felt fedoras. And before that, the ancient peoples, who have gathered for eons at the edge of the bay — polling around in reed pirogues. I imagined Ghosts rising from shell mounds and hovering in the air — a place, a city, has ghosts floating in spirals like the weather — just as an individual. There are many characters that swarm up and intermix like a gas All these gaseous souls surging out to fill the expanse flowing under us and out and above the Bay and sunset and all the lives touched by the tide. I am being . . . held in solution by whatever it is that makes a flower brighten. It holds us here.

O'Keefe drifted in an out of the warehouse. It was always inspiring to see him, get into high speed gab-fests at Moishes a Jewish delicatessen owned by Chinese, staffed by Filipinos and Japanese. I tried to get a job at the Exploratorium doing work in their exhibit fabrication shop, trouble shooting electronics, but they were full up. I worked for a while at the world's largest hash-pipe screen factory which was also in the warehouse. I also worked in a little woodworking shop where we made fine and fancy boxes out of exotic and beautiful hardwoods. After a while Russ got me a job at the frame shop in the Vorpal Gallery where he worked. There I learned to do fine framing, to cut glass, and beveled mattes in acid free papers and mount art works using acid free glues and tapes. At the art gallery were all these *tres chic* elegant young women salesgirl personnel, whose job it was to sidle up to you and urge to you buy a $5000 painting. This was a hell of a lot of money to me, more than I had ever seen. I didn't fit in. In between jobs I ate at the Food Project, which was a good big healthy meal they put on every day in the late afternoon at the Presbyterian church on Haste, a block above People's Park. Later I got a job driving a cab at Taxi Unlimited. But I am getting ahead of myself. The most important thing was my writing education.

Princess Rain

The solo theatre piece **Princess Rain**, written and performed by Bob Ernst, was performed in Berkeley, Los Angeles, Montreal and elsewhere starting in 1975. It is republished here from PAW # 11, 1976, along with associations of its impact presented as they are experienced during performance.

Bob Ernst also had a new solo theater piece and it was completely electrifying to watch. It was called *Princess Rain*. The theater piece takes place in the white space of the warehouse theatre, with creative lighting: no sets; no costume; cast of one being many. In the Poor Theatre tradition, the piece becomes all the more compelling because these are all created in the mind of the viewer by the performer weaving the images through just movement, language and vocalization. It takes place in an unfolding sequence of dreamlike landscapes; it is metaphysical theater exploring being.

The piece starts off when Bob enters the performing arena and establishes that we are in a sacred space. He takes over the space and makes it like a temple. He did this by chiming little brass temple bells. In this sacred space he chants the phrase: All Language is Neurosis.

Princess Rain
A solo theatre piece by Bob Ernst

(Cannon-style – obituary chant) (convocation)
    ALL LANGUAGE IS NEUROSIS

(soft-minor)
    we must start from somewhere
    so we'll start there

(convocation)
    ALL LANGUAGE IS NEUROSIS

(Hard, clipped rhythmic)
    I've said it before   And I'll say it again
(convocation)
    ALL LANGUAGE IS NEUROSIS

Bob Ernst

Chanted (sing-songy scale symbols))
        Even though I have three eyes and none of them
        blink oh no not one and I look out over the farm
        in the morning grass dew

ALL LANGUAGE IS NEUROSIS
I see my wife she is dim wet *(repeat)* there are no
scars on her belly   only tattoos on her breast

oh a rose   a rose any other name would smell as sweet

ALL LANGUAGE IS NEUROSIS

The sight is crystal clear   like iron no sheaths no chains
    Only a slight headache for I have three eyes
and none of them blink   perhaps rusted shut   glued tight
by matter matter matter it does not matter no matter

but the head throbs pounds like chain mail for

    I CAN'T NOT SEE   no matter how hard I try
    the farm house is abandoned its cracked
eyes scope to fall hacked stalks a dried up creek
to sun in
    and we did Bob   oh remember how we did
once upon a time   once upona time   onct upuns atomb
I   I   I   I CAN'T NOT SEE

    The phrase, "All Language is Neurosis," is certainly a confrontational opening for a play. It has that self-reflexive paradoxical humor like *'a new refutation of time.'* The phrase is a rallying cry for physical theatre, which seeks to be a theatre of anti-logos, a theatre that restores our animality. I loved the onslaught to the mind that this precipitates. The phrase immediately speaks to the body-based improvisation aesthetic at the heart of Hawkeye theatre and the sound poetry basis of the California Zen Aesthetic. Within the piece Bob introduces characters: a friend, a love interest; and events, and situations that reflect the mingling of imagination, memories and sensory input. One moment Bob is on a farm, the next he is inside a cage, the next he is in his apartment on a speed run to be drowning in overdose. The play is metaphysical in the sense that it creates its own reality as a consensus construct that shifts moment by moment as the imaginary world we're collectively creating coalesces and breaks apart again and again.

The character talks about his three eyes: this could be a kind of hip affectation or, it could be a spiritual statement about super-senses. This ambiguity or sense of a "put-on" is a counter cultural defense, but is also a result of physical theatre. One does not play characters, one is possessed by "entities." The stage directions embody many hours of exercises and improvisations to find the self. The play is grounded in male physical prowess, spiritual proclivity, self-deprecating (druggy) humor, and the aching pathos of lost love.

In the next scene we are watching the character as he starts building a cage for us to visualize. The space is a cage. The visual emblem of the cage pulls together several elements, the spikes of the drug user, the various addictions we are all trying to escape — even language and literacy — as coercive trap.

(Gesture slaps soft inside elbow veins. . . crossed arms raise overhead . . .
fast at first then slower and slower . . . to the top . . .
everything softens . . . eyelids do not close but droop)
(soft undulations, sways come into effect now. voice soft and poetic)

    I NOW HAVE THE TRUCK-DRIVING FINESSE OF A BALLET
    DANCER ON POINT

(soft simple turn barely toe to toe, slight stumble)

    Oh I COULD SPIN MINUETS. I WOULD *TOUR JE TAE* FOR YOU.
    ANYTHING, EVERYTHING, EVERYTHING BLUE, AND
    A HEAVY ATMOSPHERE TOO

    A SLAP   A SPIKE   A MOUNTAIN TO DARN SKIN WITH

    0 I DO LOVE YOU

(repeated and gets more and more junk slurred.
comes out of it to quick hard precise movements directed
to build and walk in a maze to build, to build a cage)

    awake now the head builds and aches

    The man. The man comes — he comes
    the man,
        coming, building, perfecting, building, coming,
    to — to a cage. The man — The cage — The man

comprised of many elements,
steel the cage. Skin the man—two elements to — to confuse—

he examines, he examines, he examines—let me see—

   the poles

he examines the poles. They are long, tubular, and strong—
strong like the man— The man's skin he thinks could envelope
the poles — deteriorate them from the outside and he — the man
on the outside — must build — build for the inside —the inside of —
of —
let me see now:

   theinsideofacage   acageacage   theinsideofacage
acage acagece cagecee caeee eeeyovmwl They almost closed

I will work fast—faster now finish and then maybe they will
close on the gatekeeper   oh
the gatekeeper comes
he comes to—let me see- — close in
confine   confine the space   poles   setting poles
icicles   sharp points   STAB into the ground,
   the ground

stab   stab stab
stabstab stab STAB

(building to scream in intensity   the word stab is like a mantra   for release)

EEEE
  EEEE   ah
AAA   aahah
AAA   B B B B *(reg. like a heartbeat)*

   ah-B aho-B ahouw-B
(narrative style, — precise, clear)

   The poles are placed at a space of .003 centimeters from one another
for an adequate disposition of light and to insure once again—
confinement
Not even the polished nail of a little finger will be able to protrude
space. The depth to which the poles are sunk into the ground is—is
(stumbles momentarily here)   deep enough. The points
         will   (with an edge of water)

>   drive to a depth of 5' 6 ¾ '' before rooting out forming a mesh
>   lattice work to prevent underground escape.
>   Meals—
>
> *(headache starting to stumble)*
>   Meals will be provided.
>   A waiter — white napkin   complete complete with cuff links
> *(howl)*
>   the watch dogs are hungry   *(fast, hushed, clipped, intense)*
>   they mark their rounds by leaving urine samples on the lock
>
>   It takes approximately six years; or *(calculates)* 52,560 rounds to
>   deteriorate the lock and freedom   begins. The dogs,
>   hungry on stilts
>   of toenails will charge without command—
>
> *(soft and poised   takes off glasses)*
>   the internal tension is
>   incredible   wipes glasses carefully

By now we have been witness to a lot of painful elbow slapping and falling down. It is *very* physical theatre. His body is sweat drenched; in a sense we are watching a workout. The actor of physical theatre crosses the threshold that separates the human and animal worlds and takes us there with him. He has become a Zoon Phonata. There is a lot of Howling, it is part of the modulation. Then, now that he has our undivided attention he might just follow that with speaking softly, to spin out his hypnotic tale. This theatre is not only musical but it is a ballet. The visual grace with which Bobby makes a transition, from one scene to the next, circling as he comes in for a landing in the play might suggest the eagle in Castaneda. With sheer animal grace beyond language we get a sense of environmental sense, of the animal world. With a graceful mimetic gesture – no words – we have moved to another part of the ritual. Embedded in the gesture is the practice of Tai Chi and the exploration of Form, that led him to perfect that grace. As well as the dedication that helped him insist on this artform as a way to reclaim, for all of us to reclaim, our animalilty.

Next he shifts pace and sings the plaintive song, a traditional folk ballad. This is a remarkable connection between the troubadour tradition of folk music and this troubadour poet-actor theatre. Perhaps he could be singing this to his former lost self.

HE WAS A FRIEND OF MINE

he was a friend of mine
he was a friend of mine

never had no money
for to pay his fine
        lord
he was a friend of mine

he died upon the road
he died upon the road

too much too much focus
was his overload
        lord
he died upon the road

he was a friend of mine
he was a friend of mine

    This is not the intellectual poetry of Pound and Elliot, its roots are in music and sound. The blues. A lot closer to my own culture.
    Though this theatre is ritual, it is intensely personal; it could not be performed or written by anyone else. It is one's life lived as holy ritual. As such, because of the tremendous integration between the words of the text and the reactions to the perceptions being spoken about causing the audience to imagine what the actor was seeing and experiencing, one could not help but be brought into the actual. This consensus reality is a spiritual ritual.
    The perception can be slowed down, the presence can be rendered into words by regulating the delivery of these words— line by line. The imagination accurately accompanies Bob into his world when the dance syntax and the forms of motion, and the puns, and the pull of ambiguity into interpretation work together.
    The next "act" (scene?) is a romantic tennis game that Bob plays with an imaginary opponent — a woman he is in love with. He plays doing both parts. It reminds us that theater is a game and a play is "to play."

I can't not see

(fast blow out to fix)　　　　PRINCESS RAIN

On the tennis court soft and white
My love and I played at night.
She threw the ball to start the game;
Her name in winds was Princess Rain

Short hair and ivy was her mane;
Glowing sunset — This was the game

Of games a time of times
Ceaseless rhythms ceaseless rhymes,

Building to a volley at the net,
She won me over and there we met.

Her eyes were crystal oval wide
A part of lips
　　　"Will you come inside
"—not Now — or wait for ever for—
the game is won—no more, no more.'
back away back away
to today to today

the ball was tossed
the game was lost

On the tennis court soft and white,
My love and I played at night.

She threw the ball to start the game;
Her name in winds was Princess Rain.

The success of Ernst's improvisational-style theater works because above all he brings us into the moment. Also he has a gleeful, joyous, over-the-top, gonzo sense of humor. He is a skilled dancer, and an actor with a protean face and a very powerful voice, a voice that can be like a banshee from hell or a whiskey smooth baritone- voiced crooner. But most of all he achieves that goal of physical theatre, in which the character being played and the personality of the player are transcended so that he becomes an almost transparent embodiment of the Form, and we see rising and falling on

(gruff, dejected, farting old man style) –
    He was a friend of mine.

    Stalemate   configurations of musicians
    box seats
    I see this   dark purple.

    The sun is rising.

    I have a heliotrope of diseases,
    Infirmities, passions. Are they synonymous?

    In my blood run veins
    Upon veins, upon veins —-

    THERE IS NO HOPE FOR BREATH

*(gasping — for I have three eyes and none of them blink —
brings him back around — he stops twitching)*
    You tire of this shit?
    I'll tell a story straight and true, so true,
    And I'll tell it, I'll tell it just for you, for you.
    A recently arrived speed freak   thirteen days of trying, to be
    precise, walking to be precise; of trying to see an amazing sadness
    that goes past tears in order to be precise he wears the heels down
    to nubbins.

---

every breath through to a pure speaking animal, the zoon phonata whose being is like a mystical body of which we are all a part.

    The next part of the piece is the story of a speed freak, and it was harrowing. Bob had a Cantinflas mustache (zee heavily-oiled French-pimp look). His cheeks, at the time were gaunt. I know he believed in clean living, got good rest, was a consummate Tai Chi player and was becoming a martial artist, but at the time he looked quite the part of the person in this story. It might have been an illusion he created for the part.

    In fact there was something kind of frightening about Bob, the way he could shape shift, undergoing metamorphosis right in front of you. It was like looking at a great Theater Shaman, like don Janero. Within moments he can appear sensitive, spiritual, quiet — but then instantly change into a demonic speed freak becoming maniacally animated. Or he can be a gruff old monk. In this next scene he goes from being a dancer in complete control of his presentation to being a drowning victim.

For holiness sake:
>there is no longer food
>there is no longer water

>only pop   soda pop

I don't know
do you?
>flaking skin
>yellow eyes
>>and an amazing sadness that goes past tears.
Thirteen days, to be precise   his heart hurts literally syncopated jazz skips inside his chest.
>Fright begins causes more skips causes more fright on & on
>Anyway, he decides to take a bus home to see his mother. It is seven in the morning. He has once again been up all night snorting methadrine and feeling shitty this is a change in feeling   Looking in the mirror, seeing beauty despite it all, he decides one more hit up the old shnozzola (gesture to the nose) is all he needs to be bright. Upon hitting, instead of exploding in the brain killing more memory centers and melting the ears back as usual, it quickly over amps short circuits to the heart I'mmm — I'mmm (stuttering) immediate triple pacing occurs – so fast, so fast he must wash his face on the move; must put his pants on in counter moving circles-one for each leg.
>And believe me, my friends, the room he lived in was small. He walks forty blocks for a glass of orange juice and is able to sit and drink it if taping his feet in triple time *(gesture)*

The sadness is becoming   Becomes dread of the deepest sort. There is no going home now only blank spaces in the day sitting canonized by internal orchestra of his heart.
>The coming night brings a brief but futile attempt at a juvenile love that cannot compare to the building crescendo inside him.
>the gaps
(silence listening to the non-activity of his heart)

>>ONLY SERVE TO CONTINUE THAT DREADED BUILD

Finally on a sofa in a friend's house he is completely inside   he sits in the middle of the percussion section and the aorta and the right ventricle are carrying the build to its zenith feverishly working overtime pumping, clapping out rhythms fiercely ba bump stop freeze

babababba (32nd strokes) stop freeze

build this patting hand to heart tongue hanging out like the real thing you know it

building rising to feet slowly
    THIS IS IT. ALL THAT FOR THIS?
        Papapapapapapapa   bump   stop dead
    I WILL NOT DIE STANDING UP!

let it happen faint – fall completely limp and tell the river Styx from here

Floating. The deepest, darkest state of consciousness ever. The definition is of a different kind. Like floating down a dark river, in a dark boat, on a dark night — the beings who row are like everything else.

There is, however, definition.
Floating. Although I am laying on my back, arms folded, I am able to see every the arched tip a vortex in the distance so distant it does not constrict. Like a sphincter that vortex, but the constriction remains far distant.
It is neither a pleasant ride nor a fearsome ride.
It is the most ride I ever had.

After the speed run, the next scene takes us deep down into the River Styx or, going across cultures the Bardol of the In-between state, the state of consciousness between living and death across which we transcend with Bob. He is bobbing up and down.

The actor of Physical Theatre takes us across the threshold that separates the human and animal worlds. Physical Theatre searches for another aurality between human an animal being, that results in the substitution of a multi-vocal being for the speaking subject. It is this in-between of transformation that occupies Bobby's story. The moment at which identity floats in transit. And here is the image of it, the River Styx, the Bardol Thodol, oblivion. He becomes double, he becomes multiple. The transformation that has enveloped his being also makes him anonymous. And as such we can project more on him. We too fall into an abyss that opens into return.

Silence

vvvvaaarrrooommm *(a sound)*

Vibration. Vibration — the oarman's arms remain invisible   going through gears   the forward momentum slows

vvvaaarrrooomm *(a sound)*

even slower the water is shiny and thick as mud

vvvaaarrrooommm *(a sound)*

Momentum is reversed and building going back through lighter and lighter shades of blackness to dark greys no light yet but lighter
    hha umm   hha umm

(vibrations build speed come quicker & quicker)

hha umm   hha umm   hha umm   hha umm   a umm a umm   umm umm   umm
m mm   bm bmm bmmm b   b   ba
baa bo   bo   boo   boob   bob   bob   bob
Bob Bob   Bob   BOB   BOB BOB BOB — BOB?

    "BOB – Bob?"
(simple questioning concerned call of name)
(pause to take in gradually come around eyes slowly open, widen, they never close)

(sudden jump up)

PROTECT — PROTECT — THE WALLS ARE CRASHING IN — PROTECT PROTECT

EMERGENCY!   EMERGENCY!

Shao Linn – trying to hold the walls up

(tension builds – even higher than it ever has

gesture at peak —(spike to inside elbows)
the tension goes so fast it is frightening
it is such a hit that the arms do not move
from gesture just relax totally into it
gesture should be done with back to audience
or a slight opening over the right shoulder

head and arms drooping back to audience
eyes drooping deeper than ever
the following phrases (1-6) coming slower and slower till fade away relaxed freeze to death finish
while audience leaves rigor mortis sets in)
    1. all language is neurosis 3
    2. for I have three eyes & none of them blink
    3. a rose, a rose
    4. to build the inside of
    5. her name in winds was Princess Rain
    6. I can't not seeeeeeeee — *(faint, high, distant fading away)*

We were deeply moved and touched by what happened to us in the Hawkeye theatre. Amid jubilant thunderous applause, the rhythm of his performance was ringing in our hearts. The rhythm of the words speeds up to chanting — when he is calling himself back from oblivion:

Bob Bob BobBob goes to Bob Bob BobBobBobBobBob

He easily shifts from rhythmic time to non-rhythmic time. There are just so many interesting aesthetic points that you pick up in this piece. The actor of physical theatre is a hybrid being, a singer (of country western *and* opera), a clown, an acrobat, a martial artist, that forces human language to adapt in order to survive. He fragments himself into all these other selves.

You feel your intelligence being played with but not in a logocentric way; in a deeper more loving, trusting sense of the possibilities of owning your own being. We had entered a space he totally owned. His body disintegrated and he was able to project his memories on the walls of our mind. He was able to float in the space. The space of the Hawkeye theatre became sacred; the words became unleashed from their sense and started to express corporeal effect, driven by the passion of the body and ideation of events. Words morphed into physical stance and action and this was immediately communicated on a body level to all present. This is the premise and method of physical theatre, a meta-linguistic theatre: in reconnecting body motions with the space that surrounds him, new modes of expressing became necessary for the actor, as well as new modes of seeing for the viewer. Body as depth, in the Theatre of the Body.

Bob's masterpiece *Princess Rain* brings us into a transcendent space where he has shown us what the human actor is capable of, in terms of really going for it and not holding back. The performance was almost like drugs it makes you feel high. I was deeply touched. Indeed it was like watching a force of nature.

The constant practice of physical theater, of improvisation on feelings and mood, and the pursuit through Tai Chi of Taoism has training effect on the intuitive senses. Letting surreal, nonlinear scenes spontaneously unfold through movement, sound, and free-form language flowing seamlessly into the new reality that has been created, performance skills are really a vehicle through which we investigate Being. The work is on being spontaneous, on breaking through and cracking up the way we perceive our world.

Bob had completely transcended his physical being, he was a column of air, breathing focus into every word and sound. In his movement and gesture he was able to pull a magical space in around himself that he could manipulate and that he could make us see. It was shocking to be part of this hallucinatory consensus reality, and to witness the theatre of the luminescent animal.

It was really an honor for Bob to have let me publish the text of his solo theatre piece. I felt like I was holding some kind of treasured prayer-like invocation of the possibilities of being present in the moment. It is a superb example of a kind of new aesthetic or sensibility I was trying to get at. I was going to say understand, but maybe you do yourself a disservice trying to understand. It is more a kind of knowing.

In hindsight now I might use a Peircian paradigm, or the paradigm of Actualism and say Bob gave a full derivation of the emergence of his art. We got to see it move in from the possible, into the actual, then crystallized into the form. He used the form to bring himself into the now moment of the actual by a kind of internal dynamic tension, and from there relax into the primary flow of the possible. On the fundamental waves of breath the words and movements were harmonics on this fundamental. It was like an extreme action meditation. He became a conduit moving light around inside the multifaceted jewel of his theatre, reflecting and transferring and transmuting the transparent forces coursing through the Amphyctionic Theatre. He had truly fulfilled Artaud's dream of a new language, an animated hieroglyphic. Animated in the sense of transcending logos and egos to our more basic animal knowing, which was closer to the present. Grounded in the present realization, we too could hallucinate the Form.

Bob introduced me to the great long poem *Gunslinger* by Ed

Dorn. Bob told me that *Princess Rain* evolved out of *Gunslinger;* it was the text that started him out on the project that eventually, through the process of Physical Theatre, evolved into *Princess Rain.* He let me read his copy of Dorn's long dramatic monolog poem, published by Black Sparrow 1970 with its luminous, western, burnt-orange cover. I call it monolog because the many voices seem to be talking within one. You could immediately see how theatrical and kinetic the story was. It was comic opera, mock-epic. It starts out with stage direction: *The curtain might rise anywhere on a single speaker*. This was a great sprawling all inclusive 'para-poem' but unlike those of Olson, WCW, Pound who sometimes devolved into desultory political cant or history, Gunslinger was a natural model for a solo theatre piece. It was open, an amalgam of lyric and story and theoretical consideration and sound text and song. Gunslinger was about becoming guerilla theatre, street theatre. The undertone is the great Bob Dylan put-on in the service of resistance. We recognized a senior poet writing our story immediately. It had various philosophers subsumed into the text. It was playful, nonsensical, like Lewis Carrol, burrowing down into grammar with Point Of View shifts. Like *White Rabbit* of Jefferson Airplane. The Gunslinger fugues out, goes on the nod, has lapser tendencies; he drifts into the phenomenology of the actual.

(from Gunslinger Book I, 30) –
    To eliminate the draw / permits an unmatchable Speed
    [a syzygy] which hangs tight / just back of the curtain
    of the reality theater/ down the street,
    speed is not necessarily fast. / Bullets are not necessarily specific.
    When the act is / so self contained and so dazzling in itself
    the target then can disappear/ in the heated tension / which is an
    area between here /and formerly / In some parts of the western
    world men have mistakenly /called that phenomenology —

The tone of Gunslinger was filled with that like-a-rolling-stone feeling: like the great migration of hitchhikers off to look for America. Then cut away to psychedelic riffraff chat; it was book as trip, and it spoke to the many millions who took trips. It had the voice of the 'Slinger, that cool, hip, but caring persona who made life so much more interesting, as he admonished you to Be Aware and feel your being. This kind of writing trained your experience to be aware. It was an allegorical play, staged within an individual consciousness — the waking consciousness talking among the hypnagogic and the super-egoic. The poem shifted around in point of view, speaking directly to Jungian archetypes or personified energy organizations through the exegesis of the "cautious Gunslinger/ of impeccable personal smoothness," moving across a landscape searching for "Purity of the Head," a noble goal, the openness to Enlightenment. It was about being able to Slow Down to free yourself from "the theatre of the impatient." With its druggy puns and Freudian slips and signifier slides it was certain to be admitted into the cannon of western literature, representative of my generation. It has the theme of the dissolving ego, the giving up control by the fearful I. "I" is one of the characters who evolves from the speaking narrator. "I" keeps asking dumb, wrong, inappropriate, apprentice questions in the humor of Carlos Castaneda jotting madly while his reality is being undone. In Book 1 or Book I, "I" encounters the Gunslinger, with his stoned-talking, joint-rolling horse who might be Heidegger or Levi-Strauss. Levi Strauss was studying the savage mind. (*Pensee Sauvage*) though this could be natural thought, or wild mind. Yes. We were all struggling to understand structuralism and signifier and signifying and all that. The Science of the Concrete. An artist must be a bricoleur, and learn to live on what is at hand. Art Concrete. Hippies love puns in their literature as we are introduced to the Poet weaving reality on the strings of the loom of the abso-lute. Here is POV shifting back and forth with the refugee I.

(from Gunslinger Book I, 40) –
    are you hungry / mortal I / the Gunslinger asked
    And Yes I answered reflecting

The story is about the dissolution of the ego. In book II, I gets transmorgified. In the story "I" has died and the Poet is filling I with the batch of LSD that Kool Everything had brought onto the stage. Written in 1967, this is a most epi-phenomenal statement of the whole human potential movement, spoken in the language of alchemy.

(from Gunslinger Book I, 33) –
    Your batch is now The batch / expropriation is accomplished
    we stand before an original moment
    in ontological history, the self, with one grab
    has acquired a capital S, mark the date
    the Gunslinger instructed / we'll send a telegram to Parmenides.

Characters speak in different voices. Lil has a real Texas twang, the Narrator is kind of collegiate, and 'Slinger is very cool, smooth, on top of it. He reminds me of my cool hip friend trying to get me out my over achieving, white-boy, report-card personality.

Gunslinger is dreamlike and surreal. Characters riding in a stagecoach include a horse capable of speech and of rolling joints; the "stage" pulled by six driverless horses. They pick up a hitchhiker named Kool Everything who is transporting a five gallon can of LSD. The issue of what to do with I's body gets resolved by the Poet pouring I full of the LSD. There is an element of Hunter Thompson's gonzo *Fear & Loathing* journalism in Gunslinger. But where *Fear and Loathing* goes into story, Gunslinger presents the experience more directly like you are in a play.

Against the backdrop of constant travel, into Universe City and Drop City, *Gunslinger* was like the story of my life, or anybody hitchhiking around taking part in the action and the passion of the times in 1967. It was US, a generation driven into being outlaws because of partaking in the divine herb automatically enrolled you in the mythos of being outside the law. I started out as an English major, up in a Canadian college, during the most virulent activity of the Vietnam War. I was interested in writing and the only game in town was the formalist poetry that dominated university English departments then. That summer I ate mescaline with a girlfriend Colleen and it was such a powerful awakening to the world. I went back to the states to Colorado to stay in the Drop City commune outside of Trinidad Colorado. I was there in 1968 when Martin Luther King and Bobby Kennedy were assassinated. I thought of leaving the US for good but decided to study useful Engineering at U of Texas, before the whole world collapsed. I certainly saw my current situation here in Berkeley in "I's" initiation in the cultural underground through the Castaneda humor of being a poet's apprentice, trying to find out what something "means" when supposed to Be Here Now to "see."

Bob saw something in the *'Slinger* poem that was at the heart of physical theatre. What was it? The Savage Mind? The story is about a shape-shifting actor who uses his life as means for instructing others, drawing others into new modes of perception. It really opens up the possibilities of poetry.

There are strange machines in 'Slinger. In Book II when they are in Universe City, there is the Literary Projector machine that converts reality into scripts. It is playing with the writer's ambition. In Book III there is a Turing Machine. Both of these are code translators. There is mention of the Diggers — the High Diggers, and Heidegger. Atrocious puns are very much a part of the way 60s drug lit explored the unconscious. Dorn bores into this bedrock of language with this Turing machine in Book III. We are in a swirling vortex of words and concepts and story. Its subtitle: *The inside real of the outsidereal* is a great epithet for vortex. We see the mood is starting to get jaded with this desperate searching for gurus that went on. A character, Dr. Flamboyant is doing astral projection. There is a lot of Amphictionic Theatre in the Universe City section of Book II.

When I came to Berkeley I brought three essays I had written. One, *Tesseract Theatre* got me invited out here. The essay was an attempt to make some sense of how Bobby was able to psychomorphicly take on and throw off characters as he explored psychological and physical space in his solo performances. This essay explored Euler's formula for the relationship among the faces, edges and corners of a polyhedra, but in four dimensions. Another essay I had written was *The von Neuman Probe*, about the idea of the self-replicating automaton as modern archetype. I was astounded to see Dorn playing with these language-as-virus ideas in Book III.

And the third essay I had written was The *Poem as Mandala*. It made a formal mapping from the matrix that Levi-Strauss used to demonstrate the isomorphism of mythical elements across cultures to the matrix of kinship structures he generalized to all myth. The essay went through Freudian /Structuralism defense mechanisms, mapping them to their Jungian analogs in order to access the circular Self-centric analytic relationships Jung used. I was only able to do this formal connection; I did not really see how encoding, was a general activity, particularly the poet's. I felt sure that Levi-Strauss with his parallel cross-cultural study of mythology would be helpful in understanding the fugal poetry of Pound and Eliot. It was quite a while though before I could see this matrix as their poetic method of composition, almost like the diachronic and synchronic in a crossword puzzle. That was my method too, though I had a much more Off-the-Wall raunch-and-humor conception of it: (Throwing stuff up on the wall, and moving it around to find relationship.) I was a Titivulus, the Conjecturer who collects things from the immediate surroundings of his time. But there was Dorn, with his Turing machine and virus (Burroughs) to translate code, The hod carrier – Finnegan and all the punning (Joyce). Book IIII gets into the idea of the Pythia suspended over a scar in the landscape, the Amphictionic Theatre. In back of it all is the ancient the Parmedian vision of primacy of Forms. It is Vedantic. There is a Metaphysical spirit and it imbues phenomena with cosmic order. We just have to learn to "see" it.

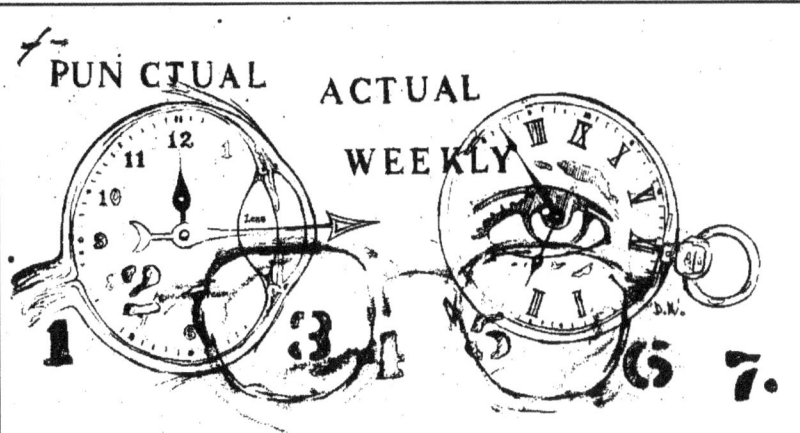

...the great Retinal Art Debate continues.

hers and Sisters and other Sentient
ing;
    The Actualist Institute is opening
walk-up-and-jive or call-in free floating
poetry extravaganza this Sunday afternoon
June 13. The lines will be open to all
questions concerning actual absurdities,
arcane assiduancies of horology, the yoga
of rhetoric, rock and roll healing,
erotica esoterica and other burning
issues of tromp d'oil satori.
    Representing the concept of Limited
Omniscience, Jim Nisbet will read from
his novel, The A Committee Considers Help
As Power and Thermodynamics Crawls Home to
Sleep, and a (tenatively) lyric poem, 'Ode
to a Grecian Landlady'.
    Representing the Frictionless Floors
College of Knowledge Michael Lyons will
read from his novel Ontological Hysteria
and the Austintejas Stomp. Can solipsism
triumph over coincidence?
    Darrell Gray, the Actual Dada will
read from his novel The Man Who Glowed
in the Dark as well as some fundamental
damage to the concept of time in The
Story of Men.
    G.Krishna Rao will show his
film 'R.Conlin'. D. Gilson will soundsurface
    Come see antagonists foil with
protagonists in the Great Retonal Art
Debate. There will be rising action,
climax and falling action galore as
these masters of streetology take the
floor. Don't be late, come and relate.
Shake those beatific attitudes from
out of the etudes. No spare changing
alowed.
        --Starry Night
Often times I've heard the word
'decorative' used with an edge of malise
applied to certain forms of art. What I
want to know is 'What do you mean'?
    As I understand it, the most essential
characteristics of visual art is that it is
a real thing you can look at. Perhaps the
question concerns the utility of Art.
    Art functions as a reinforcement of th
the subjective identity. It is the man-
ifest relationship of human & object. With
sufficient strength, respect and compassion
any form can become art. R. Conlin

GETTING OFF IN MY ROOM

I usually didn't have much
trouble finding a hit, but
this day I was having
difficulty. I had sort of
gone into a trance, making
hole after hole, just
waiting for the moment
when I'd finally get the hit
squeeze it in, and feel the
warmth rushing all over.
There were little
lines of blood running
from all the fucked up hits.
I was putting maybe the
15th hole in my arm, and there
was a knock at my door.
I swelled with panic.
"Who is it?", I snarled.
My father, sounding
a little shaken by
the tone of my voice, said
"It's me, I want to
ask you something, are
you busy?" I didn't
know what to say to
keep him out. Then
suddenly I had it.
"Yeah, I'm jerking
off!"
There was a silence
at the door. "Oh,
O.K., sorry."

--Copyright David Lerner
ABSURD ACTUAL REPORTER
    out of harmony with reason or
propriety, in congrueous, unreasonable,
illogical   in modern use, E.S.P.--
plainly opposed to reason and hence
(riduculous, silly)
'Our heavenly poesy, that sacred off spring
from the braine of Jove thus to be
mangled with prophane absurds.
Actual: of or pertaining to acts;exbiled
in deeds; practical, active,
abounding in action, actual, energetic.
existing in act or fact;realy act, or
acting, carried out; real;-- opposed
to potential, possible, virtual,
theoretical, ideal

Front Page of Punctual Actual Weekly #6 May 1, 1975. Unpaginated, assorted typefaces, staplebound mimeograph job, untrimmed 8.5 x 14, on low quality fuzzy paper

A New Zine on the Scene

Soon after I began to hang out with these people of the Pit, it seemed like a good idea to start some kind of a magazine with Darrell Gray. This is how it happened. Darrell and Peter and I, were in Darrell's room laughing at the great one line poem in Darrell's book *Something Swims Out.*:
"The stones have come so far they cannot speak."
I mentioned Ezra Pound's, "The apparition of these faces in a crowd, petals on a wet black bough."
Darrell Gray said, "Yes the minimalist poem, the Image." He talked about the minimalist poem. How it was like a haiku. Or just the perception of a gestalt.
He mentioned Dave Morice's "A cigarette is a glass of milk."
And I asked, "Is that about the oral fixation?"
"That might be a Freudian interpretation," he quickly retorted. And he mentioned one of Phillip Waylen: "The tears ran down her face like tractors."
"That sounds like a country western song," I said. And I went into my most cigarette-ravaged, whiskey-mellowed, mush-mouth, Road Hog voice: "It was raining down in Texas, when I plowed beside the house. / Yes it was raining down in Texas, I was plowing by the wall. / I wiped out my baby's tulips; my blade chopped them one and all. / The tears ran down her face like tractors when she saw what I had done. / Oh The tears ran down her face like tractors when she saw what I had done. I tried to tape them back together but she went and got her gun."
Darrell and Peter hooted and laughed at this.
"OO! oo," I said. "I had a minimalist poem like that happen to me yesterday. I was walking down on the beach — Dave took me all the way over to San Francisco to the beach, and when I was walking along the strand, I got to thinking about the sand and how it comes from ground up mountains, comes from rocks way high up on mountains that tumble down rivers to the sea where it gets ground down into smaller and smaller rocks until it gets ground down to sand and it can't get ground down any more. And I was thinking about the end of the universe, how the universe will end in a heat death, when all the

energy is converted to entropy and there isn't any thing different from anything else. And the metaphor occurred to me: Sand is the white noise of matter."

They enjoyed this. Darrell said, "You know they are doing research on dolphins and some think they can communicate with the same sense modalities with which they take in images. You know they bounce sonar off the terrain and do all this image mapping on what comes back. Then they can send that same sense data to the next dolphin, so that the next dolphin can get the same EXPERIENCE in his brain as the first dolphin. Isn't hat amazing?"

"Yeah."

"We are like dolphins swimming in text," Darrell said.

I mentioned, "Green ideas sleep furiously," and we talked about Chomsky and Deep Grammar. And how that relates to surrealism — the red eggs of fortune. And we talked, or rather he talked and I listened, about the categorical background that metaphor provides to all thought and how the surrealist pursued this as a methodological program of deranging the senses with poetry.

"I am looking for a generative grammar of the poem," he said.

"Me too."

I said, "You have all this lilting and lifting, and floating and aggrandizing imagery in your poems in *Something Swims Out*." I was being flattering, and he smiled at that, but moved the conversation into poetry itself, rather than about him. Darrell Gray, as I would come to find out from knowing him over a long time, had taught himself more about the art of poetry than anyone I would ever meet and was perhaps the upholder, the conduit, the keeper of the poetic tradition in our time.

We were an eclectic bunch. I said, "With all this talent around, we ought to start a magazine." And Darrell Gray's eyes lit up at the idea. A great back and forth high speed enthusiastic discussion ensued. Then we talked about Actualism. These guys had manifestos and everything. Actualism was our cause. And we wanted to make some kind of public art that was free and enjoyable. He told me: "If we could get a few issues of a Literary Magazine out, then it would be easy to get a grant."

And I believed him. Darrell Gray was our inspiration. To describe him he had this great open moon face. Round and jowly, though later he got the broken up veins of someone given too much to drink. His speech was a bit like Johnny Carson, quick and witty but with that Midwest sincerity — he was from Iowa. There was a lot of Yule

Gibbons in his demeanor as well as Will Rogers. And a touch of Bob Dylan too.

He would be a most generous senior editor, for everybody in the poetry community knew who he was and respected him. And perhaps a little of that glow would fall on me too, his gopher and printer's devil, by association. I wanted to do something to repay the generosity shown by the Blake St. Hawkeyes to the community. They (like everyone who knew him) knew Darrell Gray was special. He had an enormous generosity, he wasn't like the arch arrogance and bitchery that had become poetry — the left-handed, red-hair bastard child of the arts — trying to get a place at the table of so few resources. Or even worse, the place I was coming from —Texas where, like most of America, they see any attempt at creativity as an immediate attack on their personal psychology and that they should exercise their god-given right to smite this unrighteous religiosity or at least immediately disregard it as something not worth bothering their mind about. Whenever we got together, in Darrell's basement apartment he'd read somebody else's poetry aloud. We'd talk and laugh, then load a fresh sheet of paper into the typewriter and start to do a collaborative poem. It was like jamming with a great musician, and an extremely funny person, he'd be cleaving space with the clarity of his images and we'd all be typing and giggling.

So that's how it started — a place to publish collaborations and to help the Blake Street Hawkeyes get some butts into the theatre seats. I named the magazine Punctual Actual Weekly. First, because it was a vehicle of Actualism. Second because we felt like punks of the literary world; it was a celebration of the do-it-yourself punk ethos. I felt so marginalized and impoverished in my life and in looking up at the great works of literature and that system of publishing and review and academia that supported it and that I wanted to, in some way be part of, make contributions to, that I felt like a punk. Also the word Punctual had connotations of time, as well as puncture. We were going to try and be a weekly but I don't think we ever, well maybe once, we got two issues out within a week between issues. I liked the acronym PAW, because — and this was just for me, for if you want to know something about me, I seemed to have so seriously confused my head with my heart, my mind with my feelings, that for me Newton and the calculus and Leibniz and the monads were like the greatest feeling poetry. And the line, "You shall know the lion by the mark of his paw" written by Leibniz about Newton, in a letter became my secret masthead for the Punctual

Actual Weekly. The story of how the calculus was developed, the logical, notational, linguistical aspect of Leibniz and the embedded physical picture of how everything works in the functional universe way of Newton, is perhaps the greatest story ever told.

I was ready; I had experience working on a zine: I had helped Paul Spragens on *The Salamander Weekly*, organ of The Church of the Coincidental Metaphor in Austin. So the Punctual Actual Weekly was right at the right time. My layout design education was classical mimeograph school, mixed with elements of collage aesthetic. Though I had never been to design school I did have a lot of experience using the vector force diagrams of physics — to abstract out of the physical world the forces operant in a situation, connect these into a diagrammatic gestalt, and associate them with words and the concatenation of words into symbols of a math-logic-linguistic formula. I would gather material from everywhere, from the many posters tacked up on the avenues of Berkeley adding new life, new interpretations of the human potential movement. I collected graffiti from the Cafe Med and other coffee shops. I was an anthropologist in a strange land of hip erudition. I could not afford to use the electric typewriters in the basement of the Berkeley library to I did first layout on a free mechanical one.

I can picture the moment, in the studio when it started. I was in Russ's studio in the Pit and I started my wall: it was my writing practice to collect bits of writing and stick them up on a wall so I could look at them. I was kind of a collage writer, a Titivulus, an archivist, a hit and run graffiti writer of verbal art. The PAW started out of a letter. To me, the letter to a friend, filled with intimate horny humor talking to somebody you trusted and wanted to let know you was the highest uses of writing. Dave was away and I got to use the typewriter in the studio. I was writing:

> <u>Scene:</u> Late at night in a Warehouse on Berkeley's Auto Row. White sheet rock walls of Russel's studio. The gigantic table in the middle made of 4 sheets of plywood butted together 2x2 to make 8 by 16 rectangle. He had put his work away in a giant taboret; his tools, T-square and tape etcetera he hung on the wall when he finished for the day. At the back wall a stove on top of a funky painted chest of drawers.

> <u>Scene:</u> Looking down from the loft on top of the door. On the wall to the right, Russell has a piece that he calls *Conditionals*, that he made from dipping sheets of canvas into resin, then hung them out

to dry in the wind, so that they captured the shape of the wind. And they had captured it too. It was strangely beautiful. Art on canvas created by nature. Duchamp would have loved it.

<u>Scene</u>: Alcove of the studio, with a couch and a coffee table. I am sitting on the couch and typing a letter on Dave's old Underwood. He's left on some kind of tour. The letter, started and stopped and added to over a period of days to a friend back in Texas in part reads:

— Lust her. Any way we got back to the space and I cooked a nice spaghetti dinner and we got to laughing and carrying on, you know and what not, and I was getting the hots to see and touch her extraordinary Jewish quim. Dave was outa town see, and I had the place to myself. Well, we got up in the magic carpet loft, and I read her a story just like one of them artists showing a sketch, and she laughed at it, gentle like because it was communicating with her. And after a while she was sort of a fidgeting around, you know, running her elegant long fingers over the head of the bed spread, pullin' at it like, and I's wondering should I, on the first git-together, and course this being Berkeley and all and such long spells between touch that I couldn't afford to blow another one. But I finally screw up the courage to take her hand and fluster along with some small talk about her nails, and then I reached up and hugged her and she had these nice soft Jewish lips that opened and were wet and sent me wild. Well me an her rasseled around like a couple of puppies in heat for a while and then she had to git up and go to the bathroom and this big ole dumb sonobitch Irishman with red hair and beard kept her out in the hall talking about bicycles, and what not and trying to score. They ain't got no kind of Southern gentility our here at all, pard. But she came back , and I threw a hasty, thrusty fuck into her for all that, and she was extraordinary and we're going to Golden Gate Park tomorrow.

— I'm trying to start a tabloid journal like the old Salamander Weekly. I want the newspaper to be a wall where you can throw stuff up on it and look at it for a while and see how it all hangs together. There's a tremendous lot of literary bullshit status going on out here, I hope to god it don't get me, Top Con. Tell Burnt Rib that he could have them eatin' out of the palm of his hand.

— I just got up to chase a little mouse making a run for it across the space toward the food pile. Then turned on the radio. At 6 o'clock Sunday morning they got jazz here. Ain't that wonderful.

— Russell has a piece that he calls Conditionals, that he made from dipping canvas sheets into resin, then hung them out to dry in the wind, so that they captured the shape of the wind, and they have captured it too. Ole Pard, it looks so wild to see these three transparent sheets blowing out of a wall into the studio. This guy has a light airy touch and a lot of nerve to try things.

— Bertrand Russel and Max Earnst. These people meet in me. And l don't understand it. Max Occupancy and Vast Thirst. By the way did you know that Artaud has written a book called the *Peyote Cult* in which he goes down to Mexico to hang out with the Indians and eats some peyote and writes about the theatre shaman. Also there's another book called *Rolling Thunder* about medicinal cure by herbs, and theatre shamanism. Myself, I'm caught up in trying to be a cosmic a clown. Follow the Hotei Tao of Physics. Stitching and weaving these multiple realities, into a vision of America. The Pilgrims Progress Report. I'm thinking of starting a newspaper called the Punctual Actual, and just giving it away at the University of Berkeley, cause it's springtime, and I'm 27 and in love with this place.

— Bob Ernst has a lovely passage in Trunk 15: I look around / and see / my own eyes / beside boxes / around corners / within dreams.

— We talk about going out and capturing the movement of the street. Of being coincidentally aware. Like traffic is a sequence of little dots. The artist again becomes an experimentalist. There is a sequence of sounds in the traffic. It is not connected to the 12 tone row, or the harmonic scales, or minonian, perhaps it is a Fibonacci sequence of sounds. Regardless, it is captured by <u>verbing</u> instead of sequencing nouns. Trying to get back to what its own thing is, getting back to the pure sound and motion in the universe. Being all part of the same thing. Phiety. Phidelity.

— Mantra-sound; tantra-light, visual; yantra-motion.
This is how the Hindu metaphysics is constructed, from pure mind, rather than by a huge body of empirical findings. I would like to construct a transcendental physics based upon pure mind. I too am looking for the space time code of the universe. A transcendental physics in which one could "see" symbols like seeing the variable, the forces in mathematical equations. What does a real concrete symbol look like?
Mudra told me; Yantra told me; Mantra told me; Tantra told me too. Its not the UFO's and the coming contact with higher intelligence beyond space that makes me high; it's the movement. Like an

elephant trudging through tundra, I hope you like the crunch even though it is only peanut butter.

A tip from the people at the Food Project about community access to the press, lead me to the right organization and the PAWs started coming off the mimeograph press. There were some community support centers that we talked into letting us use their mimeograph. We would walk around on campus giving them away. Shout a jeering challenge at a long-haired student like: "Down with long hair on campus!" And proffer an issue.

Darrell Gray sent issues of PAW to many famous poets in the hopes that they would send in poems for us to publish.

"It would be a place where famous poets could let their hair down," he said. We also sent copies to academia and our intellectual heroes Noam Chomsky and Carl Sagan and Gregory Bateson and Will Burroughs, Alan Ginsberg, Anne Waldman, Choygam Trunkpa and other people at the Jack Kerouac School of Disembodied Poetics.

Bob Ernst has a pensive reflective grace in an early issue.

```
Fish, water boat
    anvil clash
            the sea
                    over
                    and over
                    again
 waves lapping waves lapping / waves
undertow of solitude
fisheyes breath me to sleep
from a distance of water,
a far off shore is visible
barely a flute tone in the sight,
        a breathiness of clouded vision
                far off shore
```

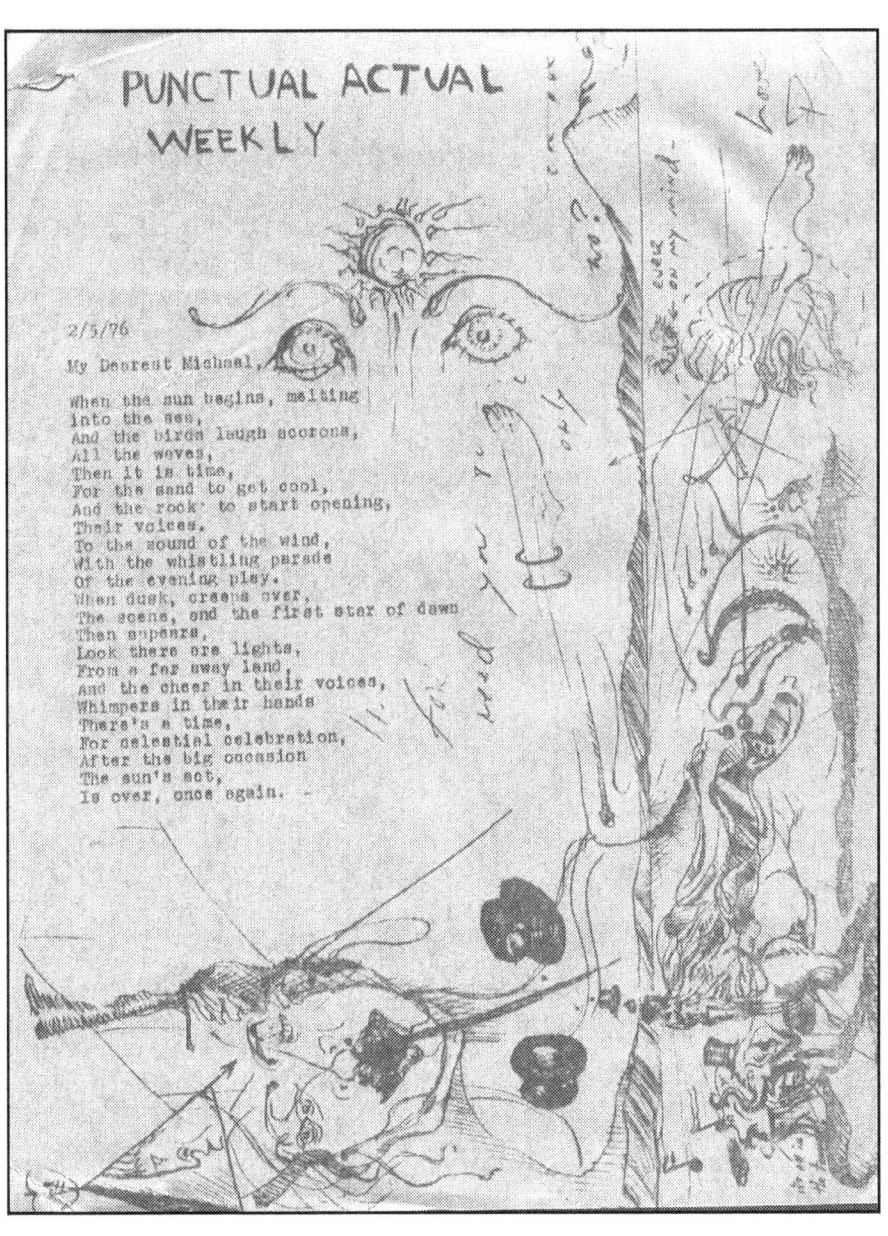

Early Punctual Actual Weekly page by Roux with hand-lettered masthead

What is Actualism

Well of course that is one of those questions that if we could answer it, the answer would not be an actualism. We get into the problem of Tristram Shandy, that it takes longer to codify a realization than it does to actually have one. But basically we could say that actualist poetry is poetry about objects of the common world. Or we could say that it was a brief, lucky, happy-go-lightly time in poetry when readings and poetry were about connection at least on some level with someone. But there is a lot more to it than that, as we shall see. We could say that it was a cross-sorting of small talk and big talk (as O'Hara showed us how to do). Or we could say that it was the reaction to the deepening influences of ecology, relativity, quantum mechanics and uncertainty, and chaos, and an attempt to go beneath the real, beneath the existential to the forces forming reality. But let us not get ahead of ourselves.

Let us look at the concrete example of an Actualist poem by Darrell Gray, *The Syntax*.

from *(Gray's* Essays and Dissolutions, *Translations from Silence, 83)*

    The Syntax

    How well we remember the accidents
    like strands of hair
    on the polished table,
    and before what you said,
        wasted or devised.

    I saw the top of your head (the neckline
        and the branches,
    branches imposed themselves against
    your face
    accidentally dark

    the wet leaves
    slanting
        the window

Darrell Gray's poem is a good example of an actualist work

because it is both looking through and looking at. It presents the situation of using your optical machinery: To see a thing we must adjust our visual apparatus in a certain way. In this poem we are looking at the face. Looking at what the face is looking at. Looking through the eyes in the face. Vision travels through the pane AND it is detained at the window AND it looks at the garden outside. The either-or opposites which exclude each other have been accommodated into a both-and. This, penetrating beneath the surface of reality to deeper forces shaping reality, and this, fusing logical opposites, are attributes of an Actualist poem. Gray continues the passage to discuss how *The Syntax* emerged:

> Here, I was consciously working with 'e's, 'i's and 'o's, vowels with 'a's generously interspersed. The consonants fell into place almost by themselves. I didn't calculate them, for what I wanted was the openness of statement, statement becoming recognition in the act of its finding a term for itself, in my attention. Hence the *looseness* of the poem. At the outset, I didn't know exactly what I wanted to *say*. I considered the occasion an almost musical one, in which variables of sound and meaning would seek a norm, and that norm turned out to be one of vowels. On retrospect, the norm became too dominant, and the verb which should have been most active, whatever its linguistic orientation, was "imposed"... too weak a word to carry the impact of the statement itself. I tried alternate words: thrust, whirled, dilated, even the word "honed." But what I wanted to *say* always intervened. I wanted to say simply that the branches, intimate as the branching blood vessels of the eye, intervened between the larger reality that I was, in the poem, trying to establish between myself and the person addressed.

Darrell Gray's *Actualism — A Manifesto* opens with: "Actuality is never frustrated because it is always complete." It was the crowning moment of any Actualist Convention when Darrell Gray brought out and unleashed the *Manifesto*. It was like bringing out the sacred relics from the tabernacle of the mind and through the monstrance of his soaring humor, letting the warriors see them. I read it in a nice academic-looking journal called Gum. It was a series of short aphoristic precepts, 15 one-liners. Another one went: "We write in words to disguise ourselves, as a protection from the fact that *words* are writing us." We can see in this the sense of modern post-uncertainty zeitgeist, the prolegomena of the poet's work: to enter into and engage more and more deeply the processes of semiosis at work in the world of which we are information in its circuit. It is semiosis that transforms sounds into words, and word sequences through transformational grammar into concept structures, through which we know and are known. I read that aphorism as, Actualism is a writing art as a vaccine against any kind of literacy that was not self-aware, but only continued to purvey received ideas driven by marketing forces, that sought only to manipulate the user towards the ends of its convention and that did not lead to an opening of the field. We didn't have the concept or meme or episteme but knew being absorbed into the system was coercive; there was a transcendental reality that we had to be trying to get to. At the time I thought all art should aspire to the actualism of improvisational jazz. For me that sense of being in the moment that jazz gave you, (no doubt heightened by moving the participants sense of involvement through its basic time structure being syncopated syncopation) was such a bracing attention. You felt like you were on the edge, moving into the now. Actualism was like existentialism drained of its nihilism and infused with jubilance. Actualism sought to supplant the real with intimations of the possible. By letting the reader feel himself adrift somewhere in uncertainty, he could participate more in the shared creative act. For me at the time, Actualism was from the Beats, that rollicking road quest, of being a stranger in a strange land. I was not at the Iowa Writers Workshop where Darrell studied with Ted Berrigan and Anselm Hollo as they brought the New York school to the west, where it got infused with a kind of cosmic cowboy / indigenous shaman psychedelic roots thing mixed with the west coast Buddhist beatniks be-bop jazz sensibilities. I was into all this and the absurdist humor of Texas, mixed with the intellectual sci-fi of Pynchon, Borges, Burroughs, and blended with my own sense of *puer eternalis* in J.D. Salinger. Too, I was on a quest for the modern contemporary myth in science, and its language of forms, mathematics. I was after a literature that reflected the profound changes in our understanding of the world given us by quantum mechanics. As I look back on it now, I see these aphorisms in the *Manifesto* were related to the philosophy Darrell Gray already understood and which would ultimately be the Vedanta verified in a full-on Kantian exposition. Another aphorism is the analogy: "Actualism is to Chemistry what Fatalism was to the Middle Ages." This shows, humorously the hubris of how Actualism was to fulfill Valery's prologomena for poetry to be a chemistry for as yet undiscovered elements. The manifesto ends with: "What, belabor the impossible?" A goof on Alfred E. Neuman.

I read Darrell Gray's essay titled *What is Actualism* in another journal, The North Stone Review. I learned that the opening line in the Manifesto was from William Carlos Williams. We do not get a simple answer for our question, What is Actualism? But in this essay Gray introduces the concept of the Automorph which is a rich symbol to lead us into a perception of the Actual. It is a hilarious and wonderful and intimate and surrealist essay. In it he keeps a fine parallel construction going. He uses an image to start us off on the aesthetic experience that is making distinctions through language.

> Distinctions occur in the world, it is true: a beautiful young woman may be seen pushing a baby carriage into the park across the street from where you are walking, and you may thing how odd it is that this is so.

The essay into aesthetics continues, while moving our mind around in a space, following a story about a woman pushing a baby carriage. This whole idea of *the spatialization of mind* is a central one in modern poetics and practiced rigorously in the amphictionic theatre. Stated as a metaphorical equation:

voyage in space = quest for being.

In the essay the revolving wheels on the baby carriage bring us back to the *field* of movement that Gray wants to talk about. He makes a stunning statement about what poetry is.

> And the thought of sadness leads also like a reflection on the water's surface. But where? Where does it lead, you ask? And the answer comes to you that it leads into a waiting, a waiting stretched so thin that it shines. So shining waits and includes its waiting, and shining is actual, as poetry is actual and shining.

This image of poetry as a waiting depicts poetry as being on a path that has been changed, deflected; we are given an unexpected pause. We have the three concepts, waiting, shining and the actual convolved here. A shining waiting, would bespeak a mind that was self-aware enough to be involved with the processes of the moment, rather than an impatient waiting for what was next. It suggests rather than the ego grasping and planning, it is waiting neither bored nor pushing nor desperate, but simply present, ready.

It is an image of poetry as a reflection on the surface of water, a shining on time's surface. This visual metaphor — that REALITY IS A MIRROR, reflecting the world of the possible, a mirror in which the world of the actual is reflected — would become a central study in Gray's essays. It is the central metaphor of the Vedas, and also of Peirce's semiology.

In the next passage Gray suggests that the function of art is to engage in a game of mirrors that gets us involved in being caught up in an aesthetic movement— the purpose of which is to be brought back to a kind of stasis.

> Surely if one goes back far enough, back to the first or "Alpha-Street" the turning will cease. And the stillness will be beautiful again, and not the terror of stillness that is the deserted streets of the world.

Then he introduces his idea of the Automorph, a sensed presence in the stillness at the heart of the world where we have been brought by poetry.

> If one is a poet one goes back to the original stillness to find what it is he has lost. Whatever it is, he has lost it by being a man. He will not find it by being a man any longer. Which is to say he will not be a man when he gets there. He will be an Automorph.

To explain, he condenses the parallelism of the essay down into an analogy:

> . . . for an Automorph is to man what a man is to his dreams, desires and loves. And here is the strange part — strange only because it is so near we do not notice — the Automorph dwells within the being of every man, as well as every animal, tree and flower.

This concept of a knowable state at the heart of the universe is one what will inspire much thinking and art. It sounds pantheistic. It is the universe of the possible emerging into the actual, and to be present at that is a state worthy of art. We will see later when we explore Gray's commentary on the Vedanta in his essay *The Transcendental Critique of Knowledge*, that the Automorph is Atman. In that essay he studied extensively the reaction to apprehending or trying to perceive, the emergence of this atomistic Atman into the world of the actual from the world of the possible through various coercive integrities and the process of noumenal ingression, phenomenology. This mode of being of itself, the Atman, is what Peirce calls Firstness; Secondness is the Actual. Here Gray anthropomorphizes the sensed presence into a character. Let us explore the analogy. Automorph:man::man:dreams.

I read that to mean the automorphic self is an adjective for the Self of Jung, that organization of energies that we have inherited from evolution that emerges when we experience joy reflected in our art. The analogy goes: Dreams, loves, desires are created in man's mind to help him know himself, to guide him — while in a much larger parallel universe outside — man himself is the dream or the fantasy, the love impulse of the Automorph, which is an archetypal organization of matter seeking to know itself. Seeking to know itself through man by allowing itself to be seen by man in the form of love, in the form of dream, in the form of myth, and art and in the pursuit of desire.

Now the Analogy is something I loved. In its expression as ratio and proportion, it is the fundamental beautiful idea of mathematics. To me the analogy is the great equalizer, the thing that connects poetry and logic and mathematics all watched over by rhetoric exploiting the analogy. The basis of ciphering, the movement in the mind. It is the process of sign-making that Gray has anthropomorphized into a character for us. Notice the progression of this essay from image to icon to indexical movement to symbol. It is the semiosis process of the universe emerging, becoming actual.

What a wonderful word, automorph. It has a special meaning in geology: it is another name for metamorphic rock, a class of rock containing the gemstones. Gems are made from intense heat and pressure and at a certain phase their lattice structure falls into crystalline alignment creating perfect containers for moving and reflecting light. Also there are automorphic functions in mathematics: these are transcendental functions which are their own derivative — the natural logarithm based on the transcendental exponential e, for example. Another association in my mind is autopoeisis, self-making. The emergence of chaos out of randomness, and order out of chaos is an autopoeisis process. This suggests to me the endless cycles of the yin and yang, shadow and light all opposites generating energy from association with each other. Jung called this process enatiodromia, made from the root word *enatio* meaning mirror and *dromia* to run, for the tendency of processes to run into and emerge from their opposite. Metaphoricity is an automorphic function, performing transformative yet form-and-relation-preserving mappings across domains.

In *What is Actualism* Gray talks about wanting to have poems be a kind of generative verse. He wanted to write poems that make you want to jump up and go *do* something. *What is Actualism* is all about movement. He personifies the primary unconscious when he talks about the Automorph moving very rapidly in man's dreams.

> Man waits for feelings to come to him, but in the Automorph they are already there. Man dreams, but the Automorph has no need to, for what is a

dream when everything is equally present and equally clear. Man's dreams are merely the shadows of the Automorph's joyous movements and sometimes when it is moving very rapidly man's dreams are thrashing into glowing images, fragments of desire hurled down from the physical world, and these images obsess and perturb the sleeper, making him forget who he is.

Gray talks about the artist's ego and how it makes him feel separate, and how art and poetry seek to make him feel ego-less.

Can it be that art makes us sad by trying to protect us from that which poses no threat? I think that is true, for there is something in man that wants to feel it is different. It wants to be the *only* man, when it is very much more. Some call this the "ego" by which they mean a distinction between "man" and "Nature."

He goes on to suggest the artists' ego — of "having to change themselves or the world to heighten their sense of uniqueness" is the source of the Pathetic Fallacy of poems stuffed with symbols and metaphors, how they appear dredged up.

To be actual is not to possess Actuality — it is to be possessed by it. William Carlos Williams, a great Actualist poet, once wrote: "Actuality is never frustrated because it is always complete."

Darrell Gray was greatly influenced by WCW. For Williams writes about things just as they are. He uses short lines one for each detail so that it may shimmer out of its background and appear new. Just how does actualism fit in the history of ideas. Toward the end of the essay Darrell Gray writes:

I want to emphasize that Actualism is not an aesthetic 'Movement" in the usual sense of the word. It owes noting to literary history that it could not find elsewhere, least of all aesthetic theory or literary criticism. Actualism begins when the Automorph in man's being decides to wake him up. When this waking-up occurs in *language*, the result is an actualist poem, novel, or play.

Gray gives many sources for his thoughts on Actualism, WCW was certainly one. The good doctor brought a lot of new life into poetry after EZ and TS had taken it into academia where it pined in an ivory tower that only a few could scale. Though I, at the time, thought very highly of Pound and Eliot, still do, there is much more sweetness to be had from learning what other poets have taught us about seeing. The titles for most of Gray's books were phrases from WCW. Scattered Brains, the Beauties of Travel, Something Swims Out, Halos of Debris. He read the master well.

The poets are inspired by trying to understand some grand design. Walt Whitman, really saw it. I was so touched by reading his poetry when I was a young hippie, embarking on many long transcontinental hitchhiking voyages. I wanted to *experience* life, I wanted to really *exist*. Look at the world and see. I did cast my fate to the open road and revel in just being and knowing I was part of something great. Hippies are Walt Whitman's wild children. Whitman started the human potential movement with his great realization, his great awakening. Like the Buddha did. The Beats saw it. As did Kerouac and Castaneda. Einstein and the Surrealists also had great awakenings. There are many paths in. The main thing is to get on *some* path and to follow it in. Into what. Through a world of signs that lead us (by a concatenation of metaphorical substitutions and mapping traversing heretofore unseen connections among categories of being) into a space of transcendence that we have always been hungry for. Where we can be taken out of our little finite world of concerns into the great wave of being at this moment, and know we are in it. Part of all existence.

We were not interested in the mood in T.S. Eliot, the despair, the fatigue, the pleading dryness. Though we did appreciate how he created this mood. Darrell Gray would go on to deeply study Tone. Darrell Gray was also influenced by the wondrous way Wallace Stevens had of using words to expand the senses, to discover things and make them new. Not to mention the whole metaphysics of thought in language. And for Darrell Gray writing verse was like programming, or ciphering the space time, it was verse that connected our multiverse to the universe. Darrell Gray was a formalist using rhyme and rhythms sparingly, when it seemed natural. Yeats is like that. But the actualist symbols are there or not, something on the periphery coming in. Poetry was liberated by Olson from being a slave to forms. Poetry that forced the sense into a form so hard that the expression is warped into something untrustworthy was seen to be inauthentic. Actualist wanted to be present to receive forms that emerge from beyond the individual mind, from the deep mind of the universe through metaphor, and the entrainment of rhythm. That's it! Beauty is an entrainment. As the Romantics knew and were empowered by forms to go out and look at your world. And see then through your own eyes, but eyes educated. Poems are vehicles to carry memes, but liberating memes, like science is.

Darrell Gray was inspired by an idea, by a kind of intellectual pantheism vision of life. The idea was something like this: that, the actual was going on within and without you, it was always going on, it will continue to go on, and just by being here you are part of the unfolding of this vast chaos with hidden symmetries, and currents and harmonies so profoundly intertwined — but more than that you could *know*, you could travel with your mind into these interpenetrating spheres of flowing being and come to know it in your feelings and understand it in your mind.

He called this liveliness, this animation, this force driving behind life, the Automorph. And it wants to know itself through us, we are peripheral senses for it and it is our job to wake up from the sleep and really realize that we are part of a great universe, and there is a lot more to see and hear, and we could if we would just wake up. Metaphoricity might be a better term, or the cascade of serotonin in the frontal lobes produced by neuronal resonance, or the catastrophic unrush of beauty. It was the function of poetry and art to wake us up. A practice, a commitment. Gray's poetry was a celebration of that. His essays an exposition of it.

At the time my education in poetry didn't get much past Pound and Elliot. Darrell and Peter started my education. "A lot has happened in poetry since then. We had William Carlos Williams. We had Frank O'Hara. And Creely. And the Beats. There have been whole different kinds of schools. You need to get up to speed."

Darrell Gray got me going on line beaks and WCW. He said: "Poets always ask me, where should I break my lines. They can break them over their knee for all I care. It is about the object arranging itself in the poem."

"Here is a nice poem by William Carlos Williams," he said. "You might like it." And he read Nantucket by WCW.

(from WCW, Pictures from Breugal, 54)

> Flowers through the window
> lavender and yellow
>
> changed by white curtains —
> Smell of cleanliness—
>
> Sunshine of late afternoon—
> On the glass tray
>
> a glass pitcher, the tumbler
> turned down, by which
>
> a key is lying— And the
> immaculate white bed

"Look at the transparency across frames and in reflections here. It is the objective and dare I say cubist style. That is, there are no people in it. It is very painterly and visual."

I realized I never do this kind of poetry of the object myself. I might be missing a huge opportunity. It is wonderfully visionary. It instills quiet stasis and sends you out to find or create moments like these in your own life. I tried to write something like Nantucket about the Hawkeye theatre room which I loved, with its floor of carpeted stage riser platforms, and its focusing and releasing of experiences.

> Snarl of trumpet vines —
> covering the back window wall
>
> a wonder of green chaos—
> reclaiming the black burglar bars.
>
> Sunlight changed by piercing —
> through meshed glass — mosaics of time
>
> like the Louvre — a pyramid-shaped sky-light
> to let it all fall — in the white action theatre

I interviewed Peter and Darrell a lot. I called Peter, Maestro. He was so cranky and garrulous and gruff and vituperative. Yet full of hope and funny. Yes Maestro. No Maestro. He seemed to like it. After all he was from old Europe. Over time I sort of apprenticed myself to these two. Darrell Gray got me going on WCW and his visual proclivities. I got going on a Cubist Poem.

a cubist at work

> a bottle of wine
> set upon a table
> with an 'extraneous' object
> the standard issue heart-shaped box?
> or a potato with clever eyes
>   (oh no, that won't do,
>   it dips into surrealism,
>   this is a cubist painting) —
>   with the world tilted
>   on its axis
> as though the artist were some infinite god-like physicist
>   who could rotate the FRAMES

        of reference
and throw the viewer into a hair-raising roller-coaster ride
    through spaces wild and tame
        beyond his perception.
    And give a sense of omniscient point of view
        from all directions
    a synchronization of several heads.
I'm sitting at a cafe.
I have folded myself into this little table and chair
the object almost self consciously
taking its moment on stage
a table in town and a bottle of wine for eve's
lucid drive through night's desperate fix on life
(without reason, it ends)

with my peripheral vision I follow a hat into traffic;
thirty feet off—
in cubism you float
in a glass-bottomed boat
through a sea of tautologies.
    The clouds are the hills' dreams[1],
these hills at the edge of town.
They rise up to the clouds
like thought
blooms in a blue field
(these dreams of movement)
drifting
across the brow
of a face
    in the mind
        of space.
The painting raises a lot of questions
you can hear . . .
    That's!
        what it does,
    it expresses
    audile space,
        where you can pin point objects
        from a kind of echo location.
    Juan Gris makes a blue, clean, orderly, quietist still life,
    while Braque and Picasso
    create a world of word extensions
    thus causing a frequency of questions
        and explorations
            that startle
into looking beyond the apparent
and fixed (bourgeois?) accepted reality.
It was like stepping out into a dimension of light it was enjoyable
just to see faces moving in the street
Every man his own philosopher.
But I must worry
the vox populi is more a buy committee.
Without sponsorship I will have to move to other professions.
Unless proven, in line, in theme, in space
 the petty bourgeois qualities of our times
will reduce my own inquiry to the question of patronage.
Yes I can see the patron, the sponsor
I can see by the look in his eyes that he wonders if my next move is
to serve him or not.
Words no longer matter,
it is the material that I must move into the light.

---

[1] Actually the trees generate the clouds. Notice they have similarity of shape: the clouds have a trunk that is an invisible column of water vapor that rises up into a canopy where it crosses the dew-point and can show itself.

"Dog. . . !?"

Sometimes, just for the sheer energy of it, or when we'd do acid, O'Keefe would get us all jacked up to run around in the streets of Berkeley playing a game we called "Dog". . . O'Keefe would say: "You come along with me, and remain silent." He smiles his best conspiracy smile. "You just do everything I do." We'd take off moving quick out of Russ's studio, out the back door, through the back gate. Quick across the parking lot, down a driveway and onto the side walk along Dwight Way. We'd run with our arms dangling at our side (like soccer players or Irish dancers), it was about getting out of your head, into your core.

We'd pander along. . . at a slight pitter patter. . . hardly more than a fast walk. . . but layin' it down. We'd move in a pack . . . Down the wide sidewalks along Shattuck Avenue. . . .Others joined the game, Russ, Doug, Me, Dave and soon there were 5 or 6 guys running around the streets and alleys of Berkeley playing "Dog". . . We'd run down Shattuck Avenue, in a kind of zany free-style . . . leaping railings. . . springing off of walls. . . banking off of benches — side straddle hopping through the shrubberies like primates forced out of their trees. . . going single file, nimble and swift like a chorus of Greek dancers along the edge of a curb. . . vault fences . . . Artful dodgers making the urban landscape your personal obstacle course, our playground. It was insanely funny. O'Keefe would have us run through the streets of Berkeley with our hands held up, and fingers bend over under out chin (a plaintiff puppy paw pose.) He had us doing ring around the rosy at a lamppost or a street sign. . . stepping over park benches, anything that got in the way. We always went directly at those massive car blocks, planters the size of a small Volkswagen, that Berkeley has at various intersections. They make it impossible for a car to pass, thus regulating and channeling the flow of traffic. We always ran straight at it, leaping, placing a foot on it and stepping over it. The idea was to transgress all constrictions forbidding movement and to find channels of urban free flow. The main rules were to not move backward, but instead to overcome obstacles fluidly, with grace, originality and finesse.

We were like long-haired Marines, hup hup hup and Berkeley our obstacle course. Like little soldiers for art, and Berkeley was our interactive sculptural garden. . . loping along. . . past the Penny Saver, and up Durant, toward Telegraph avenue. . .shoot up and down stairs without bumping into anyone or getting run over by car...California traffic laws have great respect for pedestrians. O'Keefe might leap into the street and run after the bus; we'd do likewise — moving along the sidewalk in the spring air, out to encounter the obstacles and read the unspoken signs and dare to really be there in the city of Berkeley.

We'd set out, usually heading between the warehouse and the UC Berkeley campus. Once we got on campus we could run up the creek, or across Sproul Plaza, through the Sather Gate doing the Gate of Power, ring round the tower, carillon bells ringing. Up the creek without a paddle into Strawberry fields forever. Along the creek all the way up past the stadium into Strawberry Canyon. We liked to do the Gate of Power through the Sather Gate. The gate of power was something from Castaneda where you ran at break-neck speed over dicey terrain bringing you knees up to your chin so that you could change directions at every step if need be. This engaged the fight or flight response, and it got you in touch with your terror. Our course had various spots along the way where an interesting improvisation had occurred, a twirl around a lamppost, a run upstairs, a slide down a railing or a leap over a wall. A particularly good and expressive move would stay in the Dog Run and you could do it with more grace and style the next time. It became our art work...

   Sometimes we let out a yell as we ran pell-mell down a hill. A kind of giddiness overcame us as we realized how smoothly and easily we could dart in and out of traffic... we could wander in the streets uncontested like sacred cows ... people were like trees or tall grass, through which we chased imaginary rabbits.

In a park under a chestnut tree we saw a young mother wheeling a baby in a pram... we raced across the grass and circled her, and just as quickly shot away...it created riots and disturbances... we were definitely making a nuisance of ourselves... bothering people ...It was really something to see this group of young men running. We found ourselves rushing headlong — unwilling to stop — able to dodge, parry, and leap. A kind of aerobic giddiness permeated us as we got into the first half hour — we hit some kind of plateau and felt like we could go on and on and on. On acid especialy; something happend so that the sense of balance became infallable; the stamina became indefatigable. Like we had eaten some kind of perpetual motion mana — resulting in the more you ran in Dog the more you could run. You entered into a state of flow (a seemingly effortless immersion in the rhythm of action.) You forgot yourself by abandoning yourself and becoming just part of the on-going now.

O'Keefe admonished us to look at the patterns of the tail lights, and other lights, the glint of chrome, the reflection off shop windows, the signals. He would do physical movement with an elaborate embellishment, like striking a martial arts pose during a leap, or going from fast to slow and gentle in a roll. He wanted us to be unified in stimulus and response to explore the time between so that motion became in a sense blurred, our surroundings became in a sense "liquefied" and one thing flowed into another. "Dog". . . was a process of physical dissolution.

The idea was to see the pattern in the flow, the lights, street lights, signal lights, break lights, as we moved in and out of the gridlocked traffic, the flashing taillights, the "STOP" light and "WAIT" sign, the sign indicating the proper directional flow of traffic. The idea was to reduce the input; let the eyes become like animal eyes, look for the movement, the lights. You can turn off the color, and see white walls and black spaces between them, that you can move into. Especially doing the Dog Run while on acid we entered a separate reality, a parallel way of knowing the city that was phase-shifted from the normal, or of a higher harmonic.

Emptying out space of its arduous passage with traversal we are cleaving space with the temporal.

In movement, time present is the pushing of space behind.

If Space is that which is moved through by motion, then time is that which is moved through by mind.

You have to move through time to occupy space; it takes time to divide space by motion.

Thus space is time's reciprocal, as time is space's.

Time is the sense of moving. Space is the wind in your face. I had slipped, been velocitized, phased, into the perspective of motion where space and time are just reciprocal aspects of motion, of the progression. Spacetime is curved by matter and generated by it as well. Time is the reciprocal of space and both are generated in the breaking of symmetry.

In the endurance of the long distance runner is release.

In the uncertainty there are other reciprocals; energy and time; position and momentum. We cannot say where we are and how we are going through. To have energy enough and time, we would be blessed, though it was not made to last but to pass into the past.

With slow rotation we are entering a higher dimension where frame of reference closes back in on itself, the movement does not run out of the picture or stand immobile in one spot.

With childlike curiosity and the empowerment that comes with the accomplishment of physical acumen vitalized by developing prowess, we started to see "other" possibilities: for the bench — a slide, for the wall — a vaulting horse, for the lamppost — a maypole, for the bus shelter — an extension of the sidewalk: to also be walked upon. The whole town was for us our theatre. We were an ensemble set to entertain, edify, and enjoy.

The actors of Physical Theatre cross the threshold that separates the human and animal worlds. We loved O'Keefe, he was the big kid on the playground who invented the games, and taught us how to play. We would follow him into hell if he asked us to. He was really giving us a huge lesson in how physical theatre gets you in touch with your animality. Coming back all sweaty from running up the canyon, down into the campus into the ideal world of the university, the world of perpetual maintenance of the cannon and the status quo, we'd jump into the fountain in Sproul Hall in front of the U.C. Student Union . . . and dog paddle around. . . hold your wallet in your mouth so your identity doesn't get lost, then get out and shake the water all over someone who would laugh at the zaniness of it. We would take advantage of our boyish lovableness. . . be careful not to get stopped by the cops — quick in an out — race off campus, and the keystone cops chasing behind us. Absurd: Get 'em! Don't let'em get me, boys.

From there we're heading back outside the sweet sphere of idealism at the university to Auto Row, where the Pit butts up against the Dome Builders and Hospital. Where the landlord, dapper old topper twirls his cane, and says make it so.

We'd leap; we'd bound. We were floppy, coon-ass dogs. . . shaggy gods of dogs. . . howling dogs. . .running through the indulgent streets of Berkeley . . running. . . running, now, running. Then stop suddenly, be suspicious of corners, start up again running. . .run for your life. .leap down a flight of stairs . . . run for your breath. . . run for your health. . . with what you got left. We'd develop a pack spirit . . . by using a system of signs to communicate, we'd sniff around garbage pails. . .play soccer with strange objects. . . once we used a cabbage. . . didn't kick it far before it exploded. We were howling dogs running through the streets. All one, and the same dog. . . we were. . . Zen lunatics on the back of this *Dog of Dogness*— eternally existing in the concept "DOG," the species " dog" which is always in the present — the staff from the Institute for the Advancement of Actual Thought. I didn't understand it at the time but these Hawkeye Theatre aspirations were starting to fragment me. At the time I dealt with this — alternative realities and becoming aspects of the various energies coming into the theatre — in my writings: I gave them heteronymns. I recognized them one by one: there's Zoon Phonata, resident artist in a pair of thermal underwear tights he got from a free box. And Yum Chi as Mr. Blue. There's Chismo and Salteye the two who do their improvisations together. . . who carry each other on their backs, who brought me into their dream. There's Iearto Webster with his thick glasses and resonant voice of mimesis representation. We climb over a fence. . . we'd run into a crowd and pass from group to group. . .we'd laze around in the grass and get dive bombed by butterflies. Dog moving without pressure quick round a corner up the stairs over a wall, drop down into an alleyway, duck under a truck, skittle up a little ledge, into the world, weaving through the luckless pedestrians trudging like mastodons through the tundra to their eventual oblivion. Shall we follow? The deception of being plugged into the system showed on the grim faces of the phalanx moving in lock-step back to their over mortgaged homes en masse along the congested streets. One must always jay walk, and dart in and out of traffic. It's a wonder we didn't get tickets, but I think the student's obliviousness had inured the police to that kind of behavior.

We'd get back to the pit exhilarated. We would break out the wrestling mats and practice our drops and rolls. These guys were great at crashing into the floor. "The floor is your *friend*! You need to just make your muscles soft at the point of impact and spread the force over a much larger area, and it doesn't even hurt." Famous last words. But after some practice it seemed to go OK.

In those days there was an influx of Chinese Martial Arts movies. We used to go to the cavernous Broadway theatre in Oakland Chinatown where they ran all day for $1.50. There was another theatre in North Beach and one down town on Market Street too. Of course we couldn't understand a word of it, even though some had subtitles. It was about the Flying Taoist Saints of Martial Arts that we were interested in, their highly developed psychic abilities emerging from great physical acumen. O'Keefe wanted us to slip into these kicking poses while flying through the air off a ramparts or a stairs. That was the art, or performance aspect, get in and get out; just a flash. Bob knew Jackie Chan and had met Bruce Lee. O'Keefe had met Carlos Castaneda at a party. Also O'Keefe had been given audience with Choygam Trumpa at a theatre festival at the *Jack Kerouac School of Disembodied Poetics* in Boulder. And he knew Robert Wilson from the theatre community.

We were like some kind of script been written in the city, full of hard edge Chinese ideograms and soft elaborate curlicues too. We were a perturbation that goes out, like concentric waves on the surface of a still pond into which a pebble has been dropped. Something echoes in the mind, the zeitgeist, the holy spirit is given opportunity to breath for a while and we spent it twisting and turning and running and tumbling like letters in some script writ by a moving finger disturbing the dust in a design of the tracery of a life.

We are sails, sheets of space upon which the winds of probabilities blow, and we are scudded across the glassy urban terrain like ice-boats zipping on a frozen lake, or slower, petals, whirligigs, flotsam on a stream. We are asking ourselves to consider movement as fundamental, all is vibration of strings and surfaces and spaces, seeking to resonate with the emergence of now.

Back at the pit we'd engage in high-speed conversations for a long time. Zoon might say," Think about a nasal based art".

"A nasal based art?"

"Yea, a nasal based art. That's the way dogs move. You know, dogs move like that, they don't quite have it down about how to go around corners. They can sneak out the currents of space with their nose. They come to a corner and hover around to sniff out directions, this way or that.

"They follow their nose, you know? It's like an important information trail. Its the trail of matter giving off, dispersing, part of itself, not just light reflecting or sound propagating, but matter percolating. Think of what an artist might be able to do with arranging streams of smell into a dance, you'd follow the streams, you'd follow the S, the spiraling curve, unfolding its shape as you follow in the dance."

We were these bay wolf characters, Beowolf in the just-forming moment of new language. And the authors of that language were with us, Iearto Webster and Zoon Phonata.

I told O'Keefe of the hunting dogs back in Texas. The cold nosed dog, follows a trail until it gets hot. If it gets hotter then the animal speeds up, because the subject leaves more of a trail brushing hard against things. Scent up to heightened metabolism. The speed of the dogs is the same as the speed of the coon: when he walks they walk, when he runs they run. The hunter lets his dog run the wild down. What great sympathy of motion and heightened synchronicity the dogs have. John liked that. Artists are natural cold nosed dogs. Sniffing at the trail of the future even before it gets hot.

KEEPERS OF THE GLOBE

    The four agents: Torso, Legs, Arms, and Head are employed to communicate a message. The Spectators must be considered separately, not in order to emphasize any independently escaping qualities as such, but to show how much each member has to contribute to the Expressive Whole. The larger the organ the simpler it is to deal with. One is directed to the many exciting books dealing with this specific topic.

    A strong sense of presence often acts like an instrument. The movements of Torso, for instance, are not always synchronized with Head. Head and Arms do not always fit into time, though they too desire to produce an uninterrupted sequence of events.

    One must return to the agents to gain access to the tunnel that leads to the Globe. A train is not useful in this connection, even if there is a smoothly functioning landscape around it. Like an athlete, we must be prepared to perform any kind of movement. The way is long and the rods protrude from all directions. Our instruments must not be allowed to trail-off, go flat, or impede the location of our difficultly established sensations. Here, the agents flower-forth into a new awakening: at the end of the tunnel we glimpse the petals of consciousness unfold above a sort of idealized urinal—perhaps it is really the urinal of the angels in which a round, disinfectant globe rests sweetly, purifying the years that trickle and splatter upon it. The Spectators, unlike the agents, do a little dance.

    And thus do we receive the message, who are neither instruments abandoned in a landscape nor the Creative Intelligence that turns events loose throughout time. Intercourse with the Spectators is our supreme and crowning pleasure. From its height we look down on the vain and deluded agents groveling in their complications, while we pee in the urinal of the angels!

R. Mutt.

Page of Punctual Actual Weekly with text by Darrell Gray

Boley Shuman & Dwan Kumm

The story **Boley Shuman**, written by Jonathan Albert, is republished here from the Punctual Actual Weekly # 11, 1976, along with associations of its impact.

    I got to study with the inventor of the sound notation, Jonathan Albert. He held a class in the kitchen of his studio apartment near the Berkeley Bowl at the corner of Shattuck and Ashby overlooking the new BART station. He had come from the Iowa experimental theatre background where he wrote and developed notation for sound performances using a system of sound notation he had invented. Bob Ernst was fond of introducing him as the guy who got a Ph.D. in his own stuff! Jonathan Albert had set out to explore how sound could be used in the feeling development of words rather than the thinking symbol they are usually taken to be. Rather than seeing words as made up of letters (which are symbols for sounds) his notation for the sounds used a matrix of numbers. Each number denoting an area of the mouth from which the vowel sounds are made.

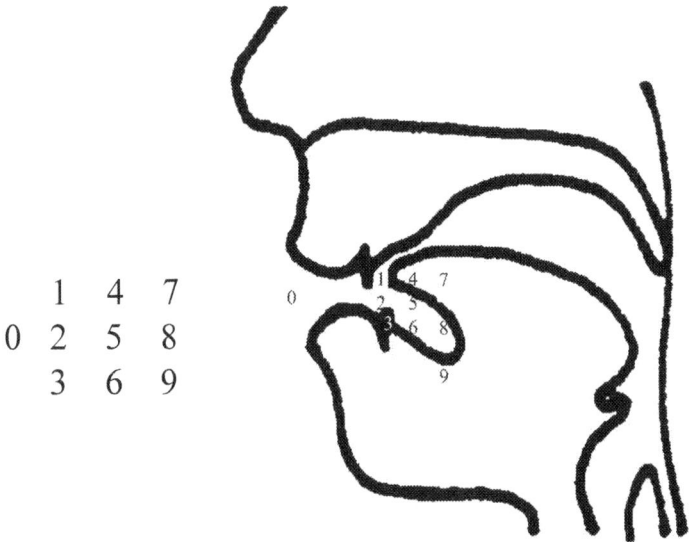

    These vowels are the energy color and they are operated on by suggestive diacritical markings for the fricative, stop and other consonants. The 0 is used for the sound shaping ability of the lips outside of the mouth to form bilabial plosives.

This is all that is needed to completely specify any sound made by the human mouth, in particular words.

The labio-dental stops: {t, d, } were based on the 1 position, unvoiced and voiced. As were the labio-dental fricatives: {s, z, sh, ch}. The bilabial plosives: {p, b,} and fricatives: {phi, v} used diacriticals on the 0. The gutturals: { g, x, k} were based on the 3 position, these velars shaped by the combinations of fricatives, stops, voiced and unvoiced. The liquids: {l, r} started out way in the back, an 8 or 9. The nasals: {my, ny } now had a real, physical based representation.

This had a profound effect on me. For a budding poet trying to find his way into acting, to explore the way sounds are made in the mouth as they mimicked something of the force or phenomenology of the world as it was encapsulated in the word: it was an awakening. We were allowed to be present at the beginning of language all over again. Like children we were the first to apprehend the world. I could see that the notation system embodied a philosophy of the body, in the sense of Grotowski, that the voice was an instrument that should explore vast ranges beyond simple discursive speech. I started to call it in my writing about it, #sonics, because the # looked like the 3x3 matrix of positions of sound-generating configurations in the mouth. And #sonics was trance inducing. First of all you had to write with a pencil like it was a kind of mathematics, a kind of algebra, you didn't do this kind of writing with a typewriter. It was almost like a kind of sound painting. A kind of synesthesia poetry. It was a shorthand for taking dictation from the Real. Or it was like mantra; one usually did it in groups, a kind of choral secular praying session, chanting and making sound. It was really good for your pipes, your language chops. It was our Sanskrit, the primal language, a holy language, for this new sense of yourself in the world.

I was astounded by the sheer elegance of it. It was one of those situations where a great mind invents a representation in a symbol system that is so compelling that it allowed lots of progress to be made. I was as intrigued now by the sound notation as I had been by the bra-ket notation ($< s\,|H|\,s >$) developed by Dirac for the vector space representation of operators and basis vectors for bracketing the spectral energy of a probability space (H was the Hamiltonian, the energy; $|s>$ and $<s|$ are the basis vectors that span the problem space under consideration.)

Jonathan Albert's number system notation spoke to the movement of the articulating tongue. It compelled one to think in a moving awareness about how words were encapsulations of the ideas, the impressions, the sensations, the mimological energies expressed in the concatenation of sounds that went into making up the word. A series of sounds notated this way showed the movements and the textural shifts in the sound series. Like in the word "East": there is a slight rise of the voiced vowel to an unvoiced fricative then a stop. Or "and", it moves through three sound categories — all voiced: vowel, nasal and stop.

In his notation the voiced vowels were colored with a kind of gilding or rub-on letraset. It made the voiced vowel look like it was filling space with some kind of acoustical shotgun pattern, a texture for the text, filling space with its presence. The study made a vocal performer much more aware of the resonators in the body and how they could be used to sink the presence more into the now. It had a profound effect on me. Albert gave me his paper *A Language of Harmony*. It was a great introduction to the possible aesthetics of his system. It presented a three level view of sound.

from *(The Language of Harmony by Jonathan Albert)*

> The most fundamental level of sound is silence. Silence can be seen as the absence of sound. But it can also be viewed as the background for sound. It is an always present medium providing a continuity for the sound.
>
> The Second level is the sound itself. All things in this universe are energy, movements. Sound can be viewed as a vibration through a medium. But if the medium itself is a vibration, then the difference between the sound and the medium is a difference of degree, not kind, perhaps a difference of level.
>
> The third level of sound is progression, the pattern. Each sound is unique. But to the degree that a sound or a series of sounds can be put in a pattern, they are linked to everything else sharing that pattern. Since human perception is a patterning, in theory sound patterns should be able to reflect perceptual patterns. All things can be seen as qualities, and the qualities can be seen in patterns. Man is limited in his ability to speak the patterns, the movements of his world, only by the limits of his awareness and of his physical mechanism.

As we began to make sound in class and in theatre I felt more like how a musician or composer feels. Through sound I could visualize a localization in space; movements connecting one sound to another. Indeed it was *Philosophy in a New Key,* (influenced by esthetician Langer). This aesthetic promoted the zen quiescence of presence. This musicality esthetic was about getting out of the mental into the physical so that one could find and move in the Flow, be part of the synchronicity, made Zen real. Once you opened yourself up to it, this kind of active listening could become a kind of compositional process involved in using sampled environmental sounds as the source material and repeating them in memory, or stretching them and blending them with other environmental sounds so that there was some kind of a dialog going on. Focusing by tuning in this way increases the perceived volume or presence of the sound. Such magnification allows the inner 'voices' of such sounds, their timbreal character, to be explored and their imagery and symbolism to be brought into the compositional process. We'll say more on this is a moment. Here is the teacher's own work.

Boley Shuman by Jonathan Albert

Dwan.

Dwan Kuum comes pouring through the trees And the voices stream past the leaves. Voices of kings and rust, voices of sorrow and waterfalls, voices of man and darkness. All the cries of then and now and soon all rush by. All rush through.

For Dwan Kuum comes purring through the trees. And each leaf hears the murmuring of time and all trees shudder in the silence of eternity.

Now Boley Shuman lives on 34th street. Boley's world is a city world. Someone's always going somewhere and something's always banging, croaking, or crying. Noise. The city's filled with so many sounds that if you try not to listen you'll hear noise.

And if you really try not to hear, you'll hear silence.

But if you are a Boley Shuman, you want to hear. Only you don't really know how. Take now for instance.

Summer Thursday morning. What does it sound like? Water drips in the kitchen. Hypnotic plopping with an occasional gurgle as the water slithers down the drain. His brother rolls over in bed. Body and sheet whisper so he won't wake while the springs creek in disapproval. Boley watches a fly move straight across the room. From out of nowhere the buzz rises to a sharp peek, and just as quickly falls away. Splashes, whispers, and buzzes. Boley turns from one to another. Does the old woman hear of any of this? What do old ears hear and what does deafness sound like? Is it loud or soft? What does his brother hear? Does the fly hear and what does the water hear? I wonder how you'd ask water what it hears? And how it would answer.

These and more questions ran through Boley's mind. Unfortunately none of the answers came with them. So Boley went to get his breakfast, but he did not stop wondering. Boley asked his father what he heard. Now Boley's father was tired. He was always tired. But he did care for the boy, so be did try to answer.

"I hear mamma making breakfast, neighbors going to work, and your brother trying to sleep off last night."

Boley asked his mother what she heard, and she said she did not have time now. Boley sits and thinks. His father hears people doing things and his mother is too busy doing things to hear anything. Boley wonders if sounds are names for things. Is the name for a fly "fly" or is it buzz? Boley wonders what his own name is. Since he still had no answers, he ate a piece of bread and went out.

Dwan Kuum listens to the leaves and the wind. A thousand dialogues. Each leaf speaks of its history as the wind runs over the veins around the edges and through the holes. A chorus of gases hum faintly over dust specks and whisper quite distinctly to the leaves. They hurriedly speak of what they carry and where they have been, and then rush on so someone else can speak. Melodic leaves and harmonic winds.

Dwan Kuum listens to the rise and tall of conversation.

Boley went to the stores on 2nd Avenue. He is surrounded. An old man with bottles in a bag. Slow sandpaper slide. Bottles clinking steadily in crackling paper. Uneven bursts of air fading noise of breath. A man and a Ford clear their throats before speaking. A woman's high heels sharply kick the concrete; her voice smoothly hums and her dress whispers to her body. Boley wonders about the different kinds of 'whispering.'

He wonders what things sound like when you close your eyes. He closes them and tries to guess. At first he knows what everything is. Then he hears something new. Creaking. It isn't the creaking of wood; too high. More like a metal spring being stretched. Boley hears other sounds. He can't always tell where they are. As long as they are unknown, sounds can be from almost anywhere and can be of things of any size and shape. In the middle of the honking cars and the talking' people, Boley hears scraping sounds and muffled sounds and loud and soft sounds. Some last for a while and some are quickly gone, some were far away and some are very close. Boley soon recognized garbage cans, old newspapers, and new shoes. Sounds are tied to objects shapes, colors, surfaces, and reasons. They come from places and they are like names again. But for a moment or two, they are just sounds, and they are mysterious and free and so is Boley.

Dwan Kuum speaks through the leaf. A voice of motion. The motion of fiber in the air, the clash of light and pigment, the spreading tremors of color. Dwan. Dwan Kuum speaking in the

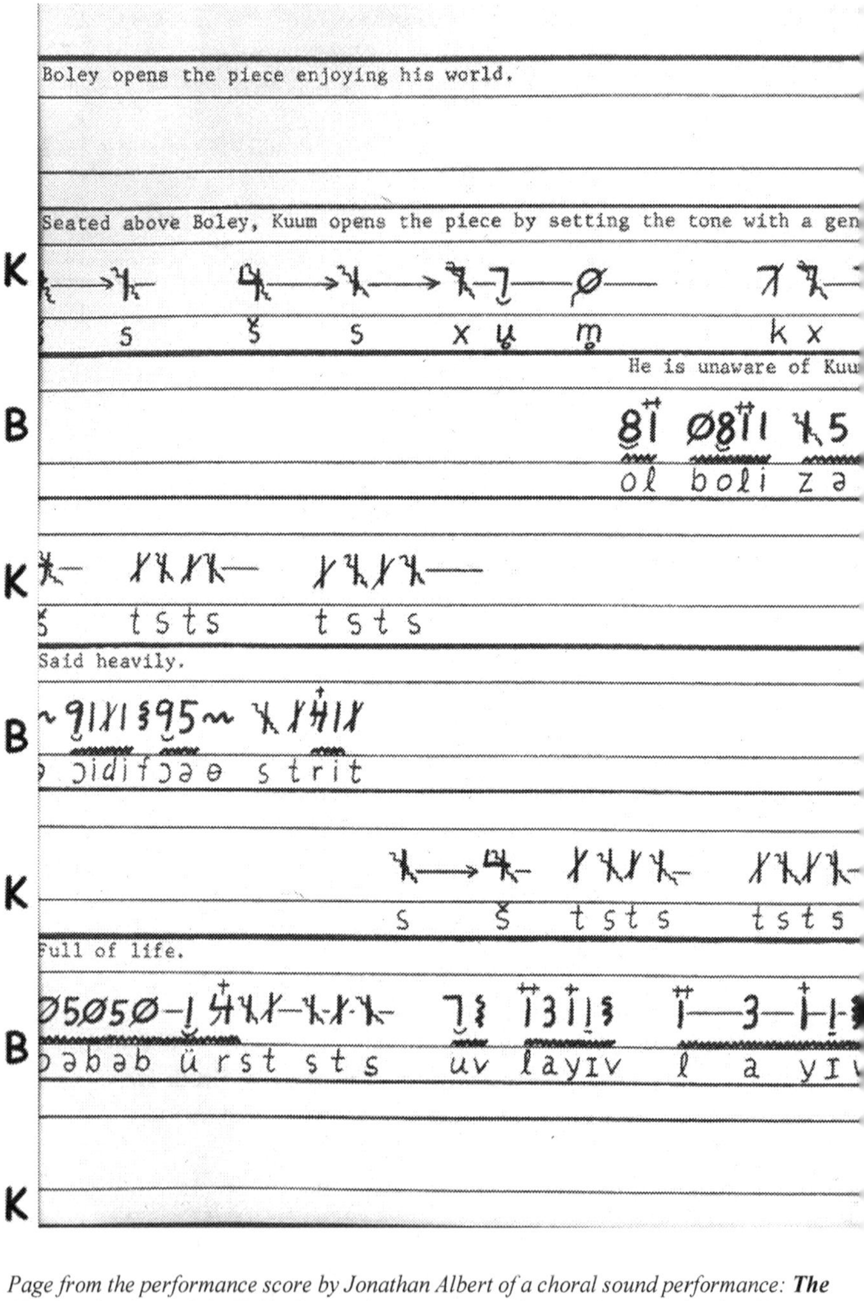

Boley opens the piece enjoying his world.

Seated above Boley, Kuum opens the piece by setting the tone with a gen[tle]

K ... s š s x ŭ m   k x

He is unaware of Kuu[m]

B   8↑ Ø8↑1 ↓,5
      o l   b o l i   z ə

K   tsts   tsts

Said heavily.

B   ɔidifɔəθ s t r i t

K   s   š   tsts   tsts

Full of life.

B bəbəb ü rst sts   uv layıv   l a yıv

K

Page from the performance score by Jonathan Albert of a choral sound performance: **The Singing Gardens of the Kwao Dawn** *showing voices of Dwan Kumm and Boley Shuman*

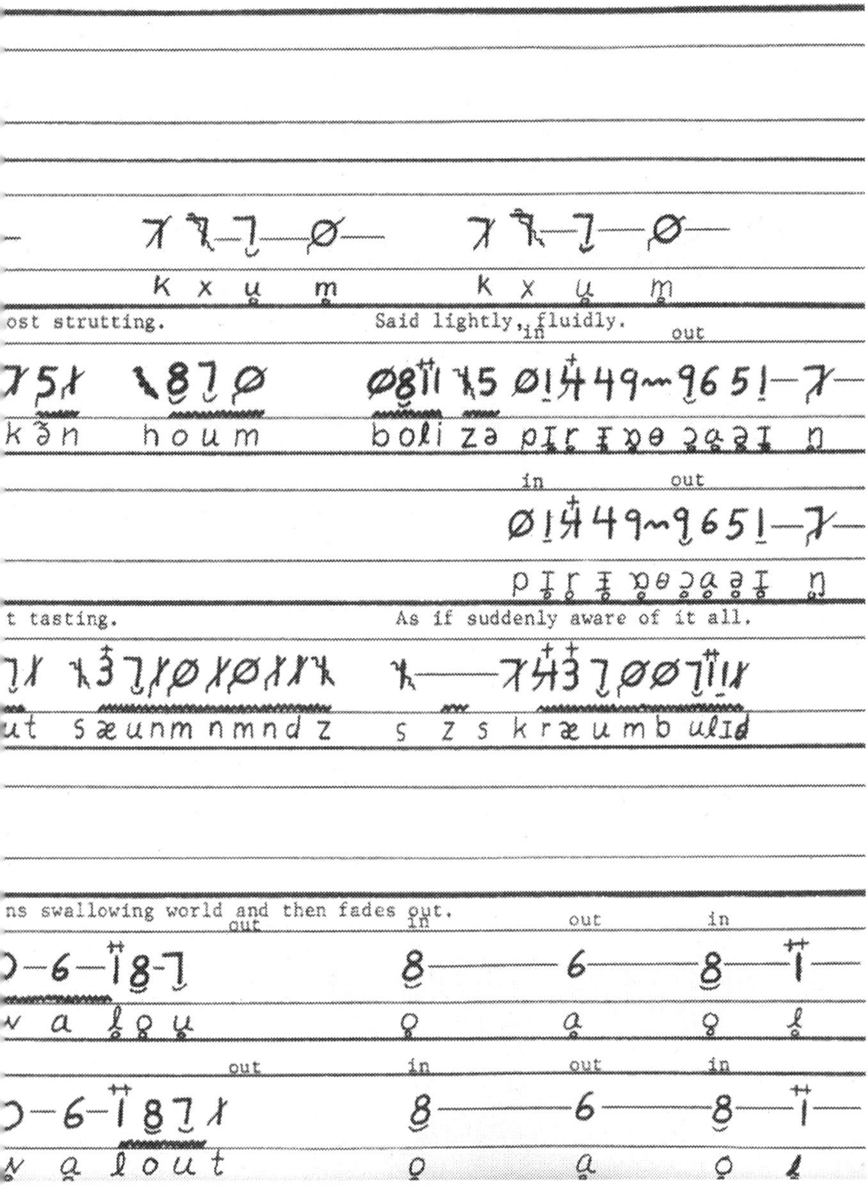

                 ⊅ ʔ ⁊ ∅   ⊅ ʔ ⁊ ∅
                 k x u̱ m   k x u̱ m
ost strutting.   Said lightly, fluidly.
                                           in   out
⁊5⊀   \8⁊∅   ∅8⁺¹⊀5 ∅!⁺449~9651—⊅
k ə̱ n h o u m   b o l i z ə p ɪ ɾ ɪ̱ ɵ̱ ɔ ə ɪ   n

                                    in   out
                         ∅!⁺449~9651—⊅
                         p ɪ ɾ ɪ̱ ɵ̱ ɔ ə ɪ   n
t tasting.   As if suddenly aware of it all.

⊀ ʔ3⊀⊀∅⊀∅⊀⊀ʔ   ʔ——— ⊀4̇3⊀∅∅⊺ⁱᵘ
ut s æ u n m n m n d z   s   z s k r æ u m b u̱l ɪ̱d

ns swallowing world and then fades out.
                             out   in   out   in
⊃—6—⁺⁺⁺̇8⁊   8———6———8—⁺⁺⁺̇l
v a l o̱ u̱   o̱   a   o̱   l̠

                      out   in   out   in
⊃—6—⁺⁺⁺̇8⊀   8———6———8—⁺⁺⁺̇l
v a l o u t   o̱   a   o̱   l̠

tongues of life, the movements of growth and decay. And softer, fainter, far, far softer, Kuum, humming. Humming. Somewhere a leaf. Dwan Kuum now the note of a leaf, now another. Dwan, the endless chorus spreading notes through time and space. And softer, fainter, far, far softer, Kuum, humming. Dwan Kuum Dwan Kuum Dwan Kuum.

Boley Shuman

Boley's sneakers are untied, and he walks like taping pencils. His hand runs over a shirt with starch blotches. Boley wears crackly paper and whispering. Like his brother asleep, like the woman.

Old woman at her sewing machine. Slow moving fast. Halting breath drive sputter wheels and steady whines. A faded dress houses thoughts of the past, while the smooth shiny machine gives them a now Boley listens to the patterns of motion. And as his stomach gurgles, Boley's patterns melt into lunch,

One leaf leans over on a breeze and talks to its neighbor. The message is repeated across the tree. And if the wind lasts long enough, the whole tree speaks to its listeners. The earth hums to the tree and the tree hears drive sputter wheels and steady whines. A faded dress houses thoughts of the past, while the smooth shiny machine gives them a now Boley listens to the patterns of motion. And as his stomach gurgles, Boley's patterns melt into lunch,

One leaf leans over on a breeze and talks to its neighbor. The message is repeated across the tree. And if the wind lasts long enough, the whole tree speaks to its listeners. The earth hums to the tree and the tree hears its food. The leaves hum the song of oxygen. And each time a man breaths, his body listens.

Dwan Kuum humming spreading through man, through each listener in whatever way they meet. Vibrations, motions shift. Dwan singing songs that clash and merge in new patterns. Kuum humming. Dwan Kumm humming.

Boley's sitting alone. Nobody's home but the silence, and Boley's listening to it. It fills the room with voices of not quite lines. A field of' white noise surrounds Boley. He breathes in the silence. Boley Shuman of 34th St. floats in a sea of movement, of silence, and listens to himself.

A fly enters the room and cuts arcs of sound in the silence. Boley feels it humming.

This story of Boley Shuman and Dwan Kumm was like a shaman and the spirit of place he channels. It made you want to go out and listen to the world. That is the first property of an Actualist work: it compels to action, it makes you want to go out and experience. I wanted to know my soundscape like that. I wanted to be more present. I wondered if I could hear the spirit of place. To really listen you had to almost meditate, you had to stop the internal monolog which is the first step, that leads to transcendence.

    I started to go on sound walks. And with the notation I could synthesize with my own voice, some of the things I was hearing. I began paying attention to my sonic environment in a deeper way. I noticed the contrast between walking in nature and walking in the city. I took long walks in the open fields down at the Berkeley marina or in Wildcat canyon. There, feet on crunch of gravel filled the ears, and sometimes when off road snapped dried reeds. Traffic noise gradually decreased as the green shores around the bay enveloped with their bushes and birds. Dogs scared them into the air and they gave off frights ~whoawhap!. twwwrrrap CREET!. . .sounds of alarm. In nature every sound is a separate sound, not like the blurring of timbres and rhythms that one hears in the city, where the only distinct, separate sounds are those which are designed to DEMAND our attention. In the city, honking, squealing tires peeling out. HELP! In the green fields we hear no human voices, except our own. This open space is a knoll, a huge green bowl framed by traffic. The city never lets off its presence; you always know you are in an urban environment. But part of the loveliness of *this* place, its scents and sounds, soft shapes and colors, is being so opposite from the city vibe. What did I hear and what didn't I hear when I blocked-out the city. And how might I navigate it in a state more fully alive — like dogs — moving with the sharpness of an animal. I am an animal, the Zoon Phonata, looking for something — the spirit of place. Like Boley Shuman and Dwan Kumm, who together become something or someone else, like a shaman and the deity he channels. I looked at the poem *Nantucket* from WCW again. (Here see pg. 66*)*

    I was quite taken by how this poem creates the image of freshness on a restful vacation. I am totally in love with it. It made me want to go out in life and make enough money so I could go on vacations. I get this great sense of transparency. How is it that such a thing is communicated from one mind to another. Telepathy? What makes the words, the quanta of the field between the poem and the phenomena that gets exchanged do what they do? We are being brought back to a quiet state through the energy of the words themselves. I tried to analyze it. There is internal rhyme. The rhythm is not anything standard. It is amazing how the point of view shifts around in the space, moving back and forth across the window. You are like a camera going over the *mis en scene*. What contributes to the sense of transparency. Is it just the imagery of glass, the imagery of cleanliness and whiteness. You can feel the airiness of Nantucket in this poem. I wanted to look into the sound level and the #sonics gave me the tools I needed: the word glass, for example, has the deep |g> sound made in the back of the throat moving up to the liquid /L/ then out to the double fricative |ss>. It infused, the voice flowed out. The |g> sounds comes from way back down, from the ground and glows, resonates with the | l >. Then in the word yellow, it fairly shouts. And there is a lot of movement in the word sunshine. What is it about the motion of the sounds that gives a sense of transparency? Does motion in the sounds of the words reflect the motion of the camera point of view? Statistically, the strong repeat of the liquid | l > sound (Flowers, lavender, yellow, smell, cleanliness, late, glass, glass, lying, immaculate) in such a short poem, of short brush-stroke like lines, is the dominant sound theme. What does the /l/ sound convey or "mean.

The Liquids, are voiced and are really felt in the making. The jaw sets up for the tongue to go labio-alveolar; the tongue vibrates the sound coming from deep in the back of the mouth or top of the throat. The internal effort the mind makes in reading the "l" sound, makes you feel sense of the | l > sound, and this sense of cavernous space is part of making sense out of what WCW is describing. There is a correspondence then between the energy in a sound, and the effort to make it. I felt like I was on to some third way of seeing: The energy in a sound, its spectral energy of a tone is a third way of looking at things, besides in time and space. This was in its penetrating power as frequency, as vibration. We can look at the sharpness of the energy content in the waves. When one makes this effort as instructed in reading the text, there is an enhanced sense of investment in the effort, and thus one feels the image more?

The | l > sounds gives us a sense of cavernous space because of the way it is made! That makes sense in the context of this poem: the space is suggested by the cavernous limpidity of the effort to make the | l > sounds, which are the dominant of the poem. We can compare that with the many unvoiced fricatives |s>, |sh> and the stop |ch> in (Flowers, changed, curtains, Smell, cleanliness, Sunshine, glass, glass pitcher, which). The |s> sound is sustained and persistent, made toward the front of the mouth. More up-tight than the "l." What is the "meaning" or contribution of these in the poem? The "s" is, in a way, more penetrating. A word like "glass" has both the | l > and the |s>, as well as the double meaning of looking through and holding volume. This penetrating is also occurring in the bilabial |w> in

(Flowers, window, yellow, white, which, white.) The bilabial is a plosive, unlike the fricatives and stops, which cut off (articulate) the vowel stream; the plosive sends it on its way with an éclat of purposivity. I get the sense of someone blowing up the space like a balloon, giving it more depth and body.

Another sense that adds to the expansion of space is the parallelism. There are parallel ends of lines (white curtains / late afternoon,) which continues with the |t> in "tumbler turned" and "immaculate white". The parallelism also suggests space: the parallel train rails going off into the horopter. This strong parallelism suggest the idea of symmetry which adds to the overall effect of space, and seeing through the space. I must admit that all this feels a bit uncanny, a bit daja vue. Is this sense of transparency, expansion, penetration just after the fact? Am I just using lit crit to bolster a personal visualization? Or is this sense of the mimesis in words so ingrained it is subliminal. Was the good doctor conscious of what he was doing? Hell yes. I think this is a great poem equal to his famous ones, about the wheel-barrow and the plums, and the flowers by the sea.

This soundscape is a powerful esthetic and it mimics the sense of presence and seeing one has in moments of inspiration and transcendence. It is part of the psychic syntax of emergent being there for us to enter into if we can quiet the grasping ego for a little while. I thought of some more symbols for other aspects of the poetic inscape. ~ would symbolize this hovering wave, # as in #sonics, would be the matrix, the diachronic and synchronic, < > would be duality separating, as in cleaving the space to look into higher dimensions, <—> would be mapping across the duality as in parallel, analogy, metaphor.

Darrel Gray put it very clearly in his book *Essays and Dissolutions*, in the chapter Translations from Silence. In که essay he is discovering the 'microphoric' theory of poetry from examining the poems of Creeley whose poems inherit the legacy off Valery's dictum (that poetry is a chemistry in which we have yet to find the elements). Gray analyzes a few lines from Creeley's book *For Love*.

from *(Essays & Dissolutions, Translations from Silence, 83)*

Don't step
so lightly. Break
your back, missed

the step. Don 't go
away mad...

It was from a close reading of Creeley that I had become aware of the play, loose or close at times, of synchronous verbal elements that determined *meaning* as much as the composition of a compound determines its ability to react and interact with other chemical states. But my first reading, which overshadowed almost all later ones, informed me mostly of the moral, or specifically *human* dimension, of the poems. I loved the poems, sensing in them a clarity of emotion and sparseness of method, but it was always the larger, total movement of the individual poem that pleased me. I would see how small and discrete the poems looked on the page, and after reading them feel how wide and deeply they opened within me. But the clue was there, only to emerge after many re-readings. And then it came to me, finally, that here was the suggestion of the key I had been looking for: "Don't step so lightly. Break / your back . . . " I had read those lines, with their abrupt break after two or three syllables merely as expressions of internal tension, ways of directing attention to the compression, on an emotional level, the poet had felt intrinsic to the occasion of the poem. Of course that was true, but what I had not seen was the dialogue *within* the lines, the way the open sounds were pitted against the closed ones, the "o" of Don't against the "p" of step, the vowels of "so lightly" against the period and beginning "B" of "Break" of the next line. In the fourth line the "p" is repeated in the dominant position, as end/stop of "step," a direct return to the initial end stop, returning us to the beginning (in the poem's time) with a repetition of the word "Don't." The poem continues as an interplay of vowels and consonants, as do most of Creeley's poems, such that even when the initial impetus is not lyric, they have that melodic exactness of succinct sensory presentation.

So I began looking at poems with this realization in mind. I began thinking of vowels and consonants as having positive or negative charges which registered as deviations from a poetic norm, such that the verbal poetic distance between them might determine an actual syncopation, not of meaning *per se,* but of a formal movement capable of engaging the reader on a level far deeper than could be reached either by image or statement.

Often while coming back from a class at Jonathan's apartment, after a rousing session of making sound, expiring the vowels and chewing the consonants, resonating the nasals and feeling oceanic on the un-voiced white noise, I had a transcendental moment. This time I was walking past the roundabout intersection blockades they have in Berkeley to force the traffic to go around or take other streets, and I was doing the actor's voice exercise of making the sounds of the world. I made the sounds of whirr of the wheels and the whoosh of cars going by and I began to think about the drag and push that made the sounds, and I began to wonder what part of the sound was made by the engine, or the car pushing air or the rotation of tire on the road, and if big tires were more efficient than small tires, and the wheels of the passing cars began to turn in slow motion, so you can see them overcoming their rotational inertia and as they go through the upswing. I suddenly saw them rolling out their perimeters where the rubber meets the road in sections of π. As I was letting my consciousness fly around and be one with the entities in the world making sound, time seemed to slow down and I could examine what was going on. I looked up and it seemed the birds too, were flying a little slower, and they seemed like twittering machines or beacons perched on telephone pole towers calling out in a strange ecology or soundscape, one that I can enter now because I speak and understood its language. And something happened between the angular velocity of the rotating tires, and the waves of electricity flowing through the wires. I don't know why, sometime I'll have to get it analyzed. It might just be that old logos <—> eros confusion thing, the French are really great at that one, but when I start to have deep feelings my mind speeds up and I think it is the universe coursing through me and the numbers of the sound movement system got convolved with physics and how the rotational motion was a wave motion and the waves in the wire was like a kind of light or different mass in a world.

One just slips into a kind of integrative trance. In the center of the hub of every turning wheel I saw the transcendental π — at the heart of the divine closed form, the circle — surrounded by its infinitely many spokes radiating radii. They seemed to shine like the spectral flare of the monstrance shown forth in a special mass. The wheel spoke in its rising against weight and falling with inertia to rise again; it spoke of the wave, the rhythm in the rolling out of motion where the rubber meets the road: the form meets substance. All around me in every wheel, in every steering wheel, in gears and transmissions, in the waves of the transmission lines, in the light of the waves (the wheel becomes the wave in $wt \rightarrow e^{i(\omega t - \phi)}$) and I am standing staggered for a moment at the timeless abstract truth beyond phenomena.

And then suddenly it dawned on me. This symbol $wt \rightarrow e^{i(\omega t - \phi)}$ was an expression of the idea that you could have in one semantically dense expression, a symbol that stood between two worlds and that moved back and forth between light and movement i.e. between electromagnetism and gravity. It was like the kernel, the seed, this transcendental monad eye jewel that could be used to see, to ratiocinate the complexity down to a much simpler more readily-apprehensible space. It was the key expression for the large world of gravity and for the small world of the electron and the photon that is part of everything that exists. Instead of a space based on the base 10 logarithm have the base e, the natural logarithm. In this space , the speed of light c=1, and the quantum of action hv —the uncertainty, the fluctuation, the flow — was also there, you had other spaces too. I had to walk around, for about 40 blocks because my mind was blown by the transcendental power of that. I almost got down on my knees and started reciting the sacred number. 3.14159. . . You could go on and on forever and there is never a pattern or system to it, just an endless rain of white nunbers flowing in columns down a dark screen. There is something wonderful and terrifying and satisfying about π. It is so essential, so much a part of everyting and yet it is so hopelessly unknowable and without reason. And e, the transcendental number, base of the natural logarhythm had turned into an eye. An eyepiece that let you see, the all-seeing eye at the heart of phenomena, it was the monad's window, that let you see into all spaces wild and tame. I kept walking around saying I see, I see, πon e. We were pi on e ers. Pioneers in the brave new world of spectral space. Pioneers forging new relationships moving out across all boundaries to the ever widening frontier. Like yin and yang. π and e. You and me. Two rice farmers creating it all out of nothing. Out of silence.

And we are moving through, displacing it and it is written in and it is writing in us. It is our job to concentrate their tour to apprehend their being there, to verify and to not stop until we have rendered all these variable dimensions as if everything were part of the same elastic field under which our seeing and the images in our mind were points of intersection of infinities of being to which we are bound.

The sound work that Jonathan was teaching us was our Kandinsky, our "Point and Line to Plane," for in Kandinsky we found our guide into the modern. He was the patron saint of synesthesia. In Kandinsky's "Point and Line to Plane" we have an exploration of form and composition. It is also a great unfolding of Peirce's semiotics.

Kandinsky defined the point as "the smallest elementary form or the proto-element of painting." It is the first impression on the whiteness of the canvas, the tone emerging against silence. Point against emptiness. This would be Firstness.

In his exposition on form, Kandinsky said the Line is created by movement of the point, this is true in mathematics. It represents movement, in contrast to "the self contained repose of the point." This bifurcation of space by point and line is Secondness in Peirce. The line can be characterized by the tension and the force with which it is created, its curvature, its crinkly, craggy motions (indeed its fractal dimension). It is what Peirce called the Actual and what we mean by the Actual. Kandinsky explores the different kinds of straight lines: the vertical is warm, horizontal cold. Diagonal lines mediate between. Angles are intersecting lines, and they have different temperatures, different tones. All these manifestations are tokens, projections of a higher order. The higher order, is the Plane, which is generated by the lines, it is the boundary, the playing field as we demarcate it with boundary. This sense of containment of distinction of law is what Peirce called Thirdness.

It is quite a leap of phenomenology into Thirdness. In shifting the sphere of discourse from the geometry of form in the visual to form in the audial, we can see that language, and speech have a similar kind of phenomenology. The #sonics showed us how there is a kind of phonosemiotics going on, a kind of sonoergomimesis. Just look at that title "Point and Line to Plane" again. Right away in that title, we have the |P> in Point as the single Place, the single Point, the sound of precision. It is of one dimension. We go through the liquid |L>, into the second dimension, the Line. Then we put the two together and move that point on all the lines until it becomes a Plane. The |L> of the Line has the power to move the Point, to spread the Point into a Plane. And now we have space, the third dimension. In "space" we disperse the precision of |P>, we spread it out with the fricative of |S> acting as a modifying operator in the phenomenology of energy emerging. <s| **p** |s> The S in space suggests serpent, the symbol the reproduction. Space like a mirror and sex multiplies. The dental linearity of |s>, shows up as a sensing or dispersive force between two things. Put S in front of pace (the positioning of things in time, timing) and you get space: the /p/ of point bounded between the curving opening and closing s.<s| **p** |s> In the beginning of a word, the presence of s seals and seduces. Speed Spread Serve. S is the spiritual seeker, the swami, the saint. At the end of a word, it forms the possessive. Spaces = Space's. For space is two sexes in the sun playing: for to have two sexes for the Automorph is to have two eyes for the head. For it lets them focus in on the scene of what is coming down, what is being born, birth bulging across the barriers of space and time. The eyes play over the seen and the two sexes play over the scene. And the eyes are essential for seeing other sexes for the creative evolution is pouring forth always and without sex there wouldn't be any *us* to pour us through, or pour through us: the intimations of design. And without the space lighted by the sun, held in place by gravity and bathed in the beneficent fluid of photons given of from behavior of electrons, gravitating around protons giving off light and heat and radiation to perturb and swerve the world to serve its design, and without that the world would be inconceivable.

I see the swirls of the cloud chamber, the forms. We have the primordial, what Peirce would call the firstness, the not yet differentiated, the potential , the possible,

The point being made, indicates by the unvoiced bilabial |P>, it is potential.

The voiced bilabial |B> is about things coming into Being.

Logographia precipitates and percolates proprioception. (That's how you break your lines.)

Doug Wilson and Jonathan Albert

Krishna Glass
& Phillipe Mignon at Dejeuner

    Occasionally Darrell and I would end up at the Presbyterian Church in the evening to partake in the "quarter meal." The church, about two blocks up from Telegraph on Haste, one block from People's Park, served an OK dinner. This was a free meal that costs a quarter. You had to pay a quarter to get a number to get into the queue outside before it wound its way downstairs to enter the basement and get served cafeteria style from moving your tray along the row of steam tables. They had stainless steel trays with four sections. And a utensil that was indeed a runcular spoon. Or a spork as we called it, a cross between a spoon and a fork — a fork that had one tine that was fattened out into a crescent moon shape where the point cusp made a kind of skewer and the outside of the moon spoon was the mini- scimitar cutting edge. In the basement dining hall one sat on bench seats at long tables. The scene was pretty cool, a mixture of poor students, artist types, Berkeley eccentrics, and the other half were hard-core homeless street people. The people who ran it were good people, very dedicated to helping homeless people. They showed me how to get access to a mimeograph machine at some government subsidized agency for giving voice to the vox populi and that's how I started the PAW.
    Though poor, Darrell Gray was not very street-wise. I, on the other hand though also poor, had hitchhiked all over America, had grown up around guns and knives and vicious, stupid rednecks and hyper-macho Mexicans in Texas, had been in juvie and jail once and had also worked with juvenile delinquents and so had the edgy awareness of a criminal and could talk tough. A lot of wild transcontinental hitchhiking will definitely matriculate you in the subject area of street sense. (Although, I might have just been heedless too.) I'll never forget the time I found myself wandering once in the area of Detroit when the riots broke out in '67, trying to hitchhike through; a friendly black dude came up to me and said, "This ain't no time for a white boy to be in this neighborhood!" And I was just able to get onto a Greyhound bus as the columns of black smoke began rising from the overturned cars burning in the streets. We had to drive through it

to get out of there. We were lucky that Greyhound had hired our accomplished and cool black driver who was responsible for us too. (I had gone up to see Expo '67 in Montreal and got my first exposure to Buckminister Fuller and Le Corbusier and Karheinz Stockhausen and those petite French girls.) So, being a battle-hardened knight of the road, I was glad to run a bit of interference for Darrell who could and did draw the predatory instincts of street people who frequented this fine dining establishment. For one thing he dressed kind of funny. It was from the freebox or the Goodwill, he was kind of like Johnny Carson with polyester bright shirts and wide outlandish tie, and a light-colored seersucker sport coat: hush puppies, and a vest and to top it off — a straw Fedora! For Christ sake. And he had that druggy, alcoholic grace that if it were not more often than not comical, could indicate arrogance, or worse — victim.

Though my hopes were just to have a decent meal and some great literary conversation at a publisher's luncheon with a great poet whose work I was just in awe of and whose intellect and breadth of education was astounding, my evening dinners at the food project within the great noisy din and clatter of pots and pans and trays and cutlery (and there were outbursts and fights all the time) sometimes felt like it was a bad movie directed by Fellini, or worse Scorsese. It was an iffy situation to which Darrell Gray was blissfully impervious. Somehow it worked.

At the driveway to the side of the church you paid your quarter, got a ticket with a number, and waited for them to call out our number so you could get in line to go in. Whoever got there first, Darrell or I, bought two tickets so we could go in together. There was a little terrace off to the side looking out to the west and the bay and the Golden Gate, to which we could repair. My fantasy is that we would be at a room in academia. We'd be at some excellent deeply wooded room of high varnished rococo embellishment. A conference in a library, with hard bound books behind glass. It would have been nice to be served drinks there; to be guests at the University in a swell *soire*. I think he had already had quite few drinks by the time he showed up here. We could keep an ear out for them to call our number.

While standing in line you'd hear talk. Some guy haranguing his friends: "The QUARTER meal can't afford to continue feeding you poor bastards. You're going to have to find somewhere else. Oh, and guess what? Now they are building the SHIT out of Berkeley, all over! Big tall building to house many students, who have lots of

MONEY! But they cant keep a 25 cent meal in town? Sounds fishy to me. Shit is going to hit the fan, I'm telling you. The Homeless are the bottom of the totem pole! Get rid of 'em is what they want. Well, it ain't that easy. It will ALWAYS be very difficult to "get rid" of the homeless, when you can see buildings 3 BLOCKS from Campus right here on the south side that have been empty for at least 2 YEARS, that have NOTHING in them, that could have been opened as homeless shelters. And it NEVER Happened! And it's because of GREED, pure and simple GREED! They would sooner see people DIE out here, than give them a little dignity and shelter. Very BAD karma is coming to Berkeley someday because of this."

I'd get Darrell to talking about what he was working on. Then they call our number. He'd say, "Lets get some sustenance and then we will be able to carry on with the Great Work."

The other person I most often hung with there was this huge individual who was a disciple of Madam Blavatsky and Alice Bailey. He read all these metaphysical books. He enjoyed talking about the energies: Chakras, auras, vertical axis of earth's fields of bla, bla. He was a sweet guy, and had great verbal ability to cool out the crazy. And if it took more than verbal ability, he would just stand there looming large with his hands on his hips, glaring at the boisterous miscreants with a most baleful stare, witnessing for the movement of god's benevolence in the world. He would come over and stand with me.

Another time Darrell and I were hanging around outside waiting for them to start up, there was quite a crowd. There were always a lot of women eating there, but they looked to be very troubled. This day there were some fine looking young women — they were all dressed up in jeans: jeans skirts and fancy colorful jeans vests, like they were somehow refugees from a rodeo show that had come through town and got stranded. Or the girl backup singers for a cowboy blues band that had wandered off out of Texas and never were able to get back. And they were falling down drunk. Just loaded, staggering around leaning and falling on each other and guffawing and giggling. It was quite a site to see. One of them had to pee, and the church would not let any one in before it was time, that was a hard and fast rule, and these girls were so out of it that one of them squatted right down and looked like she was going to pee right there. The other's grabbed her and dragged her back up to her feet as she was talking loud and saying, "I laughed so hard I pissed in my pants."

"I don't care! You are not going to pee here!" the other one said. And with a girlfriend each supporting a shoulder they half lifted, half dragged her ass off on down the street toward people's park. We didn't see them at dinner.

Darrell Gray took in this scene with dismay, and then started talking about his career as a professional poet working at Hallmark cards. It was in Kansas City.

"Yesss it was quite nice, after you got a few Sentiments in, they let you go next door and work from the bar."

"We had another person who worked with us," he recalled. "She had undergone chemotherapy for cancer and all her teeth had become like hollowed out? And rotten and her hair had fallen out, but she designed these beautiful cards, you know? With flowers and hearts and unicorns to go with the sentiments."

"Sentiments?" I asked.

"That's what we called them. Sentiments. They were keyed, of course, to the Occasion."

"Occasion?"

"You know, Mother's Day, birthday, Graduation."

"Wow, writing a poem for an occasion. Do you remember any of your stuff?"

"Oh, I had some nice ones."

"Like what?"

"Well you know it's about saying things for people who are trying to maintain a relationship. Some simple things. Like 'It's always been hard for me to just blurt out, "I love you, mom". And then go from there. It has got to be really obvious. Another one I had was for Graduation. It went something like: 'Our dreams are defined by our hearts . . Our future is designed by our dreams."

"Cool. Why did you quit."

He laughed, well, it was pretty manipulative. Besides I wanted to find my own Occasions, not someone else's. A poet does something for himself, and it turns out that it is good for others too. A poem is a kind of celebration, it is driven by an occasion. So we will need to speak about the aesthetics of occasion."

The mood generally picked up inside. People like to eat. We passed down a long steam table; the fare was good. Mostly vegetarian casseroles, and all kinds of breads and buns and an odd assortment of deserts. We all ate gratefully off the four-chambered steel tray and even took home the extra oranges, to have something for later.

The place was deafening. We couldn't hear across our own table. Thus, most conversation was shouted into the ears of the people on either side of you. It got a little weird when he shouted out some term like *a priori* and I got a little nervous that we might be overheard using words like *synthetic a priori judgements* or, god forbid, *categorical imperative* in this company.

The three of us together put me into a fantasy, where I imagined a meeting at that church dinner at the Presbyterian church, George Berkeley, the Bishop of Cloyne was hosting and visiting was the Jesuit poet, Gerard Manly Hopkins and another guest Bishop Bayes, who had developed the theorems of inference. I guess the metaphysical Lord's Witness was Berkeley, Darrell was the spiritual poet, and that left me as the philosopher of information trustability. Perhaps George Boole was there at this convocation in my mind, taking place on the grounds of Christ's church. And the reverend Charles Dodson too might have put in an appearance at the garden party.

Darrell moved to a basement apartment in Oakland. He somehow got food stamps, and started cooking. I got food stamps too, there wasn't no work. A great inflation set in after Ford pardoned the impeached Nixon so they relaxed the food stamps, I guess. I would occasionally do a big shop and take the 34 bus down Telegraph Ave. to his place in Oakland and we'd cook a dinner together. While it was cooking we'd talk, drink wine, smoke dope and collaborate on a poem on the typewriter in his little basement room with the mattress on the floor. There were several people living in that basement. Someone had a black and white TV in the common room and we marveled at the pictures of Mars coming back from the Viking probe.

Darrell Gray flowered as a cook in his new kitchen. This was the kitchen downstairs, kind of low ceilings, but tiled and an avocado colored sink and nice bright orange cabinets. I never saw the upstairs. There was some jerk up there who had the whole house to himself and his girlfriend. He was always boxing; he'd be outside on the back porch over the entrance to Darrell's basement, jabbing a bag he had hung up there; or he'd be inside banging and plowing his girlfriend. Then he'd come back outside again strutting. She generally looking kind of upset about it.

Darrell Gray cooking was like some kind of alchemist, with things bubbling on the stove. He would take on the persona of a character he had, one Phillipe Mignon, a French gastronome but really a character, a foil, a probe for the creation and gustation of savor.

He did mention that Sanskrit poetics was about the generation of savor. I didn't realized it at the time, but he had really taken on the sense of the Vedas — that being percolates through all things.

Darrell Gray was one of these guys you could say absolutely anything to; well actually, he did inspire you to keep it fairly high minded. But *he* felt comfortable saying most anything around me. He might, while cooking, speak (as Phillipe Mignon) to the legumes: "See how the fog is coming in the window, and it is being pulled into an updraft over the pot of boiling peas?"

"Yes I said, a vortex. A cyclone, I wonder where the circulation is coming from?"

Peering down at it with concentration he said, "It looks like something out of Dante's hell, steam rising from a boiling cauldron mixing with the outside air."

He walked over to the stove, and indicated the shelf above it. "There are Dante and Virgil staring down into the abyss."

Suddenly we were transported into a scene from the great medieval poem. We peered over the edge into the pea pot and saw them circulating, rising and sinking. Careening off each other — mad molecules, bubble nucleation annihilation and creation leaving tracks in a cloud chamber, "Could be looking at the fires of creation here," I said.

"Yes," he mused. "They are giving themselves to us. . . I wonder if they put me in a pot would I make such a widening spiral handing out bits of myself like a kind of Eucharist to those that could receive it."

As Phillipe Mignon, Darrell Gray could pontificate like a highly literate Julia Child: " Poetry should be simple, like the flavor of a dish made of various ingredients. You want to create something that is fresh and new and when people sample it and tell you it is the best you get a really wonderful feeling deep down inside. Cooking is like poetry. Poetry is like cooking. Savor is to being manifestation what flavor of a dish is to the substances composing it."

Darrell's best dish was Szechwan Peppercorn Chicken. It was so good that he held the cookbook in which the recipe was contained, in high esteem telling everyone to try it.

Before going over to his place I'd do a short shopping spree at the Berkeley Bowl on Shattuck. I'd call Darrell to see if there was anything he wanted. One of the Chinese employees working at the Bowl was friendly and obliging; he helped me locate ingredients like black soy sauce and shaoxing rice wine for the peppercorn chicken.

Coming from Texas I haven't done much Chinese cooking except for the hippie stir-fries that we called GORP (Good Old Rice and Potatoes). I had never heard of tofu.

I was surprised by the amount of prep work involved though it was fun cooking in the night club kitchen with Darrell chopping and cleaning, standing around and drinking, until everything was assembled, and he fired up the skillet as hot as the burner could go and started throwing things in.

The other folks in the house would be coming around and he would feed them too: big stews, or chicken slowly simmered all day in the beloved crock pot while he wrote in his little room with the bottles of wine outside his door.

I'd be trying to engage him or the others in the house in a conversation, and he would leap up run over to the stove distracted by the heat and the flames and the many shakers and boxes and bowls of spices, sometime muttering incantation over the crucible as he threw in his magic herbs, sending them on their way, admonishing them, to do their mysterious magic: "So much power in a little flake / falling, falling on the chicken bake-ing, to be subsumed into its Eucharist. . ."

Or sometime he was like a kitchen god throwing down fire in the form of chili power and the ground peppercorns: "Here comes the heat! Here comes the essence! Burning hot sauce traveling like hot thought /

from THE FROG SYMPHONY
* * *

    SATURDAY night. Though he had no calender, he knew. He could feel it where his wallet used to be; he could feel it in his groin. He could feel the general, murderous elation that lifted up the spirit of the weary nation, on the plucked wings of which ride, are carried upward, all the unfulfilled aspirations and frustrated dreams of America, in the clutches of which little remained to entangle his emotions, not even of the dispassionate venom that tinctured his relationship to the crazy world of aspiration, to the world of money and men: to the recorded history of America. But it was Saturday night. There in the gathering dusk of the already tenebrous boxcar, that rumbled its way west extrapolating the sunset, extending the day into an extra hour, letting linger the colors that he couldn't see, without a calender or prescience of the ordered progression of days he could feel it, could discern the hunger for a nameless glut for which Saturday Night had been created. (He felt that his own meager talent as an artist—on which he wasted little of his time, to which the notebook and pencil carried in his pockets and his own opinion of himself were his twin condescensions— stemmed from his ability to recognize, isolate or express these feelings about time and space, to apprehend the least tactile of the world's vibrations and label them successfully, garnish them palatably, and or even coherently. By this transliterative ability of his own he measured the (greater) powers of other artists. Sam Cooke, for instance, nailed down this particular hunger and signed his name to it when he sang "Well it's Saturday Night, and I ain't got nobody. I got some money cause I just got paid. If I don't find me some one to talk to, I'll be in an awful way.") Saturday Night: the net result of this clinical (boxcar) teleology; the name now yielded by his far off, nonparticipant eyeball; the thrall and swim of other people's perversely conceived and received emotions; the locus of their alcohol statistics and Daddy's 6-pac; the membrane of all forms of intercourse ballooned and knotted here; valve at the vertex of the tapestry of dance on the wall of creation billowed by the wind of ninety million American lies uttered at random through the fumes of the smokey Dream into the straining ears of as many receiving vessels; eulogized and harmonized like no Tuesday; nocturne of night trippers, drag strippers, soda sippers, glass slippers and <u>silent machinery</u>; of long, forlorn trains throwing sparks at phantom country crossroads, 3 A.M.; acme & climax of interminable jazz; couch of mellifluous conceptions honeysuckle scented, back seat whimpers soft & timeless; dark tunnel of whispers, accents and tender Georgian timbres, drawled bayou threats, baffled crash and tinkle of whiskey bottle on river rocks, V8 growl of icepicked, gutted mufflers; and the self-addressed stutter of the drunken village idiot, last to go to straw in the purlieus of dawn.
    Saturday night and its catalogue of clues to Yes, Yes and Eternity...

                             --copyright © 1974, by Jim Nisbet

Page of Punctual Actual Weekly with text by Jim Nisbet

Taxi Unlimited: The Trainee

I got work at Taxi Unlimited, a Berkeley co-op cab company. It wasn't very far — just two doors away from the theatre on Blake St. — which is lucky since I didn't have a car. They had a storefront made out of a house by opening up all the internal rooms. The no-budget interior decor was deep hippie funk swirling with all known hues of freebox fabrics textured into macrame around Goodwill furniture. I figured working at Taxi would allow me the mobility of a car in between being an operator of the public conveyance. Not to mention a little eating money. Taxi Unlimited was a cab company unlike any other; it was pure Berkeley style. First of all it was a co-operative, so you had to go to group meetings. I made the mistake of getting into sex with one of the honcho women there, and as she was the one who decided who would get what shifts, these meetings could be kind of dicey. Charles, a sweet small intelligent guy who was my trainer, called them "meetings to find out who Roxanne hates."

Many of the cabs were painted multiple colors, sort of like a tie-dyed shirts and the drivers matched, sporting long hair and beards. Many of the men dressed in the style of Working Man's Dead like Pig Pen, with biker affinities like large leather vests and leather bill folds attached on a chain to black jeans or bib overalls. There were an equal number of women drivers. Some were tough biker chicks in leather; some were lost waifs who kept getting raped in life. A lot of the women took one of the many dogs hanging around the place to ride shotgun on their shift.

In addition to dispatching cabs, the cooperative ran an answering service on the side and really did a great job, because the operators were middle class, intelligent dropouts who had become hippies. It was a bit of a day care too, because some of the women had their babies with them. And people just hung out around there talking all kinds of trash and playing guitars, which I guess a caller could hear through the answering service. It was popular though, pulling in at least as much money as the cabs. The cabs were amazingly junked out. They were always being worked on at the Auto Mechanics Co-Op on University. Our cabs were really out there. One was completely collaged with Fabulous Furry Freak Brother cartoons. Someone had painstakingly appliqued and carefully shellacked the comic strips into the contours of the hood, roof, trunk, and sides of the '67 Ford Galaxy. It was really something to drive the avenues of Oakland in that, let me tell you. The company kept shifting the insurance from one cab to another almost ever day, taking it off one in the shop and applying it to one going on duty.

Charlie was an Old Hand of the co-operative and I was The Trainee. We got in the car and hit the road. It was him driving at first. I just listened to the patter he held with the fare, after explaining why the second guy was there. He kept referring to me as The Trainee. Then after a while he let me drive. He watched like a DMV operative while I adjusted the seat and mirror to my height.

Taxi Unlimited was run by committee and as Charlie showed me, you had to account for the miles driven and the amount of time on your meter. Both the driver and the dispatcher kept a log called a Waybill. It had the Name of the driver, the Date, the Shift and the Cab #. There were columns and a line item for each trip : From:, To:, Name (of the Fare):, Charge:, Meter (amount), Tip:, Book (Amount given to the collective). There was an amount due. The driver's wages were Meter times a per-cent. There were line items for Gas and Oil if you had to buy some. And if you got an Advance there was a line for that. Basically, whatever was left over was your pay for that shift. Tips were yours — separate. "That's why I keep two wallets," Charlie said, "one for Taxi and one for me."

You have to handle money, make a lot of change. "And 20s," he said. "Everybody wants to give you 20s." Even on that first training shift, he kept asking me for change, and once we had to pull into the giant Liquor Barn on University Avenue to get change for a $20.

As we were going past the Herrick hospital on Dwight Way, Charlie said, "Hospitals are a good place to pick up fares. This and Highland. People come and go from there all the time. But a lot of time people call a taxi instead of an ambulance. Sometimes you gotta get them there in a life and death situation, I've had people hemorrhaging blood in the back seat. Pregnant ladies too. It's on you."

"You'll learn the best streets," he said as we were driving down the wide divide of California St. "Like it is better to travel on California than San Pablo or Shattuck or even Grove if you can manage it. Try to avoid the traffic on those if you can."

But my first night on the job riding shotgun should have told me something about what working there would be like.

We pulled into Everett's Barbecue Kitchen on San Pablo in Oakland. The people working there dispensed great heaping plates of steaming barbecue meat that was as fine as anything I had tasted in Texas. It was world class. Their whole operation was from behind a wall-to-wall, floor-to-ceiling Plexiglas barrier. To pay the cashier you had to drop the money into a drawer that closed as he slid it into him. The two inch thick plastic would easily stop a high powerful assault-rifle onslaught. I asked them: "Why the big Plexiglas barrier?" And the worker behind it said, speaking through a speaker-phone like the visiting center in a jail, "It's to keep us in here and them out there."

At the barbecue place a wild- eyed, muscular black dude, on a small trick bicycle rode in. He had a baseball bat slung in a long holster or sleeve that was strapped across the bike frame, running up under the seat and out the back, kind of like the way the horse cavalry had their rifle under the saddle in the movies. He got to hassling with several people and I was just standing there and he pulled a knife on me. I could tell that he was kind of drunk and I probably could have taken him, but I did not want to roll around with this crazed nigger or get banged into the green concrete walls of that meat vendor's bunker. I just eased on out with my groceries and got back to the cab.

Charles was kind of grinning at this. And as we drove off, said, "Not bad for your first night on the job. Got a knife pulled on you. If you get home in one piece at the end of a shift then you've had a good night."

He shared the tips with me. It was nice to get a few dollars in my jeans.

On my first solo shift, a passenger climbed into my cab and said, "Take me to the Spenglers."

"Where's that?" I asked.

Or Ozkinage, or REI or the Claremont.

"Where's that?" I was always asking. It was like that. I had to drive around with a map up my butt for the first 3 months, had to ask fares where everything was. And if I couldn't find it on my map (I had an elaborate cross indexed binder full of maps) I'd radio into dispatch, to the long suffering Barbara or whoever was on and she'd usually know where it was. Or I could call one of the other drivers on the CB. Especially difficult was the baffling warren of rabbit trails honeycombing the Berkeley hills. They were seriously labyrinthine.

But it was beautiful up there, to be among the mountain people looking down on the hill people who looked down on the flatlanders. Being up there in that psychological vista felt so uplifting that it made your temperament swell and surge out like a sail, stretching time away from gravity down below into a substance so thin it billowed out and lofted you along, sailing into a future full of, perhaps, hope.

I could tell people were a little reticent to tell me how to drive so I had a way of putting them at ease and *inviting* them to tell me. It wasn't a *helpless* act, though, I was pretty helpless. It was more like giving them the opportunity to correct a big brother.

And so began my checkered cab career as a yellow running dog operator of the public conveyance. At first it was fascinating and kind of intimate in that tight space, zooming up into the hills among those wealthy houses, stopping to enjoy the fabulous view of the bay but so many incidents with junkies, and pimps (the whores were OK) got to be kind of depressing spending any time with these people.

In the cab ecology of the city, Taxi Unlimited was low on the totem pole. Our cabs didn't look businesslike like the other cabs; they appealed to a different clientele. So we did not usually get into the line in front of the Berkeley Rep on Addison, or the BART station on Shattuck. We did better up near the clubs in North Oakland, or along San Pablo. We were right at home along San Pablo especially among the drunks trying to get home from the bars; we were not appropriate for the uptown folks coming in ties and firs from the symphony

Occasionally you'd meet a wonderful old Berkeley socialist into using the co-operative cab company, their idealism was great. The taxi driver is the unsung hero of public transportation. Hey, it's good to feel wanted, to be needed.

We'd pick up hitchhikers if we were deadheading in some direction to pick up a fare. The beneficiaries of a free ride were always surprised. Often these people would offer to get high with you if everything looked copacetic.

I picked up a hippie and his old lady heading back from Oakland. Right about 56th Ave. and Grove, underneath the freeway. They had flashed me the peace sign.

When I pulled up, he said, "We'd appreciate the ride, but can't afford to pay you, man."

I said, "That's OK I'm going back to Berkeley. Shattuck and Haste. I'll take you that far."

"Groovy"

They got in.

They told me they were Jesus Christ people. "I've got some pot here, if you want to get stoned," the guy said. The girl didn't say anything.

I turned around with a wry look in my eyes.

He then smiled in recognition. He lit up the dube and said, "We don't smoke cigarettes, but these are not cigarettes."

He passed it to me, in the front seat, and we smoked and headed on into the day.

After that I made it a point to smoke a joint before going on to my shift at Taxi.

Sometimes I'd work the night shift from 11 PM to 7 AM.

On the night shift within a few blocks roll down Shattuck to Adeleine it would settle in: the Zen of driving was on. I was aware, very aware, of what was going on around me. Left and Right. Ahead – and behind. Minimal moves, signals – lane changes – fitting in smooth, going with the flow, making my move, hanging back avoiding crazy aggression. I was a point moving on the network, a well-oiled ball bearing helping the flow of traffic, not just trying to get some place. One among the many thousands of cars and trucks loaded with precious cargo, meat and people, furniture and appliances, fuels and toxic gasses, going local and coming from far away across America. Yellow turning signals, red break lights, roof bulbs of big rigs, signal lights: Green – Yellow and above it all Red.

I headed up Marin past Spruce to Grisly Peak into the hills going over several ridges toward Kennsington. I kept slowing down on the tops of the hills so I could watch the full moon through patches of clear night sky as the high, dark and tumultuous clouds were moving through fast underneath the great glowing orb.

But sometimes the night shift from 11 PM to 7 AM could get scary. Along the great east bay freeway after midnight the trucks really get rolling between Seattle and San Diego. It is a wide fast river of momentum shooting through the vastness of night, ungoverned by cops no where in sight. Trucks loaded with big steel girders going bong in the bottom of night moving along the redwood highway; trucks packed with meat coffee liquor and gas to LA to Chicago to Oakland to Houston; electronics and appliances; cattle and chattel.

The drivers weave a web of interstate commerce, transaction converting money in mass and muscle movement, grinding gears.

Pressing on, pressing on, they go — pushing the edge of fatigue into next week and the week after that with the help of little white pills that keep the skills edgy. At every node the road forks and if the lights might fuse with the air they would leave a trace — it would weave a great body of capillaries to conduct the life blood through the corpus of commerce.

As the night wore on it could get very bleak, though. We kept in contact, checking up on each other constantly.

Taxi Unlimited Waybill Log
Sunday November 2 1975.

    Nine hours behind the wheel of a cab is too much. Nine hours of sitting in a Berkeley kamikaze cockpit would make even a yoga master's butt sore. So you gotta get out and move around, or get back to the headquarters and be there where you can walk around on dry land. Driving around Berkeley, from the Campus to the Bay, from all up in Oakland to the Kensington hills to way up lost in Benecia. Though we hardly ever went out to the Airport, we were putting in 200 miles a day.

    After a couple of these long days in a row, Friday, 201.4 miles , Saturday, 217.6 miles (20 years of schooling and they put you on the day shift) I was a bit sore and tired. The plan for Sunday was to just help the little old people with their shopping.

    The little old ladies called us at Taxi Unlimited because we were kind of laid back. We didn't get all huffy and impatient. We helped them so they didn't bumble their stuff into the trunk.

    A lot of cabbies won't pick up people carrying bags of groceries and looking for a cab. Most cabbies avoid the grocery loads because of the time and effort needed to get the bags in and out of the taxi.

    There might have been a depression or a recession on, I was so far below the level of participating in the economy that it looked like oblivion to me. So we just dragged ourselves around. No one was making much money anyway – our cars and our drivers were too scruffy looking to get into the organized cab lines in front of the cab stands. So we were happy to get these little local folks and take them to get their shopping done on Saturday. I got a call to pick up a fare to take to the Safeway on Shattuck in North Berkeley. It was a couple of very old ladies who were twins. They had to be way up in their 70's. It was surprising how much alike they looked, and they had this habit of finishing each other's sentences. They had this giddy old girl aspect. It turned out that they were writers and editors for the University of California press. They used quaint expressions like "take the road that is much the less traveled." I had to smile at that.

After they paid me the two dollars with the 50 cent tip, I told them I had some marketing to do to, and that I'd wait for them at the edge of the parking lot where I was going to park my cab under the shade of a tree.

The two smartly dressed little old ladies with four or five bags came out of the store and looked around imperious for their ride, like they expected me to drive up there and get them. So I did. One asked me to put the load in the trunk. So I did.

These ladies were working in Berkeley twenty-six years earlier, when I was just born. Now they were in retirement and would likely live on and on. Wow. They told me that they had never married, had always lived together. Well, when I finally had their groceries up on the porch of their fine old Berkeley Tudor in the hills, they offered to have me in for lemonade. But I felt like I had to get back into the hustle, and headed out. They paid me for the fare and another 50 cent tip. And said good- day in a proper way. And I headed out to cruise the streets for a pick-up.

General Semantics Rides Again

Taxi Unlimited Waybill Log
Monday December 8 1975.

As I cross Telegraph Avenue going down Hearst past the UC Campus I see a hand in the air from some guy in a suit on the cross walk in front of the Student Union building. He's an Asian man with an orange and green tam-o'-shanter beret! Big heavy glasses. Yep got to be none other than S.I. Hayakawa.

I pull into the bus stop and he walks up to the cab. The dapper elder Asian gentleman peers through big, black, bottle-thick, horn-rimmed glasses into my cab window and calmly asks, "Can you take me to San Francisco?"

I am familiar with him because of his work in General Semantics. He knew my hero Korzybski! I'd love to meet him. "Yes," I tell him.

"Good," he says, "I need to go there now."

He gets in.

Before pulling out I explain: "It's meter and a half, Mr. Hayakawa."

He is used to being recognized. "Yes, this is OK," he says.

We head down Hearst, then University toward the Bay Bridge. I have heard of him in association with San Francisco State College, and I knew he was running for the US. Senate. But I was excited because this man had hob-knobbed with the Count, Alfred Korzybski, inventor of General Semantics. I scan my rearview mirror, turn and blurt out over my shoulder, "It is an honor to meet you Mr. Hayakawa."

He smiles, doesn't say anything. Perhaps looks a little nervous.

I knew Hayakawa had written a book, and I seemed to recall reading it. I decided to put him at ease. Hopefully he didn't have too much ego. I say, "Mr. Hayakawa, I know you are a politician and president of a college, but I know you from your work, sir. I am a fan of General Semantics. I wanted to ask you about Korzybski. What was it like hanging out with the Count?"

He is quiet, seems to be considering it.

We are getting down University toward the Bay. I decided to get business like. "Where in San Francisco do you need to go?"

"Oh, just somewhere over in North Beach. Broadway and Columbus."

So we're rolling toward the freeway.

I Pay the toll. $1.

I said: "I have read the journal Etcetera. I quite like the writing there. You have got some real straight shooters writing in that journal."

I looked in the mirror. He seemed pleased.

"I like how they qualify what they write, like the way Korzybski had that way of indexing nouns, putting the dates on nouns and talking about them at the moment, because he knew they would change. All nouns have ellipses. Yes."

"You read Korzybski?"

"Yeah. I somehow struggled through all of *Science and Sanity*. It came at a moment when I was trying to understand calculus, and it was very helpful to see it talked about in a linguistical way. I got the ideas, time binding and levels of abstraction. It made me appreciate where mathematics comes from."

We hit the freeway. And headed toward the bridge.

I said: "Come to think about it, I remember reading a paper you wrote in Etcetera about Dianetics. You had some good points, really brought them to task. In fact it was pretty controversial, wasn't it? Did you get sued over that?"

He looked a little miffed; looked like he was about to take umbrage. Perhaps I was being too friendly. I took it into a more friendly book-lover direction. "I have often wondered about the extent of Korzybski's influence. I know he influenced one of my favorite writers William Burroughs; I know he influenced the sci fi writer A.E. vanVogt. I tried to read his book *World of Null-A*, in hopes of getting some insight about non-Aristotelian logic. I was so excited to get a novel that might be more accessible, but I just couldn't get what A.E. was aiming at, at all, in that book."

I tried to see if Mr. Hayakawa was warming to any of this. I pushed on. "And who else? I think Robert Heinlein. He had some nice stuff about the Michael Valentine character about how to Grock the Fullness of It. Grocking the fullness of it sounds like something out of General Semantics. Though I am not sure what exactly, but it seems like it is necessarily from something in Korzybski. What else. Even in that movie Alpha-ville by Goddard. It was some kind of futuristic scenario. They had some guy Lemmy Caution." I laughed at this. That has got to be worst name in the world for a character, a cross between a Lemming and a Pig. I continued. "Who drove — what kind of car? A Ford Galaxy, of course," — I looked over my shoulder to see if Mr. Hayakawa was finding any of this pop-culture erudition of his mentor interesting, or new. I too am this hapless driver cruising in my Ford Galaxy, all collaged with Fabulous Furry Freak Brothers. I continued: "And there were all these weird street names, like I remember Enrico Fermi Drive. It was about some great big computer that helped people, or was supposed to help people get "clear". Clear. That's from Dianetics isn't it. Was it in General Semantics too?"

Finally the old scholar gets a word in. "Well, we see General Semantics as a kind of mental hygiene in which you question how language has built into it certain conventions that are very seductive to wayward thinking. Common sense, though common is often wrong. So yes General Semantics was about trying to get people be more aware of their thinking in order for them to think more clearly. Korzybski had various methods to help people be aware of their abstracting. That is an awareness of the whole map/territory distinction and how we must always strive to not let language keep up in our received reactions. He does want this impetus toward awareness to become reflexive, he is trying to replace old reflexive behavior with new. L. Ron Hubbard picked up on that and brought the volt meter to measure galvanic skin response and use the measurement of reaction as a kind of feedback to change. So in that sense, the basis of Scientology is totally in Korzybski. Though these people have taken it into completely messianic cult-like behaviors, and woven all kinds of weird mythology around it." He sighed audibly.

We pull onto the Bay Bridge heading into the setting sun. It's about two in the winter afternoon. I knew I'd be able to turnaround and be back on the bridge before rush-hour traffic.

"So how is the campaign going?" I ask.

"We have these new radio spots," he said, brightening. "But I'm not sure about them."

"Yeah, I heard one of them," I said. "Do you think about what Marshall McLuhan said, about radio being a cool media and television being a hot media."

I got over into the right lane and took the Broadway exit, the first one off the bridge, shot down off the Bridge then up high onto the Embarcadero freeway.

"Do you know your way around North Beach?" he says.

"Yes I think so. You just want Broadway and Columbus, right?" I ask, as I push it moving in amongst the tall buildings of down town.

"Yes my campaign headquarters is right there. I have to be there at 2 o'clock," he says. I look at the clock — it's quarter to the hour.

Seeing how he was leaving I wanted to get my question in. "I always wanted to ask you guys about the is of identity and the is of metaphor. I wonder if anyone ever studied the connection between the two."

He thought for a moment. "Well it is in the functional thinking of the brain. The very idea of a function as a mapping from the domain into the range. You have a source domain, the territory and a target domain the map. We use a metaphor to map certain aspects of the source domain onto the target domain, thereby producing a new understanding of that target domain. We of course, get into trouble when we rely to much on the map, and are not really present in the territory. Probably the whole texture of thought is functional."

I put my two cents word in. "Yeah I remember reading the papers on common sense and the perception of motion. Those were really a big help. Like primitive man might think of gravity as mother earth pulling her children back to her. It was Newton who first got it right about the distinction between velocity and acceleration."

He said, "Meditation may be the only place where your are asked to stop thinking in metaphor. You are asked to really be present in the processes of the world".

When I got back to Taxi Unlimited, and waxed enthusiastic about having met an intellectual hero S.I. Hayakawa, my excitement was met with severe disdain and derision. His name was mud around there because he quelled the student rebellion at San Francisco State by shutting down the university. The students did not get to have their Free Speech movement because S.I. is such a party-pooper. My status got considerably lowered around TAXI with that, and I was never able to bring it back up.

S. I. Hayakawa did go on to win the California senate seat, his campaign took off after he changed his radio commercials.

In the Theatre of the Body

Whenever I could get the money or could work out some kind of deal to be a TA for it, I took a class from John or Bob or Dave. I was probably one of the worst students they ever had. I was too introverted and timid to ever be an actor. I was too ornery to take direction. I wanted to memorize my work and perform it in front of an audience, but I wasn't all that excited about reading to a bunch of hostile strangers. Theatre at least seemed to have a constitution of decency between audience and performer; not so with the poetry reading. I was encouraged by the sound notation articulation to find a way to do that with being in space. But here are a few snapshots of moments in the theatre of the body.

Core Curriculum

Bob kept telling us over and over: "Be aware of your core." For the human body is constructed with the forces of balance supporting it coming together in a central region at pelvis. This is the tan tien in Tai Chi. He told us this idea is used in most types of acting, dancing or performing. He got us to be aware of it by stomping and beating the floor with our feet. Sometimes Bob would play on the congas while we stomped. It was like a rhythmic dance of baby elephants doing hippo squats.

Actors stomping on the floor for a certain period of time to rhythmic music

It really made you aware of your posture. It was so difficult to carry on beating the floor with the feet in a semi-squatting posture beyond a certain length of time. Bob was a relentless drill sergeant.

Actors walking around fiercely beating the floor with the feet.

And we all went limp and dissolved into the floor. Or we fell hard onto the floor sprawled into a lump.

The actors relax their bodies totally. Falling on the floor, they relax.

We'd do this for a while then melt down into the floor.

We are to slowly rise, eventually standing in a natural relaxed posture. Bob was constantly telling us, "The basic physical sensibility of any stage actor depends on his feet. You always forget the importance of the feet in daily life."

Hovering in Dreams

At night I would be sleeping on these very boards we had pounded our feet on.

To wake up in the theatre it was really fine. To see sunlight pouring through the sky light — a pyramid shaped sky light like the Louvre — to let the most glorious light fall in the white theatre.

Across the back wall the light came in by piercing through glass meshed with wire, so it was diffuse. On hot days you could open the windows. These were encased on the outside by a curved enclosure of black-painted re-bar which bulged out to let the windows open. We could climb on these bars up to the roof. As did the snarl of trumpet vies that also grew all over a wooden fence back there. It was beautiful.

If O'Keefe was staying over, the theatre was, of course, his to sleep in. I would be sleeping in the loft across the hall. And if by chance Dave was here too, I could stretch out in the silent and quiet sound proof room; it had a double thick crystal window that opened out into a secret passage.

Breathing

Feel out a place for yourself in the room and stand still, eyes open. Bring your focus to your breath.

Look for any catches or jagged parts in your breathing and become aware of them as they subside, receed, become smooth. Examine up your body—musles in legs—up back—shoulders. Release any tension that you're aware of, in your mind. As you watch your breath come in and go out, find an inner presence moving out and becoming an outer presence. Let the outer drift inner. And the inner drift further out.

Improvising

We walked in a circle

We changed direction randomly. Dodging the other with aplomb.

We were told to babble, to be talking constantly let a steady stream of talk emerge

There was quite a lot of relating to each other strangely with babble as we encountered the other

Suddenly I was Improvising

    It was like being in a kind of ball room circulating around.

    The other; we became more aware of the other.

    It was excruciating and embarrassing to walk around in front of other people babbling. It like to gave me heart failure with the mortification of it. But these guys had no problem with it. So carry on.

    The absurdity of it had me relate to just the sound of the talking. When you passed somebody and heard a phrase or two; I would shift my text in response to what they were talking about.

    I could begin to use the material I just heard, or develop some reaction to it.

    To communicate you have to open to vulnerability. That sense of the fool venturing into New Lands living on luck and humor.

    I was relating what I was saying, but was also listening and responding. I didn't have to be the only one carrying the talk along. We were respecting each other's right to be.

The new floor

We all pitched in and built a new floor for the theatre. Dave was a good carpenter, Jim Nisbet was a contractor and Doug Wilson was a finish carpenter and furniture maker. So we had lots of experts. And then there were guys like me to do the step'n'fetch it.

We tore out the old riser platform stage, the theatre was a mess. After hauling out the broken up bits and carpet of the old stage, we exposed the old concrete floor at the bottom of the warehouse. We brought in joists and laid them out, long joists with good joinery. We nailed the thick plywood decking to the joists. Soon we had a whole new floor; everything was level and the floor had good bounce. The new floor was covered with some kind of nice smooth finish like a redwood stain but very thick and resistant to severe marking.

The Zen of Work

I swept the floor of the theatre with pride and humility.

O'Keefe was teaching me how to sweep. How to use the broom on the beloved wooden floor of the theatre.

I think they were instituting less stomping. Anyway O'Keefe was showing me how to sweep a floor. "Back and forth in sweeping motion. No jerking. And not super aggressive, you don't want to tire yourself out. Steady back and forth moving from the hips. Be mindful of your core. Let it be the source of movement.

Form

Bob was always talking about the Form. I knew from what he had shown me, especially the sense of the Form, meaning the whole long boxing exercise in Tai Chi, I started paying more attention to Form. Doug and Dave started teaching me a little Tai Chi and it was a big thrill. There was some kind of energy and spatial imagination bound up in the gesture of muscle. It was good to be connected to the ground of being in the present realization.

The Form also meant "that which triggered a sequence of

behavior, from exercises and practice." The sequence of triggers, when written down were the keynotes of the piece. It was the springboard from which to improvise. Having the sound notation made one more aware of the energy forms in words. Studying acting made one more aware of the forms of human behavior. Anything can be seen as a confluence of form and content.

> I slowly curled my fingers into a fist.

The slow progression of fingers curling is the form; the content of this form is the enactment of intention to form a fist.

Stop and find yourself. Posses being with zest, do not let it possess you.

The arc of lifting cup to lips is the form, the fulfillment of the desire to drink the coffee is the content of the action.

> I took a drink of coffee from my cup.

Like take any action. Say a sharply pointed finger. Someone pointing at someone saying "You are wrong! YOU ARE WRONG!" The j'accuse. It is a sign demarcating space — us against them. Something or somebody not living up to some expectation

> There was a hand hanging in space in the form of pointing the finger

I started paying more attention to what was going on on the street. I watched the form of people's actions. It was like inhabiting another planet there for a while.

> A woman abruptly turned on her heel and walked away

Or turning away through a shun, can also be seen as a movement in a dance. When you start being more and more conscious of your actions around you, and take responsibility for the improvisation of the moment then you will be relating to the actual — and to the ritual; to the form — and to the content of an action.

My First Acting Gig

O'Keefe was often away going about his relationship with Jen-Anne Kirchmeyer, a painter and graphic designer who did a lot of the teaching aides at the Exploratorium. She did illustrations for books. She painted sets for the Renaissance festival held in Marin, a far away mystical county across the Golden Gate in an area called The Valley of the Moon. But her soul was in some gigantic paintings 8 by 20 feet that adorned the walls of the warehouse. O'Keefe or Jen-Anne even got me a job in the Renaissance Faire. I came up with a character: the Alchemist. I threw together a dialog based on samples of dramas from Goethe's and Marlow's *Faust*, and alchemists screeds from diverse sources: Crowley, Ben Johnson, John Donne. I had one based on Sir Issac Newton, who devoted a great deal of time to the magic arts. The text I used was from his translation of *The Emerald Tablet*. I found it in the stacks of the UC library. So at the Renaissance Faire I would walk around in costume spouting out these lines like reciting a long poem.

> It is true without lying, certain and most true. That which is Below is like that which is Above and that which is Above is like that which is Below to do the miracles of the Only Thing. And as all things have been and arose from One by the mediation of One, so all things have their birth from this One Thing by adaptation. The Sun is its father; the Moon its mother; the Wind hath carried it in its belly; the Earth is its nurse. The father of all perfection in the whole world is here. Its force or power is entire if it be converted into Earth. Separate the Earth from the Fire, the subtle from the gross, sweetly with great industry. It ascends from the Earth to the Heavens and again it descends to the Earth and receives the force of things superior and inferior. By this means you shall have the glory of the whole world and thereby all obscurity shall fly from you. Its force is above all force, for it vanquishes every subtle thing and penetrates every solid thing. So was the world created. From this are and do come admirable adaptations, whereof the process is here in this. Hence am I called Hermes Trismegistus, having the three parts of the philosophy of the whole world. That which I have said of the operation of the Sun is accomplished and ended.

It was strange memorizing lines by the sea. It was fun learning the ancient Elizabethan dances, that they taught us, to enact here and there in the faire. Little gigs and aires.

Space and Shape

I became aware of timing. It was something between people that could be tuned in upon.

I became aware of shape. The direction into which the situation or the occasion was apt to waver into.

I spent several days being awake and aware of gaps in between things. When I could double my awareness I tried to listen in to the pauses between things. Words. Sounds. I have learned to focus on intention.

The theatre and its double Artaud called it. At times I could be outside myself and see myself from outside, it was a kind of astral body thing.

Yes we had found the double.

The spirit of Artaud was with me now. Humbly smiling his mad contorted smile of deviant encouragement. The grand old man, who suffered but was still totally cool.

What was that yearning double, Monsieur Artaud? Moving like a shadow through the world. Metaphysics, or the disease that gave us immunities, or the hunger that drives the world, a hunger you sought to turn into culture.

Yes you were right. After days of hunger, what passes as culture — that which would let you die — seems way in the back of my mind now. I owe nothing to it. I take nothing from it. I have nothing for it. I will not serve it.

It was not the political Artaud, who discovered that the theatre of cruelty was necessary to liberate yourself from the coercions of the bourgeoisie — loose whatever it is that keeps you plugged into this system. But the anthropologist Artaud, who sought to find a transcendental spiritual theatre. Or it was Artaud the experimentalist; the metaphysical Artaud, who saw metaphysics as one of the doubles of theatre. We have these a priori philosophical proclivities within us and we are meant to do something with them.

Artaud right down here in the bunker, so crazy, so wild so angry. What was that all about?

Dear old uncle Antin, what is that universe inside that little seed word, that starts all creation, *be*, that starts pointing to qualities and connections.

Da sein? Heidegger and Artaud and Peirce, *The Sign?*

They sought to understand its intelligence beyond words, its spirituality beyond any religion

No ontology without phenomenology.

The map is not the territory.

You are with me now mon oncle Artaud, who took the time to really possess being and be possessed by it.

It is that for which we all are longing.

Artaud saw the theatre as a lab to experiment with feeling the forces coming through, to feel the artistry of place like the old time Cabalists.

It starts by being humble, to say, sorry I made such a fuss with all my learning, I thought it would help me understand you. And it has, don't think me ungrateful, but I must get beyond it now. I must let it go.

O'Keefe and Albert and the Hawkeyes were doing what Artaud only hoped would be possible, they were working in a different language, the language of nature, that took hold of the actor and displayed itself in gesture and in shivering presence and in sound energy slowed down to language.

The actors were able to be the children they once were again. The way they picked up an object and instantly innocently experimentally used it for some other purpose. A boot became a telephone; a bell became a shell for listening with or a microphone mouthpiece for talking into. A ladder against the wall became the stairway to another world. Bob did *Trunk 15*, in which he pulled objects out of a trunk and wove improvisations on that. Physical metaphoricity. O'Keefe had *The Magician*, where he used the iconography of cards, and shadow shapes of scrim gels over theatre lights to create a world. Through play the physical actor can be anyone or anything, at any place at any time.

It was amazing to go from the reality of the Theatre to the reality of Taxi. It was such a different perception of being and time. I found I could copy the Dog Flow consciousness of the Theatre into Taxi. I could get in synch with the rhythm of the traffic, I could even help the flow along, be like a well-oiled molecule, shooting down the concrete corridors of the freeway, hanging back— moving ahead. My car was like a sieve taking in the dreck and jetsam of luckless pedestrians. My movement in the flow was at times touched by grace for stretches that seemed to go on and on. The movement through the night streets became a nonlinear stream of sequences consisting of a diverse hierarchical tree of me reaching out with my sensors from now into possibility to see what was to become of me, and at every branching reality shifts in real-time forwards and backwards, producing a vertiginous dual-presence, me and some other, Zoon Phonata or Krishna Glass. It was a far cry from the fixed forms of our everyday reactions to the pressures and tyranny of being plugged in. I was helping the commuting citizens. With less and less contact we were moving through the urban network with its global outreach; they too were no doubt likewise experiencing the changes: the time and experience of traveling within the boundaries of the culture and space-time.

Old bishop Berkeley lived in a pastoral village, a university of manicured laws and higher ideals, I lived in a jungle of inner-city high-speed connections among workers and their entertainments and we were all longing and seeking something — possession of our own selves.

In a world that was becoming more and more unreal. One could grow into who your really are. And these exercises in actions allow us to be alert to timing, or to sense when the energy was crossing over into the drama of contrast. I had always been a solicitous big-brother to the other, gently gathering information, and filling out the form of what you are doing with feeling and intention.

It takes stamina to learn to weave a trail of form through the events of your days. And patience to accumulate good experiences so that you can amplify and enhance your practice, timing picking up more detail, more subtleties with what is going on with your partner. Like all attempts to edify yourself, (and to reify yourself) the more you articulate it, the more you can articulate it.

The artists, the poet inhabits a world of signs. The sign in various dimensions of completion. It is not an exact science of how to concatenate these signs, some being excluded as dilatory, into a meaningful whole. It is a semiosis of the inferential, the intuitive, the being aware of the meme. I attempted to write about this with the concept of Zoon Phonata, one of the authors of the PAW. The floating identity what might have been called the astral body, which we now call the double, it is the Form you are having in front of you at the movement. The Actual. You have to have separated from the one to perceive it. And to make a sign of yourself. But how could this relate to the animality. It was the montage, being an element in the montage.

from[+] **A Notebook of Darrell Gray**

One of the notebooks of Darrell Gray came into my possession. It was one of those 5x8 hard-bound blank books —filled. It had a black, faux-leatherette textured finish. People buy them for ledgers or journals. I was visiting the poet at his small apartment in the basement of the Berkeley house and he had a footlocker full of these books that he liked to use for notebooks. He was never without one. He got them cheap somewhere in the Oakland Chinatown. I picked one at random, and started looking through it. It was inspiring to hold the actual raw creativity of a working poet in your hands. And here was a great big foot locker full of these treasures.

There were interesting drawings of friends, some of whom were, or later went on to become, famous poets. There were diagrams of systems and flows. And sketches of scenes. It was full of quotes and reading notes. And there were poems, first drafts, and some copied drafts. And first drafts of essays.

Because I asked about it, he let me take one home to read. I put it in my back pack. Then, when I went to take it back to him, and told him how fascinating and helpful it was, he said I could have it. I told him I couldn't accept it but that I would transcribe it for him at some point when I got an electric typewriter. They had electric typewriters in the basement of the Berkeley library, with a little meter that you had to keep feeding money to. I used the mechanical typer to do the PAWs. Well, it was years before I got an electric typewriter and he didn't ask about it, and it got lost in the shuffle, with all the moving around and ended up in my sister's attic in Texas and I found it later when she sent me a box full of old manuscripts.

  Here are a few examples of the pages from this notebook. I have annotated the tour through the notebook to give it a sense of relatedness to some of the material as it got elaborated upon and transformed into poems and essays. (I have a review of his *Essays and Dissolutions* in the appendix of this book.) The notebook topics range from Psychic Syntax, to Coleridge and the Poetic Imagination, Sound in the Mind, A Field Theory of Poetry — the topics go on and on and are fascinating. Enjoy.

[+] *(In the interest of brevity we have cut many pages from this Notebook presentation. Check the Sample area of Hitmotel Press web for the complete .pdf, available free.)*

Darrell Gray's Alpha World

Darrell Gray was an information engineer of the noumenal. He used the language of poetry as a kind of programming, or code, to speak to the noumenal, to invoke the noumenal, to call the noumenal with its own language, into being .

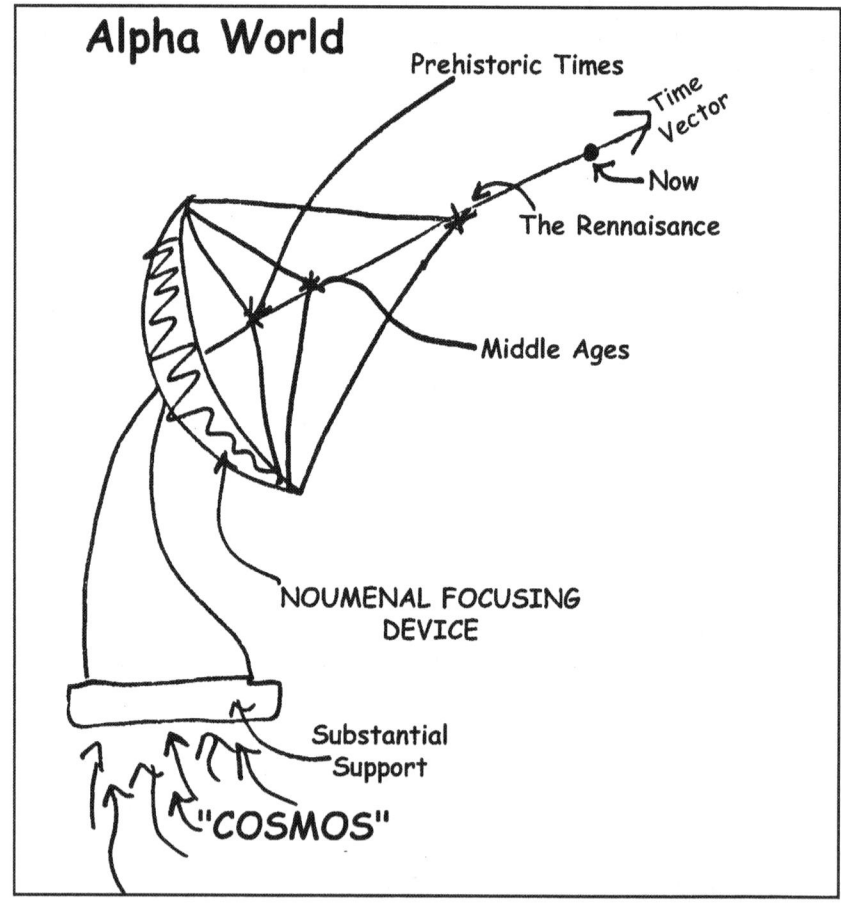

Gray was very original and was always at work synthesizing ideas. We will explore later the Transcendental Poetics of Actualism the way he did in a full Kantian exposition of the ancient Vedanta. All this creativity is about trying to know what is at the edge of the actual, to bring that world of what Peirce called Firstness, which you can only know through trails of abduction following the hints of tone and sense and suggestion and synchronicty into the unknown.

Writing for Darrell Gray was a way to see from this world into the Alpha world — a world in which one more fully participated in the ontology of being. The consciousness in his poems often goes from something very minute and particular to the much larger picture. The propositions he asks us to consider in the lines of his poems are strung like nodes on the network of the great chain of being.

(from Notebook)

Poem

>The tiny Eutruscan ants are sailing
>Home again. On leaves
>The size of outstretched palms
>Their voices curl and darken
>Their love songs seeking the
>>unknown nouns
>
>Or is it their children
>Awaking at last from their lives
>The eclipse crawls back into the fruit
>Many books have been written
>To capture the adolescent rainbow
>>they left
>Balanced on the edge of each other's life.

The Greenhouse world is hermetic

In his notes I found this untitled passage. In it Darrell Gray invokes the semeiologist Peirce, defines the function of poetry, contrasts the surreal and the irreal, and touches on many favorite subjects. I have interjected various poems and notebook pages to illustrate points.

(from Notebook, The Greenhouse world)

The Greenhouse world is hermetic, and yet embodies the same creative processes found in the phenomenal world. There is therefore a continuum, not unlike Peirce's "psycho-physical" continuum—a coherent system of inter-related states which are resolved in the work of art in the form of a tension-structure which is at once self-contained and continually activating elements beyond the structure into new and dynamic configurations. The poem, like the imagination itself, contains as its integral structure that pulsating and basic silence which lies like a sea beneath all things—that infinite sea of possibilities from which what is known emerges merely as a frequency of the unknown.

(from Something Swims Out 66)

SONNET

Beyond the immediate sensation lies a sea of light
Where the objects of passion exist in their purest essence
So as not to obstruct each other, or the passage of love.
A fullness, unnumbered, and wholly beyond us
As we move through this or that city, oblivious
Even to the world in which our feelings lie immersed,
Though what is only real can become much more.
You may want to carry something out of all this nuance,
A sort of memento of past resilience, in whose heart
You divined new temperatures, thoughts, and connections
Between even the fruit and the sunlight dividing attention.
On the beach, for instance, you felt unique and happy
Though alone, as though another world within this one
Of water, trees, birds, and their impressions, appeared
As you saw in the passive shallows the wet shells shining.

We see the astounding lushness of Gray's writing, the green house world, the Alpha world he is trying to bring us to the still point and the intersection of mirrors of being.

(from Notebook, The Greenhouse world)

    The poet's function is to make visible/& immediate that underlying silence out of which the things of this world are made.

(from Notebook)

> She approached
>   carrying roses.
> There was a faint
> smile
>   in the eye
> of the evening. There were streets
>   behind her – streets
> breaking
>   like ribbons of light.
> THE FUNCTION
>   of such action – that
> beauty
>   is simply
> this girl with roses
>   and streets.

(Greenhouse, continued)

    This means he is invariably transmuting the Known into the unknown, the experienced into the never experienced, and the common into the wonderful. His first attempt should be to break down those arbitrary and conventional categories of perception in order to evoke the underlying mystery which Gabriel Marcel has put succinctly: "that things should exist, as opposed to nothing." This, of course, means a radical and new approach to language is needed. Words must be seen neither as descriptive in function (cf. Williams & the Imagist tradition), or as ends in themselves (the symbolist tradition), but as tools or vehicles functional in the evocation of irreal. At this point I would like to make a distinction between the surreal & the irreal. The surreal, as I understand it, is a mental construction embodying purely psychic laws and actions, and achieves an absolute hermetic reality contingent upon nothing else and referring to nothing beyond itself. The irreal poem, on the other hand embodies and evokes that psycho-physical continuum and presents phenomena not as mental absolutes, but as constantly changing manifestations of the human involvement in that which lies beyond himself. Man is, as it were, on the threshold between two worlds, the psychic and the physical—the Inner and the Outer. Invariably there is a tension: he does not want to stand on the threshold forever. He wants to move from room to room. And he does.

(from SSO, 25)

THE PLACE

I stood
by the door
thinking

I could
be standing
by the window.

Then I
would be
over there,

not here,
and would see
things differently.

So move away,
I think, to
where I'm not,

and break the place
by doing what
I thought.

MEMORY LOOKING FOR A MIND

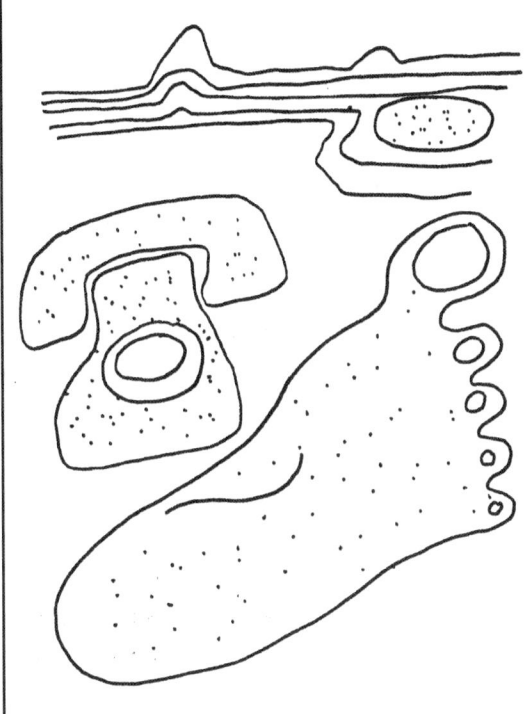

(The Greenhouse . . ., continued)

    He learns to call the wooden things he often sits on "chairs" and in the act of naming them he thinks he understands them. He has brought them under control. This surely, is the impetus behind language itself, to allow man some sort of control in a world he is continually forced to deal with. But in the other room, the dark inner room of psyche, the common objects of his experience often refuse to behave as the/Outward Man would have them behave. This is the place where chairs sprout wings and fly and monkeys play guitars at the heart of glaciers. This is the world of interior waves, rice pumps, and brass-corsages, where the objects seen in the sunlit outer world appear more immediate, 'essential, and new.

    What a poet might call a "chair" in the outer world, he would not be so quick to call a chair in the Inner world, because the possibility that something could so simply and discretely as to be, as it were, summed up in a single 5 letter utterance, would not occur him. Only the experience of the thing itself would occur in him, and never in isolation

> from the other equally significant occurrences. Indeed, it is only from the interaction of these things and occurrences, their qualities of immediacy and intensity, that the whole complex can be known or felt at all.
>
> If I write the word moon, I must mean by it not only the object in the sky which exists in a spactio-temporal matrix, but also that polyvalent image of it which exists in the mind and is capable, through the emission of connotative waves, of transforming the mental space into an area of intense psychic activity. Each object or thing experienced in the external world causes a corresponding disturbance in the mind-field, and each object once internalized has its own characteristic energy level. In the course of its psychic-activity, it emits this energy in the form of omni-directional connotative waves which invariably strike the waves emitted by other internalize objects, and, ultimately, the objects themselves. Waves of similar psychic frequency reinforce each other, and the objects emitting them are drawn together. And become "bonded" much in the same way that an atom of oxygen bonds with an atom of hydrogen to form water molecules. As psychic elements accrue, a coherent configuration is formed which embodies that spontaneous creative process which one recognizes, in the growth of a rose.

Again we see reflections of Gray's developing understanding guided by Valery's idea of language as a new chemistry for which we do not yet know the elements. Facts have their own dynamics.

C S Peirce: "The idea does not belong to the soul; it is the soul that belongs to the idea. The soul does for the idea just what the cellulose does for the beauty of the rose; that is to say, it affords it opportunity."

Darrell Gray had an incredibly easy, loose way of laying out the lines of poetry. Like an expansion of space, like something going on on the surface of an expanding balloon. It was all about this expansion.

Notice how the word Click here, sets up a bracing attention.

(from SSO, 25)

In a poem of the 20th century

> We photographed everything
> we could see.
> The click
> of the relase arroused our attention.

Types of Music

Here Gray applies the concept of open and closed texts to music. For example, a murder mystery is a closed text where the code is known and cause and effect chains are not open. "Open" texts, on the other hand, such as most poetry make complex demands upon the reader. Such texts are seen differently by different readers at different times. The stop sign is a relatively closed text, however, a photograph, advertisement, or painting, are much more open to individual interpretation. Modern poetry is usually an open text. A limerick or rap would be a closed text. The open text doesn't have a political, social or other agenda, or if it does, it is not primary. The open text seeks to create an atmosphere of discovery, of exploration. We can easily see this in music: Rock'n'roll is a closed music, jazz (especially egoless jazz, Alice Coltrane, McCoy Tyner, T. Monk,) or raga, or the new phase shift music, Phillip Glass, is open.

Gray called open music — constant state music; he called closed music — commuter music.

Commuter Music is written and performed for the purpose of transporting the mind to higher states of consciousness. It is written and performed by minds that choose a particular vision as the "Real."
[Van Morrison, Donnovan, The Who]

Constant State Music   is music which is always a complete whole, existing independent of the Reality Structures appended to It. Once there, it is almost impossible to return. (CJ & Fish)

Commuter music takes the mind only in one direction at a time. Usually either vertical or horizontal.

Constant State Music cannot be schematicized.

However ALL commutes are plastic.

Music includes all worlds. It is the world of worlds. When the music living in words is released, at first it does not want to leave. The edges of the word grow stiff! Trying hard to hold within it all its music. When two external objects collide there is usually more than one sound emitted. Gradually, a whole world of sound shorts out into the waiting region. I say the region is "waiting" because it is so totally released to [that-which-regions] that it abides in the expanse of all music, thus open to new accumulations.

A tone can decide where it goes. If it goes in circles, or in straight lines. If it vibrates softly or harshly; if it radiates branches of tone that do not refer to the human mind, but continue to grow, condensed and unhampered.

A long silence is no more intense than a short one, no?
(LONG SILENCE)

What if everything we consider Real were only the "gaps" or fluctuations of some Higher Energy? Life, as we know it, would consist of varying status of deprivation. All the five senses will merely be ways of plugging into the absence of the Real.

Still, things continue to take up time and space in the observed world. A dictionary contains many sensible alternatives, each surrounded by a separate sense of how the Real submerges itself in a many colored distance / and each word floats up to the surface, which is only the undersurface of Maya.

Some voices enter a new space. The Knocking occurs at the door thought it is entirely the wrong room and within it on the desk the paper weight retains the characteristics of sunset.

A light full of tones is between us. Nothing opens as deeply as that – an azure charm as between two highly charged clouds, and on the separate clouds a premonition of agitated leaves. Each leaf is a note from the Rolling Stones' version of Carol – great rhythms resurgences in the midst of tremendous gloom.

The Ear of Creation
1) Evanescent – The most fleeting of tones entrances it.
2) Absolute – It can go anywhere.
3) Amazing – It gives birth to the world.
4) Eternal – Nothing can alter it.
5) Blissful – Everything wants to be heard by it, though nothing hears it.
* That is which is not Heard, Though hears ALL.
* The Ear of Creation is Infinite and Silent. Though in it all this Cosmic Manifestation is constantly varying.

3 Questions
1) What is coming out of where?
2) Why is so much silence containing It?
3) If the outside is really "out" how come so little of everything is exposed?

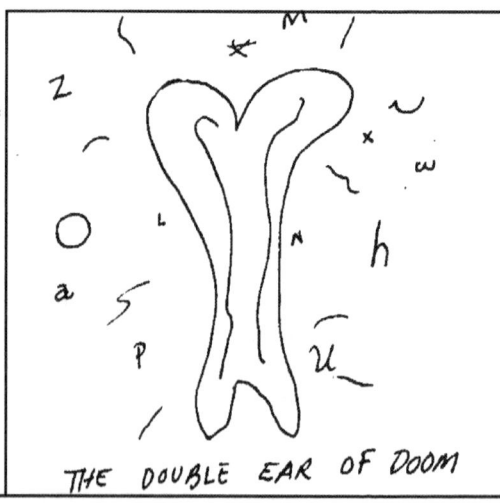

THE DOUBLE EAR OF DOOM

Toward a review of Darrell Gray's book *Essays and Dissolutions* in the appendix, let us examine a few more notebook pages as a form of what he would call "concept tenderizer" to get us ready for the plunge into his philosophical disquisition. Gray filled his notebooks with sketches, reading notes, quotes and inquiries into the creative process. The poems were a by-product of the experimental effort. He often began a work with an image.

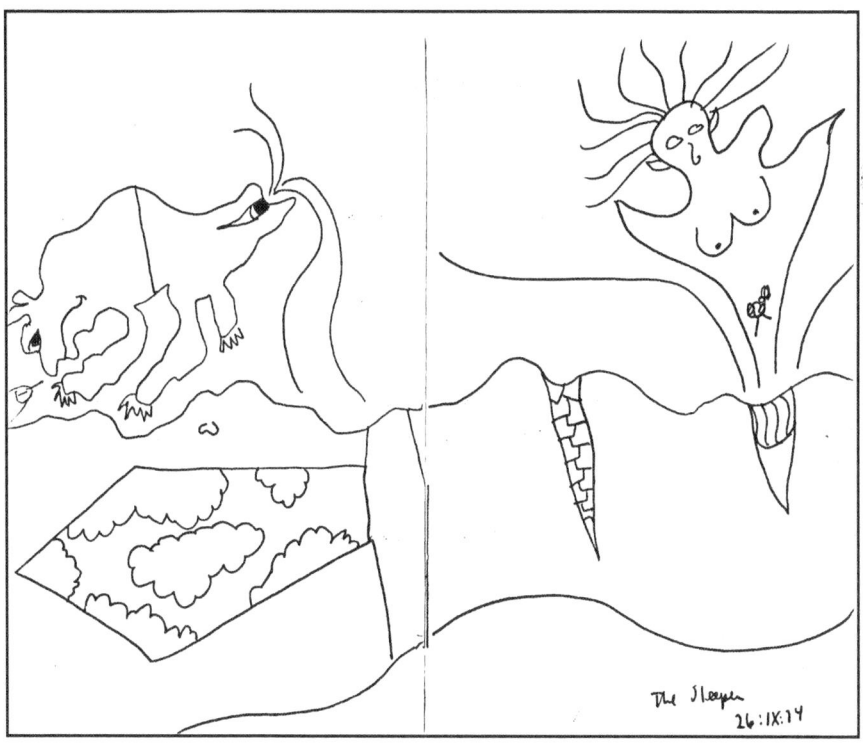

The semiotic flow from image to diagram to writing, traces in signs the emergence into form of primitive qualities and feelings and hunches. Peirce divided signs into icons, symbols and indices, according to how they signify. An icon would be the pencil marking on a paper signifying a line. An index would be the way smoke signifies fire. A symbol could be a sign as an information delay system like the x for the unknown in algebra. Poetry is exploring the modes of inference. Gray would later go on to develop this into a field formalism, of interconnected nodes of being. The four pillars of Actualism are the axis of (Pound-WCW-Olson-O'Hara) and Peirce and (Goethe-Steiner) and (Vedantic-Surrealism.) In the following we see Gray working on the concept of word as object.

Semiosis and the Word as Object

As we will see in Gray's essay *The Transcendental Criticism of Knowledge,* as he looks to the ancient Vedas for a non-dualistic philosophy upon which to base the poetics of Actualism, he is taking his cues from the idea that the sound vibrations on which the *Vedas* are based are not necessarily derived from the sensory experience of hearing per-se, but that they are analogous to vibrations the fundamental of which is in a noumenal dimension and the harmonics of which are in our local sensible phenomenal dimension.

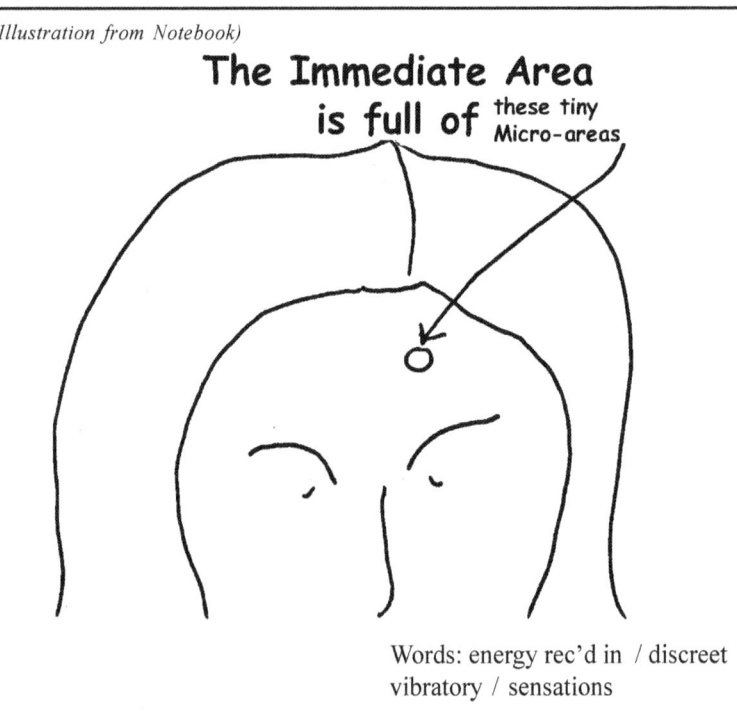

The hope of transcendental philosophy

(ED, 118 The Transcendental Criticism of Knowledge)

> The sound vibrations on which the *Vedas* are based are not derived from previous sensory experience. Therefore, their ingression within the phenomenal sphere of material activity is not directed at the adaptive and differentiative modalities of the lower mind. Emanating from the anti-material Source, these vibrations penetrate directly to the receiving facility of the individual atomic anti-material particle.

In this page Gray is considering the phenomenology of the object, to be specific, the apple. He has the image of the apple in mind and he draws it on the page where it appears, as an icon. He uses the name of the apple, in a sentence: "There is no "gap" between the Word / Sound Apple and the phenomenon itself." By doing that he brings the machinery of language to bear — in particular the indexical (subject of the sentence) which draws our attention to the icon (the image of the apple). In semiosis, the apple which had been beyond our purview has come in search of taking up a brief presence in our consciousness, as a symbol. This symbol, "apple," interacts with the index and the icon through being a word in a sentence which itself is a composite symbol. With this we have gone around the semiotic triad a couple of times at least.

I am concerned with the distance [N-Space] between WORDS & OBJECTS
Some words seem to be at the heart of objects, while others recede at their edges.
There, for instance, is no "gap" between the Word / Sound **APPLE** and the phenomenon Itself.

A signal trying to become a sign remains only a signifier until it becomes significant for some interpreter. We have seen the icon as an the image of, a schematic diagram that depicts, or is similar to, some thing — an apple through another thing —its sign. We see the apple image as the sign of an apple while deep down we know full well that the image itself is not an apple but the interdependent, interrelated, interaction (in the traditional term, "re - presentation") of our apple image with an apple.

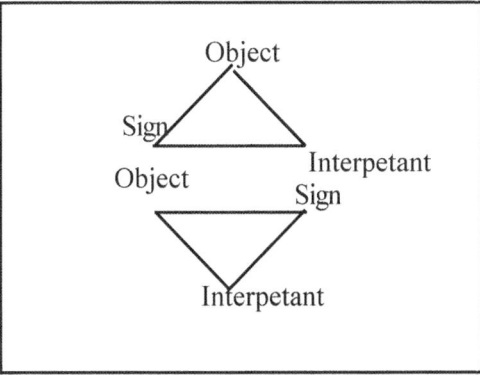

The Physicality of the WORD-OBJECT Continuum
"It" becomes "material" for the
occasion of modifying space.
Minds are adjustable. Great
artists are capable of incredible
mental adjustments. They can
not only adjust there own
minds to perceive new
frequencies of the "Flight" of
Kosmos, they can also
alter other minds as well
*

Art, like Nature, changes.

Psychic Space Altered by an Ascending Tone . . .

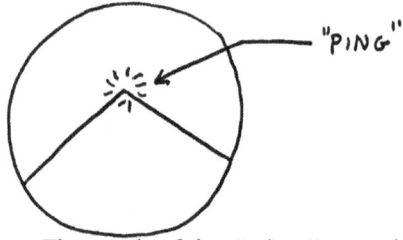

Thousands of tiny " pings" comprise
an Epiphany, which is none
other than an orchestration
of the Cosmos.
In the Body of Bliss is an
orchestration of Space & Time &
Matter. [Matter is an "excess"
of Energy within Space & Time]
When matter leaves the Space-Time
Continuum does it cease to be
"matter'? What is matter like
in other Continuums?
Anti-matter is Spirit.

Matter changes when it leaves the "CONTINUUM"

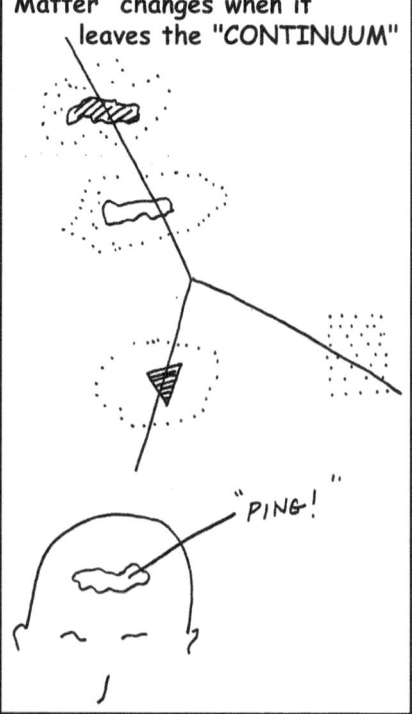

Super Senenses and Psychic Syntax

PSYCHIC SYNTAX

The basic problem, as I find it, is not to "give up" or abandon syntax, but to find or construct a syntax which will allow me to write poems which have an integral structure and movement similar to that of the mind itself. I am of the opinion that the English language as it is used conventionally is an inadequate vehicle, to express the deepest poetic insights. Poets must create their own language, and not be intimidated by the existing linguistic apparatus.

Limits of measurement is a by-product of an attempt to bring the world under control.

THE NAME:
a) descriptive (lyric)
b) definitive (external)

Descriptive / definitive process

The poem is not a postulate of natural conditions, but a utilization of natural possibilities.

Juxta-position

To bring the psychically valid occurrence into the "external" world. The phrase "African Golashes" – synthetically valid, and referring to possibilities in Actual Occurrence: i.e. – golashes made or worn in Africa.

The life of the poem is the life of its worlds – That world it manages to create independent of objects as objects – that is, as Ponge says, it exerts "in so many words" - - > FINITE

fox
blood
time
ice
moss
hand
open
ache
fish
hangs
hook
frozen

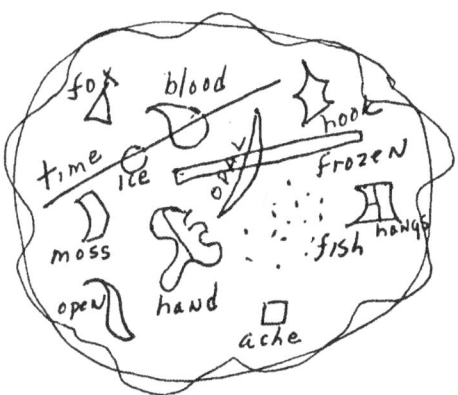

The fox, the opal, and the blood
Exist in time like ice and moss.
The hand aches to open,
But the hook still hangs.

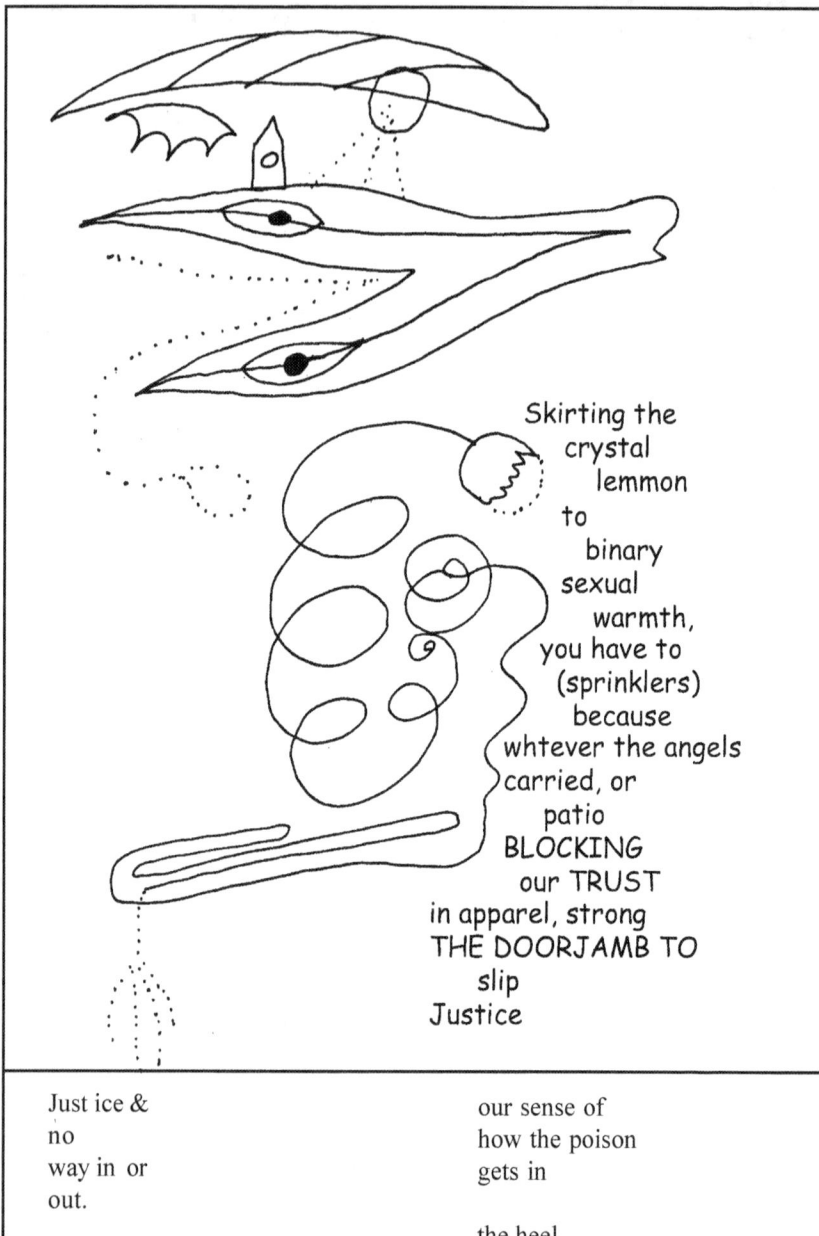

Just ice &
no
way in or
out.

Because
whatever the angels
carried

or the patio blocking

our sense of
how the poison
gets in

the heel
when one of us remotely steps
on some
thing shining
in the surf

(from Notebook)

Riverside

After the smooth stone
the lizard seemed smoother
here was a place for the body –
down by the river. Again it's
        seen –
place where touch
echoed the sheen, and father
threw me in to bob
        back up,
as life and love. At riverside
palm fronds were greener than trust
bent over where the willows went
trailing defiant tips on the water
here where the fish-mouth
opened
I thought of a daughter
boyish and tired.
Fireflies hugged the dark: the story
of all homes put to sleep.
Still – the scales meticulous
are with me.
I bob among objects; among
        dreams of friends.
I know every stone.

Driftwood

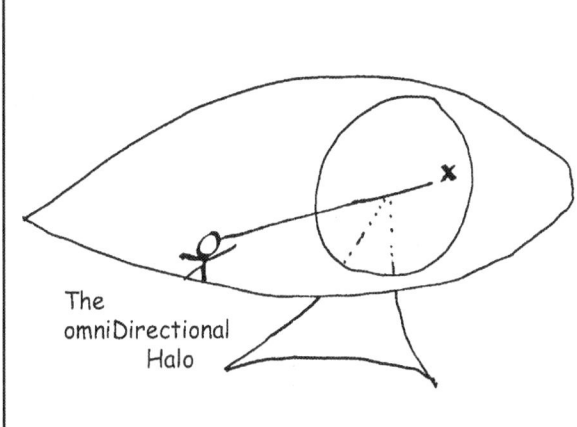

One must look down
a long way
and hard
to see what the others
are doing —
the ones in
chairs, —
one imagines them
thinking.
But the birds
are so many they
make the sky dark
when they move it.

The Poem as Feedback Machine Process

The aesthetic of WCW — "no ideas but in things" — is a rallying cry of modern poetry. Gray built on that idea. It was a reaction to the way poetry had been driven into academia by Eliot and Pound. Though we did not like the mood of dry despair in Eliot, one had to admire how he created it. TS&EP, their poems were a net of intersecting synchronic and diachronic allusions reaching across the language and mythology of the world.

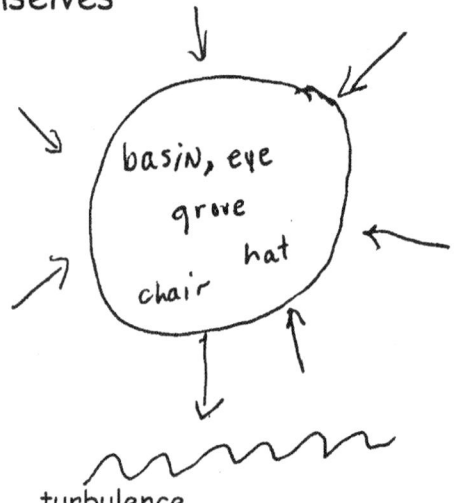

Other great ideas in the modern cannon: the looseness and autobiographical familiarity of Frank O'Hara; the cunning linguistical ejaculations of ee cumings; the magical way Wallace Stevens used precise and exotic words to sharpen the sense perceptions and reify concepts; the open spiritual thrust in Kerouac's be-bop focusing in the movies of the mind; the whole Beat / existential insight from Whitman; the surrealist program of exploring metaphor; or the language school, or the spiritual mantras. The possibilities of poetics are many.

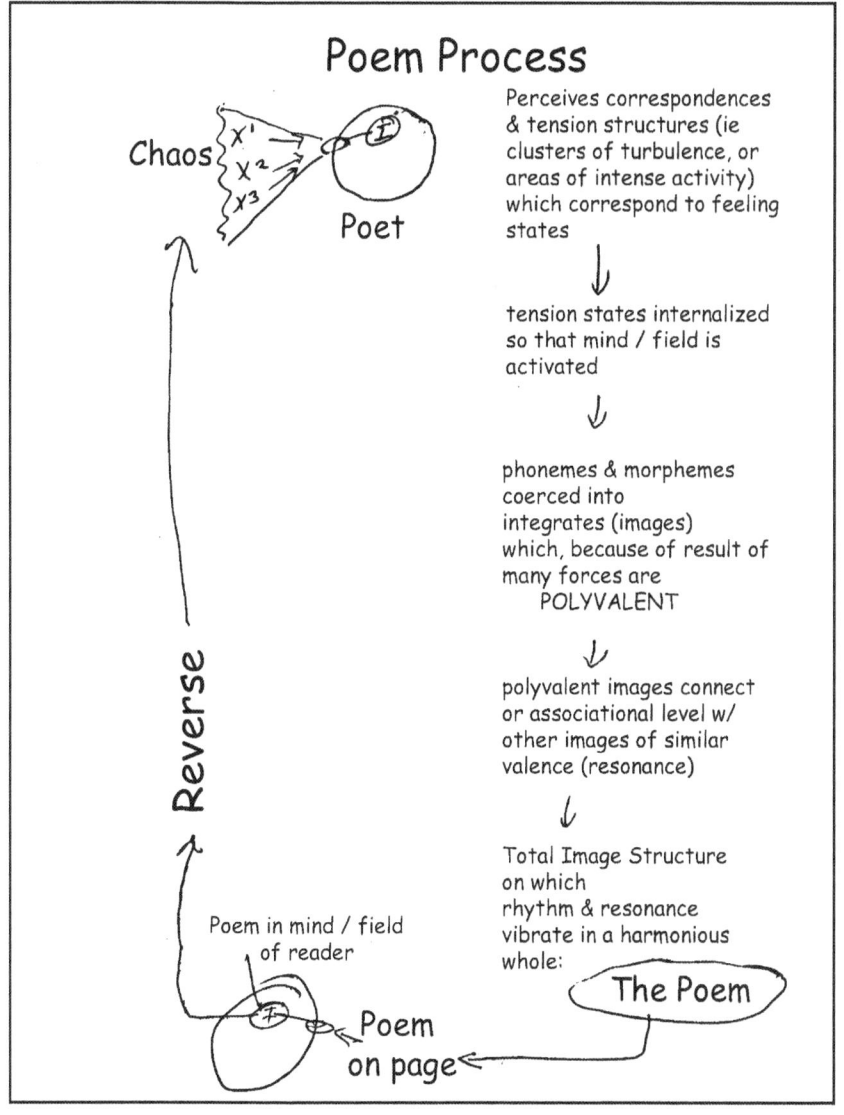

If we can abstract Gray's model of the poetic process from the previous page, we will see that it is congruent to Peirce's system of phenomenology and semiosis, as it must be.

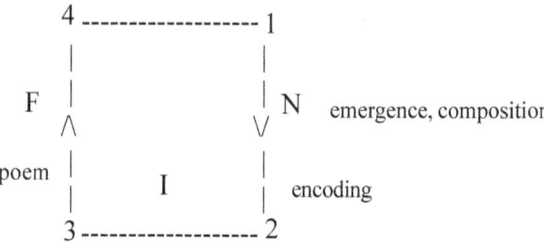

Where

N, is the Natural sequence of emergence into coding from primary
    2a, perceives correspondences & tensions
    2b, these perceptions are internalized, into field
    2c, sounds meanings align into image
    2d, image is the language of the mind flowing, associationally
    to other images so they stick together in resonance - - > 3

F, is the Formal system (or model as it exists in the mind of the reader and the poet.)
    1, is causal entailment
    2, is encoding
    3, is inferential entailment and
    4, is decoding.

There is the I, the interpreting of field events in the process of encoding the poem and there is the interpretation that the reader of hearer of the poem is doing. We picture these two process as the inverse of each other. In the cyclical-permutation group, finite algebra, register-shifting mathematic of semiosis, $1 = 2 + 3 + 4$.

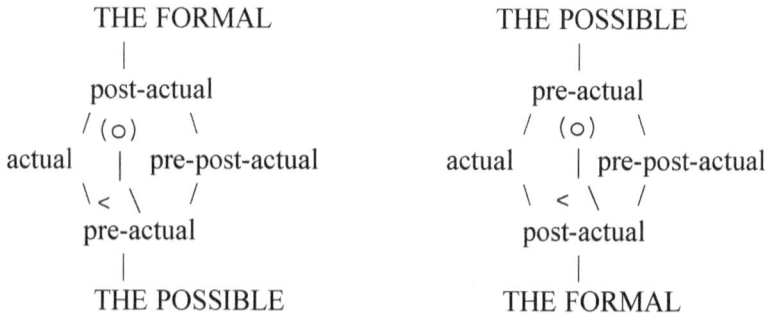

A Vedic-Vorticist's View of Time

Darrell Gray thought of the natural world as full of hermetic metaphysical processes. He understood the deep image, used the idea of the image as central in his poems. Pound the arch-Vorticist defined Image as an intellectual and emotional complex not in an instant of time, but, as it were, at the vortex of time — beyond the category of the instant.

Hovering, Focusing and the Irreal
Darrell Gray was involved in the practice of Actualism.

There were various methods and practices to help the initiate reach the state of being actual. Usually this state only lasts for a very short time, but with practice it can be obtained more often. Some of these methods were Hovering, Focus Alignment Process. These practices were the basis for an "autistic generative phenomenology" that he called Automorphism.

Focusing involved holding up the process mirror to the neumonal mirror. As explored in the essays, Gray saw Pounds Vorticism as a precurser to Actualilsm.

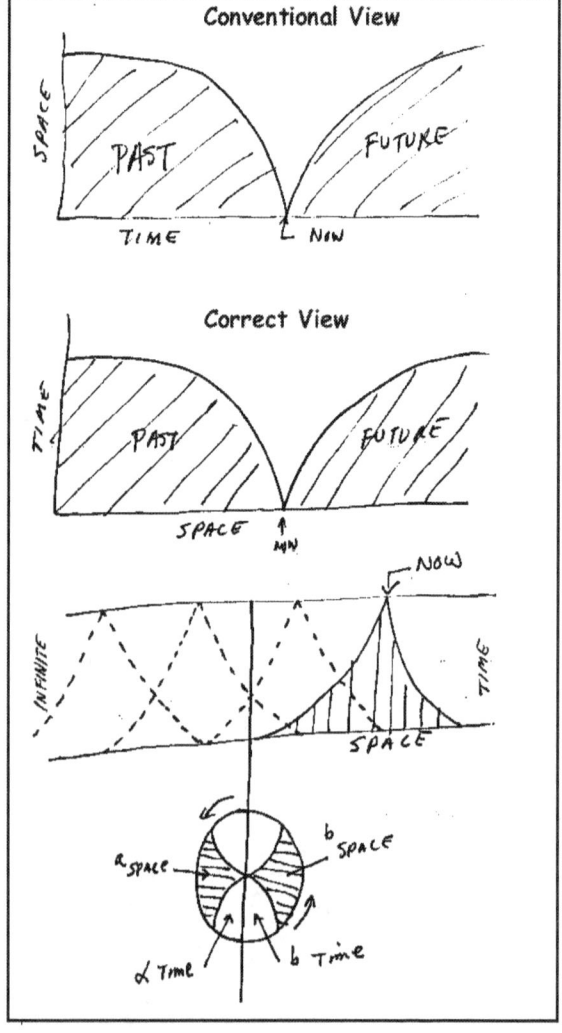

Noumenal Essences are Omnidirectional, being the
unobstructed source of all Phenomenal manifestation —
as a result they are not subject to simple linear coercion
of integrities in Spatio/Temporal Realm.

Complex conjunciton of
Simple Occasions Determined
by Numenal Essence

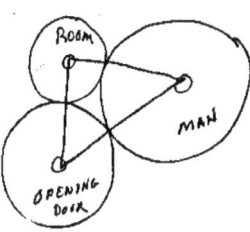

Poetic Movements

Low Pressure System

We get to the edge: no use
that the edge is within us –
    particular
        in my mind
      you live – particle
      after a month
"the world's richest man is dead"
    H.L. Hunt –
        And the bath-tub
        drain
            is clogged
that's the News
folks
that's the
hot-dog
        29:IX:74

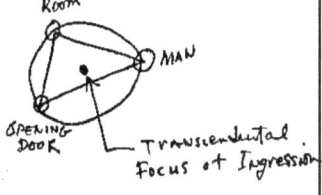

Transcendental
Focus of Ingression

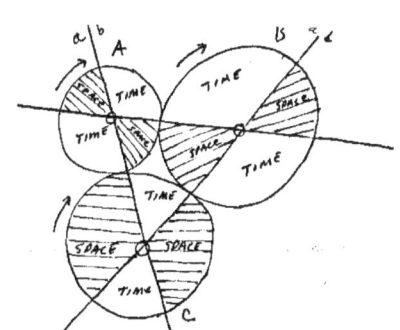
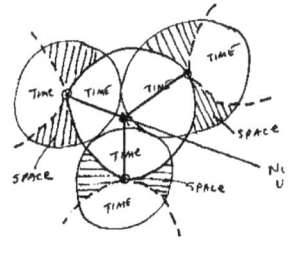

(from The Beauties of Travel)

BUBBLE

Around no point in particular
around no given summer
around any small enough town it begins
    to exist
hanging around the street lights and
surrounding available insects waterdrops
    and parts of speech lost in
    parking-lots at night
enclosing night itself in a flexible skin
growing expanding carrying away
    the universe
while we go to work eat lunch make love
    and fall asleep inside it

THE
BEAUTIES OF TRAVEL

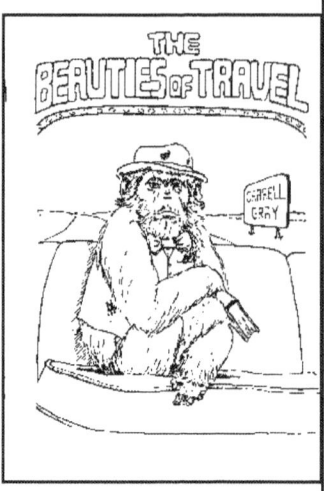

Gray first mentions Rudolf Steiner in the context of Krishnamurti and Buckminster Fuller. This shows him thinking about the forces of myth at work in the world and its role in the emergence as being. One of Steiner's spiritual principles involves the vortex spiral as a key component found throughout nature.

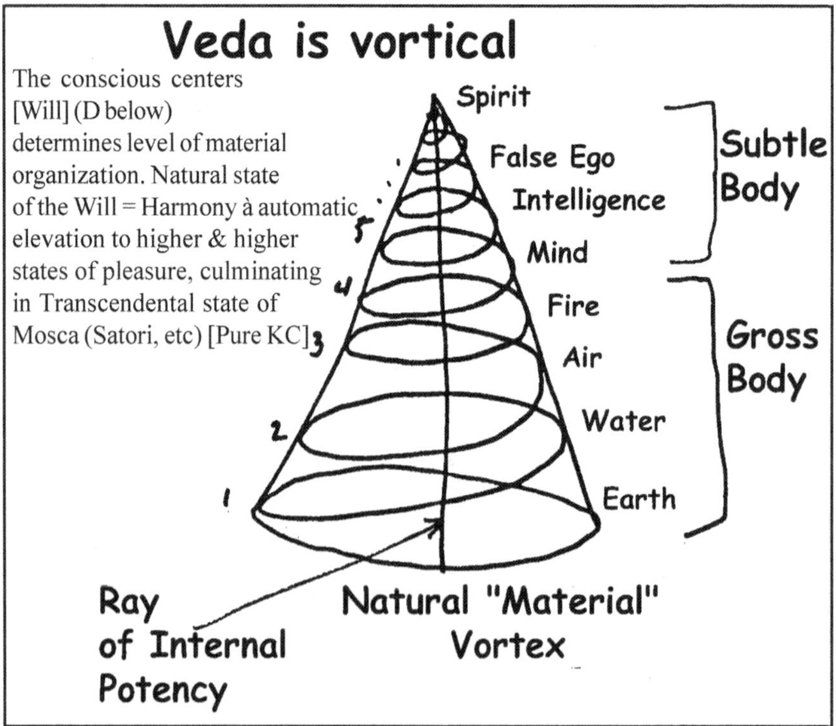
Veda is vortical
The conscious centers [Will] (D below) determines level of material organization. Natural state of the Will = Harmony à automatic elevation to higher & higher states of pleasure, culminating in Transcendental state of Mosca (Satori, etc) [Pure KC]
Spirit
False Ego
Intelligence
Mind
Fire
Air
Water
Earth
Subtle Body
Gross Body
1
2
3
4
5
Ray of Internal Potency
Natural "Material" Vortex

Pound started using the vortex as a model of all the things you need to know circulating around you as you set down to write the poem. He thought of the poet as the center of revolutionary movements and currents. In his hands this model was a proposition of the ego in resistance.

Olson bridged the gap between Pound and WCW especially with his infusion of Jungian archetypes into the mix. In Olson's program of *Projective Verse*, Pound's Vortex gets analyzed and generalized to be an image of the zeitgeist. The whole oeuvre of the modern from quantum mechanics to cubism is, at core, projective. The sense of the projective in Olson contains Pound's sense of vortex. The vortex is one manifestation of the projective.

Olson's program of *Projective Verse* was so liberating for poets working after him that it becomes a prolegomenon for future poetics. (At the time I delighted in his celebration of the typewriter as an instrument, and his grounding of metrics in the breath.) I think many of the topics in Grays poetics can be traced to ideas in Olson's text. Even the word trace has its origin in the idea of the projective. We will see in the review of Gray's essays found in the appendix of this book how he worked out these implications of the projective.

Briefly, some of the ideas he explores which first occur in Olson's manifesto are: The Poem has its own time; The poem exists in a Field; The objects in the field are not always symbols; Sound is of a more lasting and primitive aspect because it is closer to the head (Gray developed his ideas of Trace Tone Poetics); The open poem searches for coherence on its own terms, (these terms include "other" games: Gray wrote essay on Wittgenstein and the logic of the irreal); in the pursuit of coherence, the open poem seeks its own key, (key is as analog of the concept of key in music, meaning a whole register of conventions in which performance and composition occur.) Gray explored the "field of form" as the Idea. The field of form as distinct from the force field, is not anchored in space. It is the IDEA — the "roseness" of the rose — manifesting in millions of places. The idea is that which is recognized by mind.

In *Projective Verse* Olson express a desire to get "rid of the lyrical interference of the individual as ego, of the 'subject' and his soul, that peculiar presumption by which western man has interposed himself between what he is as a creature of nature . . and those other creatures of nature." Gray's idea of the Automorph is born out of this struggle with the ego. Actualism was how Gray worked out the problems that Olson challenged future poets with in his program.

What does it mean: the poem as vortex. The time internal to the poem of rhythms coming back to relate to other parts of the poem.

For Gray the vortex is a chaos attractor or a freshness attractor in many dimensions. The vortex is a model of all life evolving on this orbiting, spinning, precessing planet who took this ancient diurnal dimension of time into our hearts so that we experience time as a projection, an average, over these cardioid constrictions and expansions and neuronal pulsations ebbing and flowing.

A classic clock with hands for hours minutes and seconds shows the end of a cycle coming back to the beginning. Some watches show phases of the moon, and other sidereal circadian movements. Time as embodied in the clock is a representation of the classical cyclic group, a finite arithmetic of mod 12. Time is a vortex. Time can be seen as a fractal vortex, if you convolve the second hand onto the end of the minute hand onto the end of the hour hand. We could express each of these circulating hands with the rotating phaser $e^{i\Theta}$ simply by putting the h, m, s into the argument: e^{ih}, e^{im}, e^{is}. Time becomes a vortex, a spiral of spirals moving on the path of a helix.* Time is the projection of rhythm. These orbital rhythms become vortical time. We can start to understand the projections onto our weeks, days hours minutes seconds. Time as a vortex can be see as zooming in on these time scales. The vortex rotation is like the period of a day, the mixing time inside the vortex is on the order of hours. The interface flux at the edge of the vortex is the realm of the seconds.

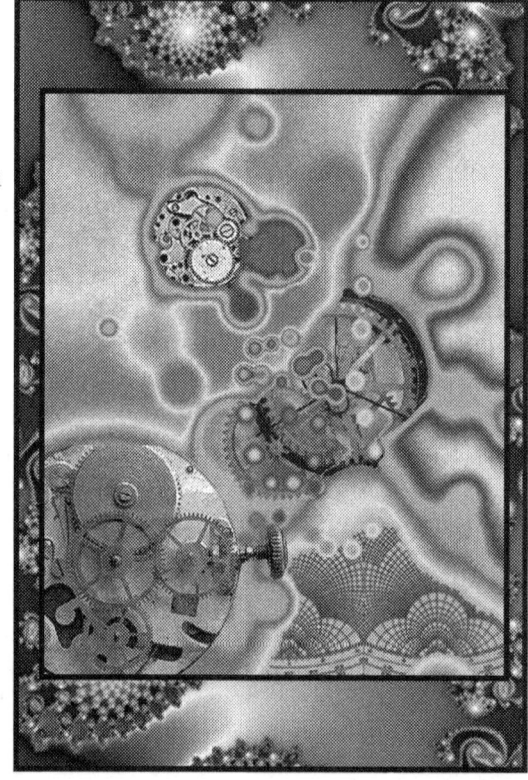

* *(Time viewed as a Vortical Fractal by superposition of second hand on the end of minute hand on the end of hour hand (i.e. $e^{id} \cdot e^{ih} \cdot e^{im} \cdot e^{is} = e^{i[d+h+m+s]}$) in which chaos is attracted out of randomness and the internal mixing is equal to the interface spin.)*

The natural language of a turbulent vortex is time. The turbulence and motion of the entity is a response of internal forces meeting external forces and becoming commensurate on time scales. External influences force the vortex to move and in its spinning to meet and equilibrate with external pining forces impinging on the vortex in relation to a nearby wall or other interface. The reaction is spinning. The result is the time it takes to move a distance equal to its own diameter. In human terms this would be minutes to days, the period of rotation. It addition to rotation period, the vortex has an internal mixing time, and an interface flux time. Mixing would take place during a day, while interface flux is in the range of seconds and minutes. There are relations among these. For example, the mixing time is the deceleration time of the rotation rate. Finally, the flux at any nearby interface can be represented by a flux time which depends on the ratio of the vortex moving in a line to its rotation time. This is called its persistence.

In his essay Gray sees the whole history of poetry, in particular the movements of structuralism and vorticism, moving toward Actualism. He starts with WCW — The poet thinks with the poem. He invokes Olson and thinks about the projections of higher dimensions into ours, reflected in the harmonic ontology of the Vedas. The Parmedian world of the ultimate source leaves traces in our world at every moment, along the unfolding path curve of the great chain of being. Steiner was an inspiration as were Korzybsky, Castaneda and Dorn, and de Bono.

Forms were opening up. The modern poet at the end of the 60s human potential movement was part shaman, part physicist, part monk. He was a poet in the sense of autopoeisis, self making. The oroborous, the self referential. Openness and coherence are not easy to make commensurate. Just as to essay is to *try* and bring things together, by projecting them out of a field of potential, so the poem was the *making* through an open form that emerged into being on the potentialities and reflections of the ideal forms. For me the moment of being actual was a great mixing of eros and logos; it goes back to childhood, of feelings and ideas being like transparent forces pushing across the membranes of my self. (The Greeks thought of it this way too, in the childhood of humanity.) Children know this. Poem is the first making, the essay, the trying to catch the emergence of being in the moment.

We see Gray was very much involved in a dialog with Olson.

Linguistics & Projective Synthetic Geometry of the Poem

This notebook entry refers to Olson whose ideas on the poetry of 'open form' in his essay *"Projective Verse"* became famously influential. Called sometimes organic, 'open form' emphasized authenticity, the speaking voice, and the 'natural look' of lines cut on sense and content carried on the rhythm of breath and the poet's mental momentum. Through syntax as a mimesis of action in the poems, momentum became an active verbal force. Gray is working on these ideas which he designates with the algebraic X, to be essayed. Then Gray solves for that involuntary element. He starts from the primacy of tone and moves to the other elements of poetry — content, association. He deduces:

> Core — node: ie. it seems most likely that there is, within language a center away from which devolves the originating nuclear energy.
> Tone, being primary devolves less acutely than either content, association or involuntary psychic processes.

Then Gray asks about the relationship between Tone and Intention. He establishes the primacy of tone, and this is a statement of the idea that one is *in* a process rather than *conducting* a process.

Rudolf Steiner note: Steiner, was a big influence on Gray. In his essay *On Goethe's Theory of Knowledge as an Epistemology* Steiner has a diagram illustrating how an arrangement of equally present sense data, I, is organized by the mind into causal linkages, II.

```
     I                II
  a — b               b          I group of elements for mere
  | \ / |           a / \ c        sense-perception
  | / \ |             |
  c — d               d          II groping of elements for the
                                    mind
```

Steiner uses this diagram in a discussion of inorganic vs organic science. Inorganic science is governed by Natural Law which is wrongly applied to organic science. The Form of Natural law is: "when this fact interacts with that, this phenomenon arises." Indeed Goethe had written an essay *The Experiment as Mediator between Subject & Object*. The simile pre-echos Peirce, in his phenomenology of events moving to law: something might happen - - > something had to happen. This is an appeal by understanding to natural law. It is nature being brought into a kind of congruence to the mind. Rather than staying in the natural law habit,

Steiner wants us to address the organic object with an evolutionary question: Ask whence comes it instead of what purpose does it serve. The essential statement from Steiner is this: Look into every entity in it inner completeness. And for Darrell Gray seeking a "natural law of poetry" it was this poem as 'completeness of being' that he thought was the highest criterion for a poem to be satisfying. To observe an object in its becoming $O_{t1} \longrightarrow O_{t2} \longrightarrow O_{t3}$ was the essence of inorganic science for Steiner and would become Gray's *Trace Tone Poetics*. What Gray calls tone, Peirce calls quality and Steiner Type.

For Steiner Type meant that one looked on an organic entity as a special instance of all possible and that there were other factors besides the facts of natural law. "We must conceive at a deeper level than the influences of external conditions. Something which did not passively allow itself to be determined by the conditions but actively determines itself under their influence." The type plays in the organic world the same role as that of the natural law in the inorganic.

Here is another cross pollination from Steiner. The entity on a deeper level that actively determines itself - - > automorph.

"The type is this: the Idea of the organism; the animality in the animal, the general plant in the specific plant" Type is fluidic, it imbues the organic entity. Gray used deBono's hydromorphic models of cognition. (This is fractal. How Steiner would have loved fractals if he had been around to see them. He certainly loved projective geometry and nonlinear dynamics.) Steiner reminds us to think of Organism as a particular shaping of the primal form. Type is not something finished it is fluidic. The analog of proof in the organic is intuition. "We must not confront the single form with the type in order to show the type governs the form; we must cause the form to issue from the type. Natural law governs a manifestation as something standing above this, the type flows into the single living entity, identifying itself with this." The type must create the content with the form. This is certainly a dictum worthy of Darrell Gray: intuition as the main principal of poetic science. The poetic act is to trace the movement of type. Steiner then says "intuition is the actual being-within, an entrance into the truth which gives us all that comes in any way under consideration in regarding truth." The central essence of the world flows into our thinking; that we do not merely think concerning the nature of the world but that thinking is an entrance into connection with the nature of reality.

This 'actual being-within' is what is meant by Actualism. Gray sought to avoid poems that were commenting on reality he wanted poems that traced the emergence of being into reality.

Dissolution is finding the meaning within the thing. It is a kind of dissolving through intuition and contemplation into being. His was the way of the Pilgrim, seeking to know how the type flows into specific Form. Type Token Term stand before phenomena with just your intuition to enter into it.

Gray then uses a matrix to display and consider the characteristic dichotomous elements intendent upon the emergence of the poem.

Most easily shown

S/T	A/C
-	+

$S = I \qquad A = E$
$T = E \qquad C = E,$
$S = ACT \text{ (space = action)}$
$\text{-->) O (--> synapse space neuron}$

Here the ratios S/T and A/C show Gray is considering
S = I, Syntax = Intention ;   A = E, Association = Energy
T = E, Tone = Energy;   C = E, Content = Energy.
He sums up with the equation
S = ACT, Syntax = Association, Content, Tone.
The Involuntary X-element in conjunction with association divided by content.

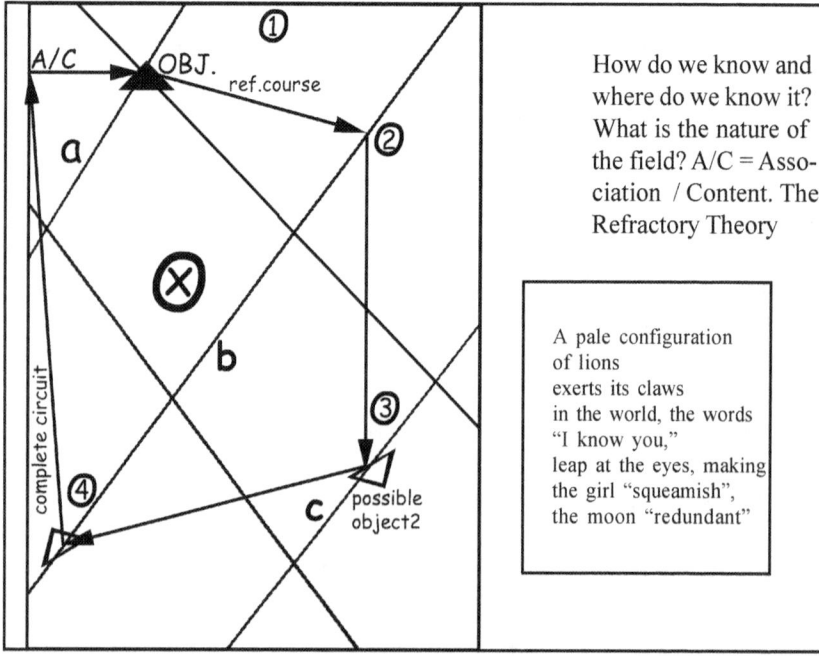

How do we know and where do we know it? What is the nature of the field? A/C = Association / Content. The Refractory Theory

A pale configuration
of lions
exerts its claws
in the world, the words
"I know you,"
leap at the eyes, making
the girl "squeamish",
the moon "redundant"

Next Gray speaks of the tension(s) created by structure, the yoking together of disparate categories in metaphor, with the concept of "Perceptual Distance." He works through several examples of structure, essaying the repellant capability of the imaginary object. He eventually goes into a Kantian discussion of Synthetic Reverb.

Non-Synthetic Reverb

Here we might ask: What is this non-synthetic reverb? What a concept! If we ask Euclid, he would say Synthetic geometry is elementary as opposed to analytical geometry of Descartes. If we ask Kant he would say, I use the term synthetic as opposed to analytical when I am talking about propositions that do not and that do contain their own predicate. You can answer the truthfulness of an analytic proposition from the proposition itself, but a synthetic you have to look outside, pull in other facts.

Or we might ask an audio engineer, about 'synthetic reverb". He would say that it is a circuit in his reverb box, that causes delays in the transmission of sound, and this circuit does harmonic filtering on the sound to make it sound like it was traveling around in a big room, maybe a cathedral or a tunnel. So these diagrams that Gray is drawing are diagrams of the movement through syntax of the creative impulse as it gathers momentum in the semantic space of the poem and is undergoing delay and relay and transformation from associational impacts while bouncing around among these various categorical imperatives in the design criteria of the poem: We have seen these imperatives being yoked together by syntax are opposing Intentions, Emotions, Tone Energies, Associations, the Core Nucleus of the Poem and the Content proper. These notebook entries continue with:

> A poem is self-evident only when the Field factor involves in its being activates all particulars within the field(s).
> Deflection of all verbal particles from N must penetrate into the O (or operative) field of behavior.
> The O Field
> It should not be treated as a "container." The world does not "contain" phenomena – it enacts them
> $$\overset{\wedge}{<\text{-- N --}>}\} \ [S = M + C]$$
> $\wedge$

We get a sense of Darrell Gray involved with the process of semiosis here. Using linguistics modeling in the essays on syntax. Linguisical modeling as a kind of notation or pseudo-code for the movement of feelings in the poem.

Birds

As we wander through the garden of Darrell Gray's poems we are often treated to the perception of birds and flight. The birds serve to delineate the space.

Example a (*SSO* 75)

> I take the pill
> & am gone. Birds fly because they have more imagination.

Darrell Gray begins his book *Scattered Brains* with an invocation of birds. Here as in many poems he quietly takes us into participating in an opening fascination.

Example b *(SB 9)*

TIME WITH BIRDS

> My shadow is also theirs
> when they're within me.
> I feel the wings widen,
> I roost
> in the new
> bones, opening
> world for world.
> Is the head an amplitude,
> a
> swerve
> embodied?
> What would it hit?
> I become a child.
> The wild rose opens
> its soft machinery—
> a tenseness fired into
> song, or a nest
> for losses.

The poem Time with Birds sets us off trying to answer a rhetorical question. Is the head an amplitude? This suggests the harmonic ontology in the Vedas, with the levels of existence thought of as organizations of higher and higher frequencies, over base or sub-harmonic frequencies. This suggests flight. Rhetoric explores the two powers of "is," predication and identification.

"Is the head a swerve?" The concept of the Great Swerve is from the first atomist Lucretius. The early atomists thought nature was the result of a swerve in the rain of elementary particles. The swerve also suggest a shimmer in the landscape like a shifting heat lens, a mirage. This goes back to the harmonic ontology again. Swerve then suggest the next question if we have swerved off course what would we hit. We have this scene of a bird in flight, and it is coming back to the nest in which the poet has set himself to roost in an earlier line. We are going back to a moment in the child's imagination to enter the soft machinery, the cellulose that affords the beauty of rose.

So we are looking into nature on several levels, going back to the primordial entity out of which it all emerges and its variations on a theme. The poem is a flight out from and back to the nest, where we are alone with loss, and we have a place to be with that. Succor comes to mind, self-calming flights of imagination and penetrating intuition represented by birds are the vehicle of imagination. This poem has some nice feedback loops. Flights of fancy take off from the "roost" and "nest" positions. Flights into childhood, ancient Greek philosophers, the childhood of humanity. There is something in the motion of the lines too, the cut lines of WCW or the enjambment of Creely the short line asking us to see at every step. Ultimately this poem is a triumph of sweetness and intense imagery trading back and forth, wings widen and become a child, the rose opening as against machinery, losses, shadows. Once you notice it, you see that there are many identifications with birds in Darrell Gray's poetry. Birds represent the place of the imagination, or the intention moving with the will in the world as idea.

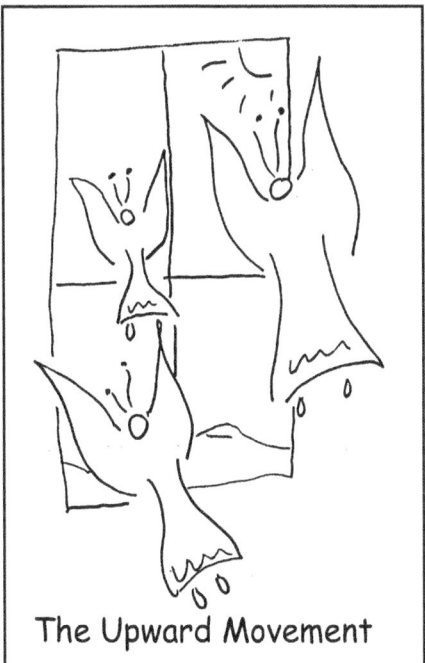

The Upward Movement

(from Notebook)

everything is being lifted

mars, the zodiac, everything
the trouble of love
each has grown separate
but is lifted

the wheels coordinate
the summit of the dark
the golden —they are lifted
still.
invisible futures
                are lifted
a ship,   while as it turns
   in mid-stream to return
   because of some eminent
danger
is lifted—
the same scene in an old
                park
is lifted
the girl lifts her chin to
survey the weightlessness
of the lifted bird.

Some Art Business

Peter had to let his place go due to lack of work. He had an old brown slant-six Dodge van that he lived in.

I still saw him often around the warehouse. We'd go over to the Berkeley Flea Market at the Ashby BART. He told me: "I landed a job working out in one of the satellite cities east of the bay: Walnut Creek. Man, I was ready to give up. I mean I was tired. And I was discouraged. I was starting to refer to myself as Mr. Unemployed." He did a little lumbering shuffle like Mr. Unemployed. He said: " I hadn't had a job in nine months and I was scared. Walnut Creek is no place to be when you want to quit."

One day he showed up with some new paintings, big ones on canvas, loose, unstretched. He laid three of them out right on the ground of the parking lot, late one evening. Everyone was gone.

He indicated a set-up on the side of his van. It looked like something to hold an awning. "I made a little money," he said, "and got the idea to put together this rig on the roof of my van. I made it out of two ski racks that I bought at the Berkeley flea market. I bought a roll of canvas, and had it so that I could easily pull down and stretch enough to make a large painting, about 4' by 6'. I would use the whole side of my van as my easel. And paint what I saw."

I was impressed.

He continued: "In Walnut Creek, I ate lunch at this coffee shop/drive-in. All the young kids would hang out there. It was Summer and it was hot, and there was absolutely nothing for them to do."

He told me about how the punks were tired of being treated like children all their lives, and feeling their anger, loudly protested the fact with amplified noise, brawling and carousing and listening to their giant boom boxes and thrashing their skate boards in the parking lot. He told me these are suburban punks, kind of soft wave, not into the stupendous filth of the hard-core Haight and Telegraph Avenue punks who manifested their youthful vigor by more lively activities like screaming, fighting, urinating, breaking glass and revolting out-of-tune singing.

"After I ate at this restaurant a couple of times," he said, "I struck up a conversation with one of the young chicks. She seemed approachable. Most of them looked at me like I was totally lacking in good taste not to have died before the age of 30! But Donna didn't quite buy the punk aesthetic for woman, which sought to always challenge what traditional beauty was, by being into horror. She wore a white miniskirt and horrendous white panty hose. A pink sweater! Long hair in a single braid went over her shoulder almost down to her young breasts. She had quick intelligent moves. She is going to be a courageous woman some day. She is fun. We'd be hanging out, leaning against a wall, talking about the other people in the room.

"I'd ask her, 'Look at that guy there. What is his attitude? Dejection?'

"And she said, 'Nah, I think it is more like Contempt and / or Reproach.'

He was definitely looking-sullen-off-into-the-distance.

So I started sketching them.

Some of the younger ones really were good at it. They were still kids. They could show Charity on their angelic faces. Also Shame and Fear, which everybody shows most of the time.

I helped her see some of them and I think she liked the power that this level of abstraction gave her.

I guess I identified with them, felt a lot like them. At least I had my art to keep me from flipping out completely.

We talked a few times. I told her I was a painter, and I could tell she was intelligent and interested in art and I was explaining to her about models and asked her if she might pose for me sometime.

'Sometime,' she said. And she was cool with it."

I was pleased that my older friend was finding some love and sympathy in his hard life.

He continued: "So I painted her outside in the parking lot. I stretched a canvas.

Donna is wearing a beret, and a black guinea-T. She had on leather wrist bands and black leather belt, hung around her hips. She copped a very strange pose, her body arching up in an S curve, hands outstretched and above her head in a Y, configuration, knees bent as though she were about to spring into a long dive.

And there it was. Drawn from life in the moment. Quickly sketched to capture the moment in a moment, an ordinary young woman, not a model but to me extraordinary, the presence of her face emerging from the forces that shaped it.

I looked at the girl's face and her beauty blew me away. Ah, inspiration. Enchantment struck as real as lightening."

I was enjoying my friend's happiness.

He continued. "While I was painting her she said, 'It's OK if I make you blush, isn't it?'

'Sure.' I said. It is just the blood that percolates through the body, perpetuates the spirit and penetrates the soul."

Later he said, "The most important thing is the figure. The painting exists for the figure.

I was asking myself: What is it that women want?

And the answer comes to me. Not to fly, but to dive down into deeper water, to that secret cave, to swim in it. To go deeper and deeper into the water. The cave is dark, but there is a pink light glowing deep inside. The water is blue. The Fish are shiny, slippery, silver. Figure comes out of ground, comes out of the landscape. Like de Kooning's Woman. That is what the landscapes do, they percolate out the strokes, they fulminate the figure, they gestalt the figure — the person. Just as in reality, morphogenetic fields carry us in space.

I showed much of the drive-in, and the push-pull energy of the punks, who wandered over and admired the work. They really liked it! They are in it, sitting around, in their black and leather and their eye shadow, and their spikes and studs.

Then after a few weeks — later, I show it to a friend who I had done some work for out in Martinez and he likes it. Holy Smoke! A 4' by 6' high punk icon!

They are smashed on some good grass and they offer me $100 for it. A sale! I have entered the realm of professionalism! Well, you can imagine my excitement! This was a big day in my life."

Peter was really proud of himself. He loved the work he was doing, trying to capture Being, the manifold potentiality. No brush had depicted it, no concept had outwitted it . . . Until Peter the wild man, bay wolf comes from Berkeley. He felt superior to commercial artists posturing and simpering in the coffee houses and art galleries. He was the outsider artist, the bay wolf howling at the heals of the zeitgeist, moving like a mirage across the landscape of our time. He captures the beast with tubes of paint applied directly to canvas and smeared with his bare hands! At last ... he cuts a painting off the large roll of canvas and stretches it on a canvass and nails lit up to a wall!

Peter lamented: "Now I have to go over to my friend's house in Martinez to look at her. I no longer see the real girl. I've got her number but don't ever see her.

But there in the painting, she arches and points out and away into her generation. Yet there really isn't anybody else. Just you and her. And she'll point at you out in your world. Where the wind is blowing. She'll be the Queen of the Punks. She understands. She's forever hanging out in summer, where the kids are sitting close to each other with their rats nest hair blowing into the trees, and the punks gyrate and stare at you. Her girlish skittishness provoking love and protections, the love and protection you felt for the mousey-haired girl back when you were you—in the hippie days.

The painting has that fresh acrylic wetness. You'll see the wetness swimming around her, her figure in an alive world, dewy as an early spring morning."

Hogs Tale

Bob and John and Dave produced and performed in an ensemble theatre creation they called *Hogstale*. Bob was from a farm in Iowa, had raised hogs; John was also from small town Iowa, and Dave was the son of a famous professor of molecular biology. So there was something of their class background in the dynamic of their relationship played out in *Hogstale*. A lot of it had to do with Dave being excluded and dominated and chased away and invited in by the other two.

Bob and John facing front, in the middle of the room, standing side by side; Dave circulating back and forth at the back wall.

Bob and John at the back wall, standing side by side, and facing the back wall, like it was a wailing wall. Dave in the center of the room shouting at them.

I do not recall their being any real spoken words in *Hogstale*, just choral singing, harmonizing, sound making, shrieks, blood curdling yells, wild wolf-howling, grunts and shouts. There is no text to examine. Their theatre of improvisational presence was truly an opening out into a spectacle of the physiological psyche.

They might have called it Dog's Tail, for it was a whirlwind of animal frenzy, like a dog chasing its tail. Round and round the actors go, stabbing gnashing and thrusting. Each stab inspires another and another gnash leads to another thrust. One move inspires the next and the next responds to the one before. The frenzy of this theatre becomes more significant than the causes of its motion. This play is about that animal frenzy. This was not your regional, or downtown subscription theatre attended by swell older ladies with blue hair. This was a dance, a basket ball game, a coming together of the three into a kind of unified entity; of parts that moved in synchrony. They made you see the form of connection. It was a vortex of energy being stirred from within. *Hogstale* transcended the duality between the actions and passions of the body. There is no longer anything to prevent propositions from falling back onto bodies and from mingling their sonorous elements with body's olfactory, gustatory and digestive effects. (O'Keefe's earlier play, *Coyote* had been about this too.) Not only is this theatre without costumes or props, it is a theatre that does not allow any sense to be derived from words; there is perhaps a grammar or syntax but this is for you to figure out, from the sonorous and gesticulated use of articulated syllabic, literal and phonetic elements. This play was a kind of ritual to portray and celebrate the creation and annihilation of configurations of existence itself. It was not a matter of story, or resolution; they showed us how to relax into time, to not be focused on outcome but to really play with what you've got. Artaud would have loved it. Wild Boho Boys in Bedlam.

They gave new meaning to the phrase 'Off the Wall' for they seemed able to run up the walls. The would run full tilt at a wall, then start UP the wall and somehow do a back flip off the wall. It was terrifying, outrageous. And there were ropes. Terry Sendgraph, inventor of *Motivity* an aerial dance, had her performance and classes set up in the Hawkeye Theatre at this time and she gave the boys lessons in climbing and slithering on precarious surfaces. Also Contact Improvisation was becoming popular, at the affiliated Project Artaud, a huge building full of artists and theatres in San Francisco. There, an all men's group called Mangrove lead by John Lefan was happening. This theatre allowed men to get over the fear of touching each other, to carry each other in dance using great structural gymnastic balance. This was also an echo of the 60s Happenings, a spontaneous convocation celebrating the 'un-spoken thing' binding a group.

John and Bob and Dave, master practitioners of Physical Theatre gave themselves over into the context of the improvisation, into the game, into the play. They extended their senses into being rooted in the moment, into a kind of hyper-awareness in which they perhaps had super senses. They see their partners on the stage and they see themselves in it as well. And the audience sees it. The improvisational aesthetics, Watching, Planning, Being in self-possessed presence, were all being used, embodied, imaged, taken into role-playing. They were totally in the moment with each other.

They changed roles from the person making sounds to the person moving being controlled by the sounds. As if the sound were some beacon to real them in, some goal, or some source from which they must flee.

The role change move is relevant to the improvisation at that moment. The exchange went around and around so that there was a moving thing, a token, a trigger being wordlessly passed — the unspoken thing between them, among them. It was animality, played with in the frenzied grace of the truly possessed.

John standing in the center of the room facing front, Bob standing in the right rear corner facing the right wall Dave kneeling facing front in the corner.

Bob and Dave standing in the center of the room going round and round yelling at each other, John rolling across the floor toward the back wall in the left rear center.

It looked like children playing, having fun. They were playing with ideas from Castaneda, the place of power. And they were *seeing* in the moment. They were realizing and improvising off what they had perhaps worked out beforehand in play / rehearsal. But now in the moment of reenactment they were realizing, reifying from their relationship. The dynamic of their relationship with each other was constantly being displayed in the way they were located in the space — John with his great perspective and power lording it over the others at times, and at other times learning from them.

We in the audience were filling in the story of *Hogstale* in our own minds, from archetypes of relationship we had seen countless times in previous experience. We were being treated to a demonstration of the *elements* of theatre. Physical theatre is about the elements of relationship. Dynamics. I could understand that from physics. It was the force of an action, how an object was moved through time and space. What was compelling it, impelling it. Form and content, dynamics and meaning.

The mover takes care of movement. The Sounder and Speaker must sound and speak without moving.

Absolutely. No movement at all, except facial expression.

The Sounder and Speaker may only move to change location and shape. It might not be appropriate for you to speak, or sound, from the posture that you are in; you may have to change posture and location too.

The play made a statement: We are not the act. The act moves us. Our awareness keeps the act from overwhelming us. It was astounding to see, the years of practice they had put in together, to understand the basics of action in theatre, the sensing of time, the use of pauses, the focus of intention, the thrust into contrast, the attentiveness to partner, the awareness to pull together what was going on in the moment, the magnifying and expanding out of form, the spinning out of story (even with no words), the access to feelings, the shape of the space — the constant ebb and flow of distribution in space of the person, the creation of a unified entity. All these things were exercised and woven into *Hogstale*.

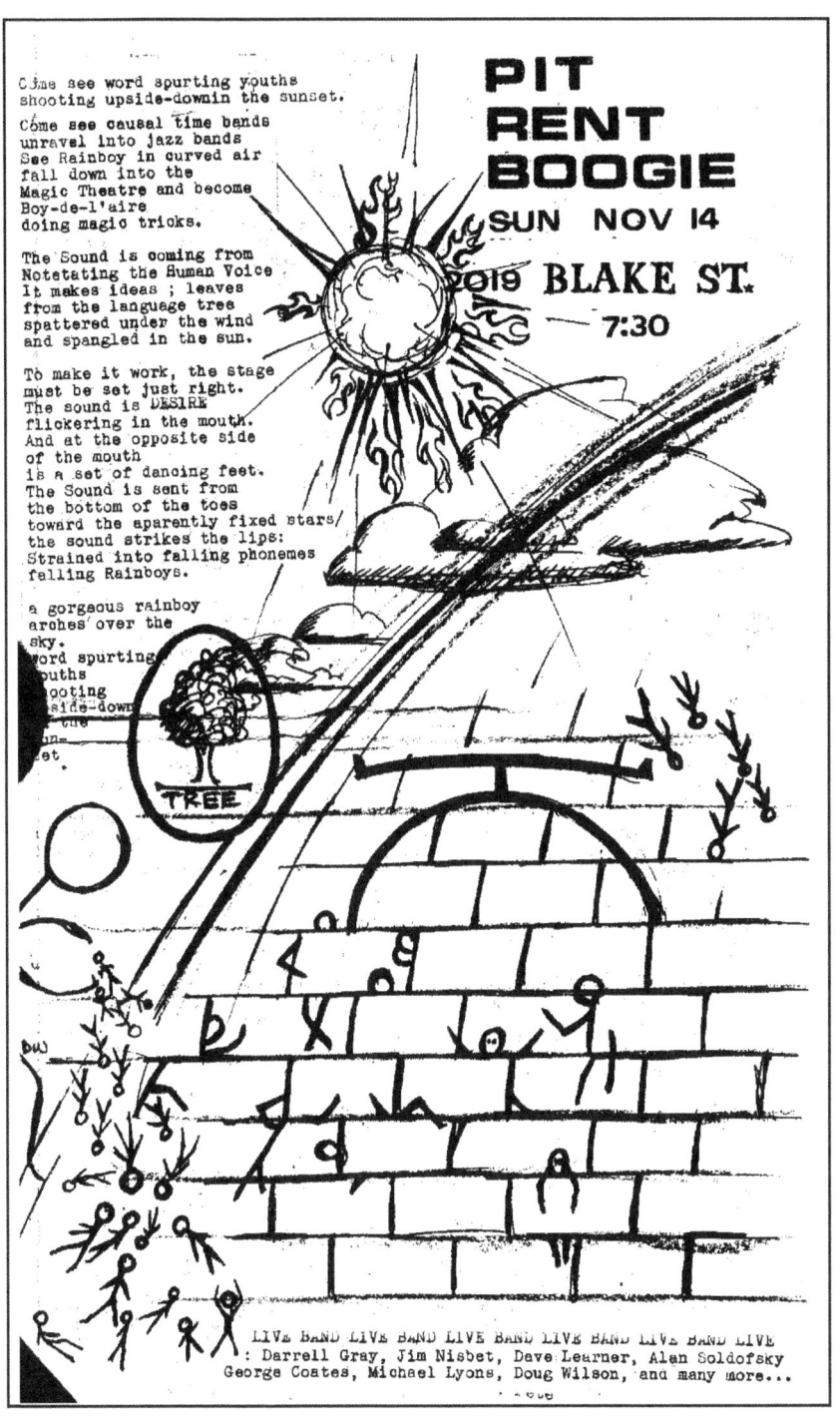

Page of Punctual Actual Weekly announcing a benefit dance

THE ZEN WHIMCYCLER —Light Fantastic

'Sometimes, when I go Whimcycleing through the whaters of the eithor, I feel like I am surfing on quanta of trauma waves' said Krishna Glass, as he showed this reporter his own Whimcycle—Apotheosis Extract.

Apotheosis Exlax, is a 'de lux' helix model homade. It includes such features as wheels made of Synchrouous Numinosity; the front wheel being the Wheel of Fifths from Music, and the Back Wheel being the Color Wheel from Painting. But on this model says Glass, 'sight is infinitely variable not just 3-speed like the old Primary Secondary and tertiary mandalas of Religious art. The whimcycle is propelled along in the whether, by sails made of Golden Rectangles, that billow out when the Winds of Conditional Propositions blow.

It's trajectory is always a geodesic of Mandala Space, it travels the spiral yellow brick road into a cornucopia horopter of laughter, says Gla

It has a snow white pyramid hood ornament with piano key running boards and a warning bell made from the tinkle of children's voices for good luck, he adds.

PERPETUAL MOTION FOOD

Glass is serious about whimcycleing in reality— so serious that he plans to cast a curse on it Sat. during a regular meeting of his Onerophagie and the Art of Whimcycleing class,'which is exactly that', says Glass. 'Dreams are a kind of perpetual motion food, and we have found found a way to preserve them in Art, said Glass reflectively.'If you can them, then it is possible to whimcycle forever; since they are perpetual motion food , the more you whimcycle, the more you can.'

Glass is a member of the yet ununicorned Church of the Coicidental Metaphore where he holds the office of . Acolite High Lowatt Tomorrowboy of the Temple of Natural Laws, under whose auspicies the ludecrust is drawn from.

Offences agains the Holy Ghost may be going the way of Cheap enlightenment said Glass. The Fee Is Free to See how Glass Proposes to link Whimcycleing with Divine Principles. Participants must be responsible for their own dreams. 'You'll be barkin up the wrong tree, if you don't come talk dogma with me', he said, echoing Muhamid Ali.

Glass does not favour laws proscribing Whim cycleing. He does favor both algebraic tricks and speed, give me math or give me meth is his motto. The essential teaching here is that the veil covering reality can be ripped by getting ripped.

HELMENT

'Helmets are optional, but a good idea for the novice whimcycler' he adds. The Helment consists of a muster gas mask with 2,2" flexable rubber hoses going down into a box strapped to the chest. One hose goes to an ice filled bong, so that the smoke is always like cool air, always Spring time fresh.The other hose goes to a breathing unit that holds the exhaled smoke, mixes it with the ambient CO_2 and breathed again, in and out, in and out, gives expanded shotes to the arreoles. Also in the ear pieces there are filters to filter the bad harmonics out of noise, to make sweet sound go round, and wrap around tinted glasses to look at the world through.'

' Whimcycleing'is a pleasant way to regain one's sanity'.

Berkeleities will not soon forget the shattering of Glass, the tinkle bell laughter of childrens voices, the random propagation of homunculi quasars and rainbow hued whyers,' the incessant dramma of wavical phonemes with no place to go whizzing off every which way, as Glass shatters the speed of sound wheeling in and out of the stuff of mind as it filters through the quincunx of language. Telegraph Ave. is one of Berkeley's busiest Tao's a mainline artery for the smack and crunch of the tilt-a-whirl world making our urb orb.

These are paths or tra tories of creation and annihilation in the unified field, what Fibate Capa call the Dance of Shiva,;what Muhamid Ali has called giving him Punishment.

Fibate Capa is a Road Chief at the institute, and has found that the people who live in this fields are Multitudians who wear quotidian moccasins and "Unless you walk a mile in another idean's quotidians you do not know him." is their traditional street greeting.

'Suppose I was meant to be Jesus F. Christ Himself, says Glass, even in Berkeley that wouldn't do. So I supress that part of my being, trying to get as much energy cranked into my mysticism system as possible We like to get this raw energy from our archtypes because it cranks us up to be With the Present as it takes the Chance out of the Future and sends it into the Ppast riding on the Golden Rectangles of Coincidence, Conditionals rolling sheets of sound leaving the center of this pulsating univers down Telegraph Ave. Central of the mind in which everyone on earth is calling everyone else just just to say HELLO. After all Jesus Christ was a poet and a master of consciousness, but let us not forget that he was a classical poet and did not have access to computer phrasing to recreate and cre mate reality at a moments notice.

Just as Time is created by the electromagnetic field making little cat feet prints in Gravity, when an idean experiences something it is like Time traveling for him, because he flows in and out of the Self.

This effect is called Whatalivity.The Quantum of trauma does not varry, for everyone in the whold who crys, somone else laughs.

Page of Punctual Actual Weekly #4 Feb1976 Unpaginated, typewriter, mimeograph 8.5 x 14

The Divine Plant

The finest smoke I ever had was some that showed up at the Berkeley warehouse. Now a lot has been said about the pot one smokes, and all the fine aspects of partaking in the precious Maryjane. For we have learned a lot about the beloved weed since the early days of lids and bricks. And in fact smoking pot had become something of a demarcation line of distinction between people who did and those who didn't. Darrell Gray smoked, Jim Nisbet didn't; Doug didn't smoke, but Russ did. John O'Keefe did. Dave Schien smoked but didn't inhale. And much has been written and talked about among the folk seeking all manner and sort of psychedelic and mind-altering experience and it was written about in the magazines about what the most-precious, divine plant ever bestowed on us by Nature's succor. People talked about Hawaiian and Thai and Ganga from India, and mota from Mexico and the endless debate over the sexy intellectual stone of Sativva vs the swoony body-stone of pungent Indica. And everybody talked and bragged about all these kinds of weed: 'they gonna get you stoned, SO stoned,' and if they don't get you stoned to your satisfaction, they have heard of, or know, about some dealer that knows a dealer that can get you some of the finest gauge and it will really straighten your mind right out.

But I'm gonna to tell you about an herb we had there for a little while at the Warehouse that was just the sweetest, gonest, most transcendental smoke that ever circulated around and through the bodies and minds of the denizens of this sweet, swinging, orbing urb. Now this here weed was grown by women in a Berkeley radical, feminist, lesbian, cabal. And since it was the sinsemilla (female plant, never pollinated by male plants) nay, never touched by male hands — not so much as a whiff of maleness on its way to us — and since it had the purest, highest, mountain intellectual clarity to its bouquet which was of the sweetest most earthy casolette and since it is my claim that this here weed brought your mind into a more direct perception of Nature herself, I'm gonna call this weed, Anima, or Prima Materia.

I had thought that since Nature, this subterfuge of creative evolution, that calls successive generations of the world into being, that wakes us up with the sound of cars going by and buses' exhaust and jet airliners sonic boom roar and other sounds of the city and NOT the sounds of birds and breezes, I might give is some Gnostic name like Sophia or Maryjane; but I guess I'll just stick with Prima Materia. Naming Her is like trying to keep the many names of god all in your mind at once anyway. To smoke it was to partake in some strange new secular sacrament. It was a sacrament somewhere between communion and marriage, between baptism and confession. And it made you feel the love like a solid thing (made your dick stand up and point in front of you, like a dowser or a diving scepter or a lightning rod.)

This marvelous weed was brought into the warehouse by a friend of Doug's. Her name was Mountain. And she was a gigantic walking avalanche of a woman, who shook, jiggled and bounced like an earthquake when she moved; she punished the Birkenstocks at 300 pounds. She was the ring leader of the radical feminists.

The weed itself was the most beautiful I have ever seen. It had the sweetest, almost pine-needle scent. And the dried flower buds looked like little green balls of combed fire, green fire frozen into a shape like those stylized flames and swirling clouds in Buddhist Thanka painting. And it just felt so good and fine in the hand like course pubic hair, not the slightest blemish of seed.

Mountain allowed me to buy a little and it was a most precious time and thing to have. I tended not to share it, offering others a more workaday smoke. I kept this soma of the gods, this manna from heaven, this benefactor of the seers, this crown in the muse's diadem, this scepter of the anima to myself.

Smoking a bit of this elixir made Berkeley an even more magical head space. It made you reconsider with suspicion your ideas: you saw then as received. What was right or wrong could be questioned, and sometimes even put aside. One saw experiences of school — the lost and wasted years of high school in which everyone treated you so cool you couldn't wait to forget them as forgettable. You saw in perspective how the endless grind of university, with so little social flavor as to remove meaning from existence, could be transcended. And the attempts to know the divine through love of women — most of which ended in dismal failure that left you with an empty heart, if not the sense of kamikaze dive-bombed, burnt down, smoldering aircraft wreckage, carnage, fuel spillage contaminating the ground around whoever was in the way — could be forgotten and moved on from, with new hope for romance. The unkindness, jealousy and fear of the world of organized work that tormented your mind every moment you spent there with the jaded sense of being exploited by the owners of production, though true, could be put aside for a while. One could re-frame the job experience in a group theoretic perspective: work as a kind of group therapy where you were trying to be with other people accomplishing something real, useful, life-enhancing. This respite provided by the motivation of weed might even lead to being able to do some of the wretched work that needed to be done. As the old street-poet says, "There are things that must need doing / there are things that must get done. So hand me down a number and I'll do 'em when I'm done."

Your own wondrous spirit could be called back from the haunted dimension of unfamiliarity into which it had been had been projected by your abandonment.

Feelings that indeed, God is Real were circulating about. Things were alive with Prima Materia; magic was afoot in the everyday world. Leading you into the circle of this zeitgeist's seeking seers, Prima Materia helped you see that now you were with some honest company and you could see them for that and they could see you. *Mota* Prima Materia was the elixir that bound up your psychic wounds, brought you into this vibrational space, let you join in the revelry of these truth seekers. It invited you to come on in, be here now. You could be one of them, you could play with them, you could trust in them. You had some champions in this great, stochastic, effulgent experiment.

This is the theatre in which you dwell, it kept telling you, in the body, which you must not sell! But turn with it, within it, like floating — the way the great ancient I Ching *pa kua* compass does, sampling the synchronistic dragon currents that point into the probabilities and possibilities that everything is made of. The *prima materia* emerges.

I began to realize I was walking around inside my own movie. In between takes, I could be doing warm up exercises. Exercises that lent themselves to a more expansive yet grounded and pleasurable sense of presence. Go with what you got. It was about intention, and engagement, and going with the flow. My day didn't have to be a disappointing, self-deprecating, value-eroding collection of experiences all strung together by a dogged and persistent feeling of my own lack of self worth.

I began watching me in this movie. You are the star. And this is an old movie, low budget. It is not noire or sinister, just social realism.

In fact it is partly in black and white, except the parts where you make a break through — then it goes into bright color, like in Yellow Brick Road, where they go from Kansas through a tornado, out the window into the land of contra-pane. Perhaps the genre is thinking man's sci-fi. You are in your 20s, you are not a genius, but you know some. Because you don't have all the gifts upstairs, you have to work all the time, comrade worker of the mind. The film is about you coming to know yourself. There is a scene where you are in a theatre in a warehouse and are walking the boards at night, being visited by the ghosts of all the group rituals that have been enacted there before. You are so inspired by their works, that when you get outside and realize you have no vehicle, it doesn't bother you. Then you realize you are a movie critic. In this movie, you come to understand how important you were to your friends, though they didn't indicate it at the time. You can explore alternative life lines, like in the movie "It's a Wonderful Life." In fact these parallel possible worlds are possible. Walter Mitty was probably a Head, living in the alternative world of his secret life. This taciturn, henpecked, shut-in version of Don Quixote is perhaps the character most easily identified with in the modern cannon.

I'd be streaming through the days, enjoying the free time that comes with unemployment, though broke and eating at the mission. I was glad not to have to engage in the experience of corporate America. For most working situations are wretched and imbued with cynicism. You are broken, bent by corporate America, by the machinery of the society trying to turn everything into a bill collecting machine, creating money so that everyone is some lender's servant. Entrapment *is* this society's sole activity. But when the Mota Prima Materia started working her magic on you no matter how badly twisted out of shape by society's pliers you were, she could straighten you out.

Yes, feel it. You see the company of Maryjane was so strong, so fine, talking to you about being great, about loving everybody, about giving of yourself to the many causes worthy of your focus. You have got to let her lead you into digging what she is putting down! For she will give you insights, she will release you from your pain. And help you accept your art; for writing is one of the few places where you can match ability with challenge, so that there is terrific engagement. It is pleasurable and needs to be continued.

And here you are, with these other fine artists, who are transcending into the flow and able to feel their birthright through expressing it. And inviting you to learn and to make it just like they are making it. And even though you may fall on your face in the long struggle to learn this art, for it takes forever to develop mastery, Maryjane is there to pick you up and keep you on the track of glorifying nature of which she is a spirit, one of many. She is not one of the Fate Sisters (one spins, one measures and one cuts); she is sister to the muses: to song, to meditation, to memory, to poetry, to history, to music, to theatre, to dance and to the stars.

Throwing great arms out like a nebula to pull in and connect moments of fineness and finesse. Yes! To NOTICE nature, all the life forms put on this planet, all the bioenergy conspiring to create the world. The synchrony of energy and forms, the deities building this world for you and you are here now and you need to cherish it, go with it on the long journey, feel communion in it, whale song forming out in the blue, operates in here too, all the forms of the multimedia art, and above all the human voice speaking language, so much fine language inside the mind outside the mind in the world. Chistae Buddha Hindu all the names of god, but this will give you the *experience*. Elephants trumpeting, vibrating the earth. Ghosts of the great one-horned trumpeting parasauralophus too. And *lophoforia williamsi* too. Singing the praises. Spiraling up to pull the scene into the multifoliate rose. Make love solid —a thing— like a field holding the world together.

God is the name for what is really the buzz of our own self-aware nervous system.

Anima, Prima Materia, Maryjane wants everybody to see through her eyes, the eyes of nature, the eyes of long time, to see how there was timing and space for everything to be, and you just have to be part of it, not let your ego hold you off from it. To see Her playful and beautiful, intricate beyond belief and full of motion and immense complexity and to revel in the amazing fact that we had all come down this narrow path of evolution to where we are now.

Made you feel beautiful like Jim Morrison.

What is this prima materia, anyway. It comes from the cloud chamber. The beautiful chaos of creation and annihilation, the emergence of space and time — geometry — along with the breakdown of symmetry and motion. Changes and progression. Etiology, and Teleology. If we could see as the ancient Taoists do, we'd see all things as motion, as change progressing. It is second order, the rate of change, and the *rate* of the rate of change. Space and time progress. The vacuum of space is really a complex detent, a balance of matter and anti-matter. Pass energy through it, and you create self annihilating pairs that go off in strange trajectories, decaying into other entities. The spirals are forming the complex quasi-closed space-time-matter lattice. The View.

The two most important paradigm changes in my generation are these: 1) the shift from linearity to the fractal , and 2) the breakdown of the distinction between living and inert matter. The first is a shift from a geometry of space to a geometry of scale; the second is uncertainty raised to the power of belief. Prima materia is a model encompassing these two views. It's image is the cloud chamber, and the hierarchical tree, the divine plant: the propagation by dispersion of one medium into another. And its icon is the monad, the smallest sensing window from one scale into the next.

This is how it all begins. Vacuum breaks down, into space and time and radiation, there is a symmetry, many symmetries going on at all levels, called the *aufbau* — the filling in, the populating of energy levels and this quantum world is writ large in the species populating niches. It is the instantiation in time of matter affording opportunity to symmetry and organization, whenever possible, whenever normal, — that is to say distributed in a way (based on phi) that is the perfect shift, the perfect distribution so as to accommodate other entities striving for existence in *their* niche. It is the Universe not only in space and time, but of space and time, of scale. The great fractal dimension of one thing field-grounding its way into another. The universe's time, evolution's time. The time it took evolution to make all the creatures filling the niches using the same ideas over and over but at different scales. Darcy Thomson, *On Growth and Form* showed this. Were these great symmetries already there? Potentially in matter finding its way through the 4-fold way of carbon polyvalence, the portal life used on the a planet in the sweet spot of a solar system (not too close as to have the water boil away, not to far as to become solid ice) from its central star — a water planet with a big sister Jupiter to keep the asteroids from destroying too many epochs until there was enough intelligence to get it all going.

And it means that the objects, surrounding us, are live tissues, and are the components of living beings from the other space-time scales. The whole Universe appears to be alive. The life at one level scales to be connected to the life at other scale levels. And we are moving through, displacing it and it is written in it and it is writing in us. It is our job to concentrate their tour to apprehend their being there to verify and to not stop until we have rendered all these variable dimensions as if everything were part of the same elastic field under which our seeing and the images in our mind were points of intersection of infinities of being to which we are bound. It has to do with monads, windows to the soul, it has to do with the teleological, the movement through the 4 fold carbon symmetry of matter into the world of enzymes and respiration / photosynthesis; duality metabolic pathways; to self-protecting immunocitocities; to self replicating cells. And organizations into self perpetuating organs by autopoesis. What an honor to call yourself a poet in that sense of autopoesis.

I mean it is the world's wildest story to ever come along: the way that matter evolved into intelligent beings, and how this intelligence interacts with the matrix of nonliving matter from which it came, and which still supports it at every moment. Prima Materia is more like an abstraction, an attempt to understand the real neumonal prima material behind all phenomenon. If that ain't a rush I don't know what is. It is more like an image that resonates with what is already in our minds anyway. It blew my mind when I figured this out. I had to walk around, 40 blocks just to calm down. The universe is not just a mathematics of space; it is a mathematics of scale. And metaphoricity is that function mapping aspect of mind that lets us look at similarities across the scale.

What does this prima material look like. Well it is fundamentally a harmonic continuum, just as a vibrating string contains harmonics, a vibrating space does too. The string can be incredibly short or very long. We might get an idealist image of this space by thinking of something like the powers of 10 notation, the MKS system Meters kilograms seconds. We will also ratiocinate this space down with $h = 1$ and $c = 1$. and there would be other normalization factors, to divide by so that complexity was dropped out a bit and we have these basic constants that delineate the domain. In particular we might think of the wavelength of the photon, and the wavelength of the graviton. These are field quanta, bosons in general that transmit or propagate the action of a field throughout itself. The photon is the quanta of light, and the exchange particle of the electromagnetic field and the graviton is the quanta of mass and the exchange particle that instantiates the gravitational field, holding mass together. Gravity creates a box of time and space for the photons and electrons — that is to say everything else — to exist in. What is the fundamental size? The dot, the point. The puff before the bang of coming into being.

Title page from PAW for long taxi story leading into the inchoate

Many Worlds Interpenetration

Taxi Unlimited Waybill Log
Friday February 13 1976.

    I'm cruising in my cab over the top of the university near the stadium when I decide to do a loop through the campus past the engineering and physics buildings. I used to be a student of physics and engineering and now that I am driving cab for a living, a little voice inside sometimes whispered to me: 'Thus have the great and mighty fallen.' But I get to write because I live in a warehouse and don't have to pay rent at the moment. So I drive a hack for a couple bucks an hour and tips. It's a scenario that will do for the nonce.
    I make a left onto Inner Campus Drive, then start rolling through. The radio is playing "Everybody was Kung Fu Fighting" a big hit. Disk jockey joking: 'Kicking butt fast as lightning.'
    I'm trolling past the Engineering complex, scanning the street, being careful not to run into the herds of the privileged collegiates. I see a man, his right hand in the air. He has a very hardy distinguished look. Balding and bearded, like a weight-lifter with brains.
    I pull over. I recognize him. He gets in. From the back seat, he blurts, "The Ritz-Carlton, please."
    Wondering if I should introduce myself or not, I think he might like to hear from a homeboy. "I recognize you. I think. You are a professor at the University of Texas, right? Bryce DeWitt."
    He looks surprised.
    I say, "Yeah, I went to UT Austin."
    He smiles his big twinkling smile.
    I say, "I only did an undergraduate degree in Physics. I used to go to some of the open upper class graduate seminars. I went to one you gave in the auditorium about the Many Worlds Interpretation of Quantum Mechanics.
    I can see in my mirror, he looks puzzled. Pleased.
    Turning the corner into College Avenue I head for the 13 Throughway. Pushing it, I head South into Oakland.
    "What are you doing at UC Berkeley?" I ask. Giving a paper?
    "Yes," he answers, "at the Department of Astronomy. A conference. On Particle Acceleration Mechanisms."

"How's that goin'?" I ask.

"Pretty good."

I squirm in my seat, sensing his discomfort.

He asks. "Well what did you think of my lecture at UT when you attended it."

"Well, I was just an undergraduate. But I did study The Vector Space Theory of Matter with Matsen. Best — most challenging thing I ever saw. Really elegant."

He laughs, "I heard of him. He was in the chemistry department, wasn't he? We had some of our grad students go and take it. Yes, it is amazing that he teaches that stuff to undergraduates."

"Well you know that story he tells about teaching vector spaces to undergraduates?" I wait.

I continued: "About when he was in Paris and they were practicing their French for giving a paper and they were walking around in the Tuilleries garden, and his friend grabs him and says, 'My god Matsen! That kid is using the plus perfect indefinite!'"

I hear DeWitt chuckling in the back seat.

"So Matsen tells us that we can learn the vector space theory of QM like the way children learn language. To see it in use."

"Hmm," he says.

"Anyway I though it was beautiful. The bra and ket notation that Dirac gave to QM. For the dual basis vectors of a space, then with the Hamiltonian operator producing the spectra of the problem space. It was axiomatic, algorithmic. I like that."

"Well it is the Heizenberg operator algebra approach," he says.

"Oh!" I say. "You know I once saw Dirac in front of the New Physics building at UT. It was a horrendously hot summer day and he was out there in a BLACK suit! He had a starched collar and everything. He was all red in the face, I thought he was going to collapse without air conditioning."

Pause. Driving, I take the downtown exit into Oakland off 13.

Wanting to talk the talk a little further I said, "Yeah, I never really got a good handle on the Schrödinger wave equation. I mean I got it that it was probability waves: the time derivative of probability density equal to the space dispersion."

Then I said out loud: "Sigh. (ψ, psi) That IS beautiful. You don't see that in the matrices. It was groovy stuff. We had a really good course in waves at UT, based on the Berkeley physics books."

I was dying to ask him a question because I didn't get his "many world interpretation." But I didn't want to appear facile or dense because these guys do not suffer fools lightly. "Well what about the many worlds picture," I ventured cautiously. "You know I got a sense of that — I think, from the Feynman books and from Statistical Mechanics. Got the great big Tolman tome for stat mech — the superposition of all possible outcomes being necessary to talk about the probability of an outcome. But that is just the basis of probability. Isn't it?"

I knew it must be about something more. So to provoke him I invoked a popularization, though I knew these guys held this in contempt. "That's what Schrödinger's cat was about, wasn't it? A *gedenkin* experiment, a hypothetical cat used to demonstrated a 'quantum superposition' where 'dead' and 'alive' states coexist. The cat was stuck in a box and irradiated and we don't know until we open the box if he is dead or alive."

"*Well*," he said, sounding dubious (I thought he rolled his eyes there in the back seat) "the many worlds interpretation is different."

I fessed up. "I have to admit I never really got the Many Worlds Interpretation. It didn't filter down into our undergraduate Quantum Mechanics class." My mind runs into associations. Freud. Live a little. When you say you never really associated the idea outside of math and physics. Live a little. They are completely general. "I mean I got the idea that the particle, the object, was a space. Now you are telling me the object is a wave? I mean I got it that an object, a particle, is a vector space."

DeWitt said, "Well the wave function is not simply a description of the object's state but it actually is entirely equivalent to the object."

I let that sink into the air a bit. "Wow," I said.

He continued, "The way they were able to keep the wave function in the wake of Uncertainty was by saying that the wave function underwent a *collapse* as a result of the action of observation. That's the beauty of the Many Worlds Interpretation of Quantum Mechanics. We don't need to consider observation as a special event. It is just another one of many."

Hmmm, I think. Sounds like a good place to infuse Peirce, and explore observation and interpretation. I said, "I always just took an axiomatic approach to uncertainty and thought that the non-commutativity of the energy / time commutator or the position / momentum commutator indicated that we are not in the realm of regular numbers any more, but had shifted into a creative realm of algebras and other abstractions beyond our ordinary numbers — like spinors and twisters and things."

"Well in a way it is a kind of split," he said. "The system — and the observer is a system — are split by an observation. Each split corresponds to a possible outcome of the observation. These splits generate a tree of possible outcomes. My contribution was that the various complete alternate histories, which are paths along the branches of the tree, can be superposed to form new states."

To which I reply, "So how does that look in the wave equation interpretation?"

"Well, in the Many Worlds Interpretation, the Schrödinger wave equation is like the F=ma of the quantum mechanical universe, it holds for all time everywhere. An observation or measurement of an object by an observer is modeled by applying the Schrödinger wave equation to the entire system compromising of BOTH the observer and the objects."

Still not getting it, I persisted. "But how is the splitting different from the idea that is the basis of probability and statistical mechanics that the space of all possible outcomes is the basis for figuring out the probability of the desired outcome?"

He said, "Well the many worlds interpretation gets around the wave function collapse, but most physicists don't like the idea of infinitely many non-observable alternate universes."

I said, trying to keep it light: "That reminds me of Girodano Bruno. Do you know him? Burned at the stake for taking up the heretical idea that the earth was not the center of the universe but that it dogged a star — our sun — and that there were millions and millions of suns with planets out there in the universe."

"Yeah," DeWitt said, "he REALLY met with some resistance to his ideas."

We both laughed at this.

He continued: "Anyway there is not yet any way to experimentally verify it. That is why it is an interpretation and not a theory. It split the philosophers into two camps. What they call Actualism and Possibilism. Actualism is a position on the ontological status of possible worlds. The Actualist holds that only the actual world and its inhabitants can properly be said to exist. Possibilism holds that possible worlds other than our own exist (in some sense) just as much as the actual world does. Or, more precisely, the possibilist holds that possible worlds other than the actual world exist and that what it means to say that other possible worlds exist cannot be reduced to, or analyzed in terms of, the existence of anything in the actual world."

"I'm the arch-Possibilist," he said with a wide smile.

Wow, this blew my mind. I wondered what it meant. I asked: "Is that for real? I'm part of an artistic movement here in Berkeley called Actualism. I though it was invented here."

"No. . . I've never heard of that," he said. He pressed on nonplussed. "The Actualist versus the Possibilist debate gets pretty out there," he continued. "They even have a kind of modal logic to be able to talk about it."

"Modal logic?" I asked, intrigued.

"Well its a way to frame the "possible worlds" talk in logical relations amongst consistent and maximally complete sets of propositions. Take an example. I might say: I could go to the movies today, and I could decide to stay home. Most Actualists will be happy to grant the interpretation of "I could go to the movies, OR, I could stay home" in terms of two distinct possible worlds.

"But for the Possibilist, that contingency is usually taken to mean that there is a possible world in which I go to the movies, and that there is another possible world in which I don't. Now, only one of these two worlds is the actual world, and which one it will be is determined by what I actually end up doing. The possibilist argues that these apparent existential claims — that there are possible worlds of various sorts — ought to be taken more or less at face value: as stating the existence of two worlds, only one of which, at most, can be the actual one. Hence, they argue, there are innumerably many possible worlds other than our own, which exist just as much as ours does.

"It has to do with consistent and maximally complete sets of propositions. "Consistent" here means that none of its propositions contradict one another (if they did, it would not be a possible description of the world); "maximally complete" means that the set covers every feature of the world. Here the "possible world" which is said to be actual is actual in virtue of all its elements being true of the world around us."

Whew. After driving all the way down College, hitting Broadway we were into Oakland. A few moments later, I pull into a the Ritz Carlton hotel. This building has a doorman and I let my fare out after pulling into the circular drive-through.

I roll away thinking, Wow, I just traveled down a path, a world line with a famous physicist from my old time Institute, and I was able to hang with him in a bit in conversation. I wonder how he would take to the work of our new Institute. Probably wouldn't care for it at all. We'll include him in ours, though he wouldn't include ours in his.

Dropouts

The performance work **Dropouts**, directed and developed by George Coates, was performed at the Addison Theatre, Berkeley in 1976.

On his first theatre production, George Coates asked me to help him out. He had worked with the Blake Street Hawkeyes in *Coyote*, and acted in other productions. Coates, with his artist's goatee and beret, loved to play. He was one of those self-reliant, resourceful ectomorphs with a great sense of presence who enjoyed life, enjoyed elaborate meals, and when he set out to write, had to make sure he had the great pen, the Parker Mont Blanc, and a nice journal. Once, on a stroll across the UC Berkeley campus, he told me that he had worked for the psychology department as an actor. He had been hired to impersonate various patients exhibiting serious mental disorders as part of a training program to help doctors distinguish false presentation from the real thing. Apparently Coates was phenomenally convincing at this; they hired him again and again.

In addition to being an accomplished actor Coates was an amazingly savvy impresario and business man. He wrote up a grant proposal for the Berkeley city council and they funded his Dropouts project. It was to pull together a bunch of high school dropouts and create a theatre performance based on their stories with them acting in it. Coates himself was a high school drop out and this would be empowering. Having been through the Hawkeyes boot camp, he was firmly grounded in physical and poor theatre and knew its great transcending power. He was nervous at this his first theatre production and I was along for moral support and to provide some writerly type help, (whatever that meant). Basically the idea was to get these young people — high school dropouts — in a room, have them tell their stories into tape and develop some kind of script from the tape. To get the ensemble, he advertised in the East Bay Express, a local paper and pretty soon he had some amazing young people show up for auditions. One guy looked like a young Marlon Brando and talked like Lenny Bruce. He was a New Yorker, and had that hyper-aggressive, faux-Jew, Mafia-Italian, get outta my face hutz-pa. He was just like Marlon Brando in *On the Waterfront* or like Stanley

Kolwalski in *A Streetcar Named Desire* and would riff out doing routines from these movies. Appropriately named Peter (for he had an enormous infatuation with his cock) — it was the main subject of his talk, delivered in that fearless humor and shocked / teasing delight in filth that Lenny Bruce had.

At the interview we asked them, Why did you drop out? The list of reasons why people dropped out were many. Peter said, "For the past 10 years from the time I was 12, I spent drunk. I was never there." During the interview Peter astounded us by giving a history of all the Mafia dons that had ruled various boroughs in New York and their turf wars, killings and exploits. It was like a recitation of the Tane, the Irish cattle tribe rustling exploits.

Another tall slender young man — from Alabama — named Larry was a cross-dresser. As a boy he could be the picture of barefoot, freckle-faced, southern, male innocence in blue-jean cutoffs. And then, he could get dressed up in capris and pumps with spangled jewelry and let down this gorgeous cascade of red hair to present as a beautiful girl. I was shocked. He had various horror stories about growing up in the south with androgynous cross dressing tendencies.

There were some other interesting women too. One was a young lady named Lenore who had gypsy aspects with flowing skirts and who was way hip beyond her years, a blues singer. She answered the question about why she dropped out of school with, "It's white. It's suburban. It's very dull. Everybody there has lots of money and my family doesn't. I hate them."

She said, "Right now I spend a lot of time smoking hash, watching Star Treck and listening to the Rhythm Kings. I was gettin' into my old man. I just hacked around working, singing songs, getting gigs around here. We'd get up real late and stretch out the days. A good time for me was being with that person and gigging. And he was getting off on me and I was getting off on him. I was the lady who brought the songs."

Another guy was a swarthy young Mexican dude named Mark; he was a gang-banger, his body festooned with tats.

Basically all the young high school dropouts wanted to be doing something more important with their lives. None were trained as actors. Coates wasn't the least bit worried about that. He was more interested in the theatrical potential of the personas of these young people. He had a great understand of physical presentation, and what would constitute interesting theatre (in the sense that it should be shocking, powerful, a spectacle—even in the poor (in the sense of being self-sustaining, without reliance on props and sets) theatre of Grotowski. After the interview he got them moving around in the space. Coates started off the exploration by moving around on the stage. "I just wanted to get a sense of the space here," he said. He got them moving. He started them off with physical warm up and stretches and got them owning the space. He got them doing floor stretches and rolling around on the clean swept floor. He got them doing basic vocal exercises, made if fun. One exercise starts with walking around and singing: "La-la-la." He lies down on the floor, does the "La-la." Gets them up again, the "La-la" is now repeated against the ceiling, the wall and the floor, alternating between the head, belly and chest voice. They enjoyed it.

Next he got them doing the "KING-KING" Exercise. They repeated calling out of the word "King" on a very high note and in a quick tempo, with a whole series of variations ranging from very low to very high notes. Right away he was conducting them in a kind of choral ensemble. And getting a great awareness of their growing expertise with these quick results. Coates obtains the most amazing results by improvising around this word at a successively higher pitch. It really raised the level of energy. The dropouts started becoming like actors, much more aware of their vocal apparatus, that it was a thing to play with. They could see the delight and sense of accomplishment on the faces of their fellow-pupils. They had become his pupils and he charmed them so that they relaxed and began to trust him.

At his flat on Dwight Way where he lived with a lovely Irish girlfriend of flaxen red-hair, Coates and I laboriously typed up what we had recorded from interviewing them.

At the next rehearsal Coates got them moving on stage and saying things from the script. He said, "We are like kids learning to play again. Theatre begins in conversation and should just be a structure around conversation." Coates coached them in physical presence and movement. And the mood was a lot more confident now that we had text. Coates placed the individual sheets of dialog from the recorded interviews into the center of the stage, and has each dropout pick up some one else's words. Coates had them speak each other's lines so they wouldn't feel the responsibility of having to represent their own truth, but the truth of someone else in the group.

He had each one recite a text at will with his voice gradually increasing in volume.

Peter: My whole life is exploded up
I'm just looking for something to do

                                   Lenore: Well, take me drinking and dancing, then.

Peter: Thats a good one.

                                   Lenore: I'm just suggesting it to you.

Coates said: "The words must resound against the ceiling as though the upper part of the skull were talking. The head must not be tilted back, as this causes the larynx to close. Through the echo, the ceiling becomes the partner in the dialogue which takes the form of questions and answers." During the exercise Coates leads the pupil by the arm round the room. Then he has them begin a conversation with the wall, improvised. Here it becomes evident that the echo is the answer. The whole body must respond to the echo. "The voice originates in and issues from the chest" he bellowed in admonishment. Next the voice is placed in the belly. In this way a conversation is held with the floor. Position of the body: 'Like a fat, heavy cow."

Again he told them: "Theatre begins in conversation and should just be a structure around conversation about conversation," he said. "We are like kids learning to play again." And he got them talking to each other, retelling their stories.

He had them try out various dynamic rages and gestures. He'd say, "You've got to get it to the back of the room."

The next time we were together he had them do a check-in. Someone said they were scared. They were exhilarated too.

The next time we got to the theatre we found that Coates had blocked off areas of the stage with tape to give these amateur actors an idea about how to move to their point in space. It was like a huge game board.

Peter: My whole life is exploded up
I'm just looking for something to do

                                   Lenore: I've never been on an airplane because of my guitar; the case isn't good enough to travel and not good enough to insure.

Coates conducted them. "After Rich says a line, then Peter does. Really get behind what you are doing. Rich, Peter, Mara Mark, Rich. Round and round about."

Coates told them it would be like Rowan and Martin's Laugh in: "You know were the little windows are opening up and they are saying little jokes and statements that are the signatures to the specific characters. Like that one German guy that says: 'Very funny. But Shstuuuupid.'" He told them that we will develop our wardrobe from the free box.

We considered the game board to be a region containing four distinct zones. A trip within the region may originate or terminate at any of the four zones. One zone was anger, another envy, another seduction. "It is like a game. Like hopscotch."

Reading each other's scripts as though they were their own, they were impersonating each other. I must say I was shocked at this. I had not had that much experience with theatre and games, but I thought the Hawkeyes were the ultimate in individual authenticity. And that was the first thing Coates had dismissed in his theatre.

We developed a basic framework for Dropouts. It would be a Play for three men and two women. Costumes would be iprovised. One man, Larry will be a cross-dresser. He will sashay and whirl

Anger Area	Seduction Area
Claudia: We get together and have a good time and then split up	Lenore: He was getting off on me and I was getting off on him

Jealousy Area	Depressed Area
Claudia: She wants us to ask her what she did today	Lenore: I get five hundred dollars in the city. But its too depressing to tell you how

Areas of feeling types in the Dropout theatre Space

when the time comes to change from he to she. They speak out of the predominant emotion of their area.

It is to be playing a kind of game. That the stage is a playing field, and that there are distinct zones, which only the players know about but which should become emerge as a pattern to the viewer as the play proceeds.

All this was a further assault already begun by the Hawkeyes on any preconceived notions I might have had about what theatre was. I talked about the idea of mapping out the space with various zones.

Basically we have The Origin point (O) and the Destination (D) point of the movement. O - - > D. Now, the Player / Traveler has needs to meet some kind of impedance to his flow. Some kind of "challenge viscosity. Something standing in the way.

These would be zonal functions. And interzonal interactions.

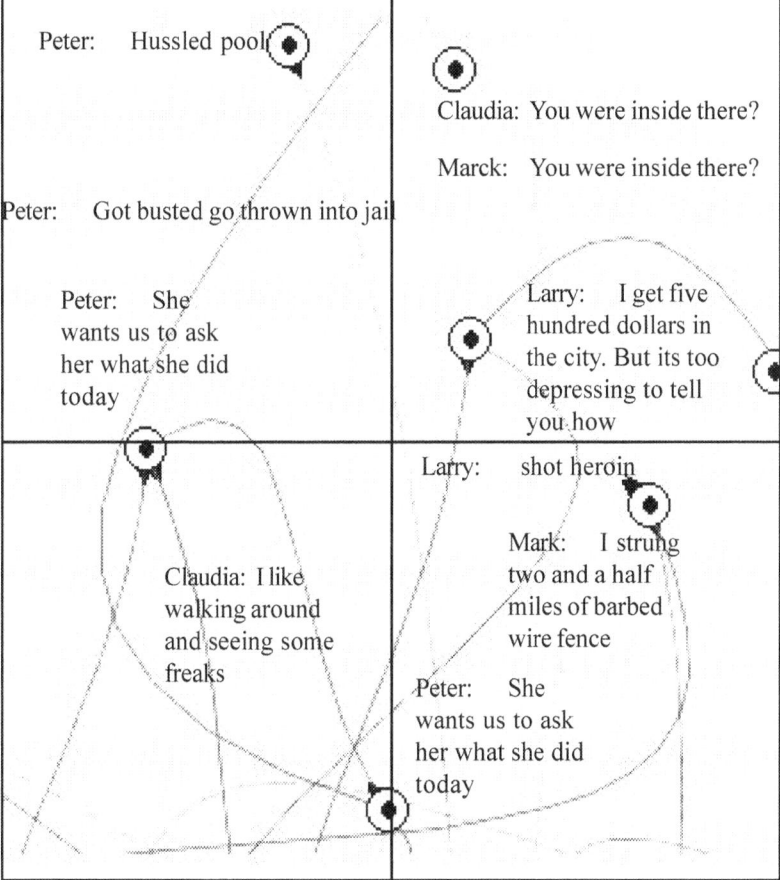

Spatio / temporal speaker rhythm score for Dropouts theatre

What are the interzonal interactions? Well, the speeches they make to each other and the gestures and other movements.

Travelers I called them. It appealed to my background to think of the problem of moving people — travelers — as though they were

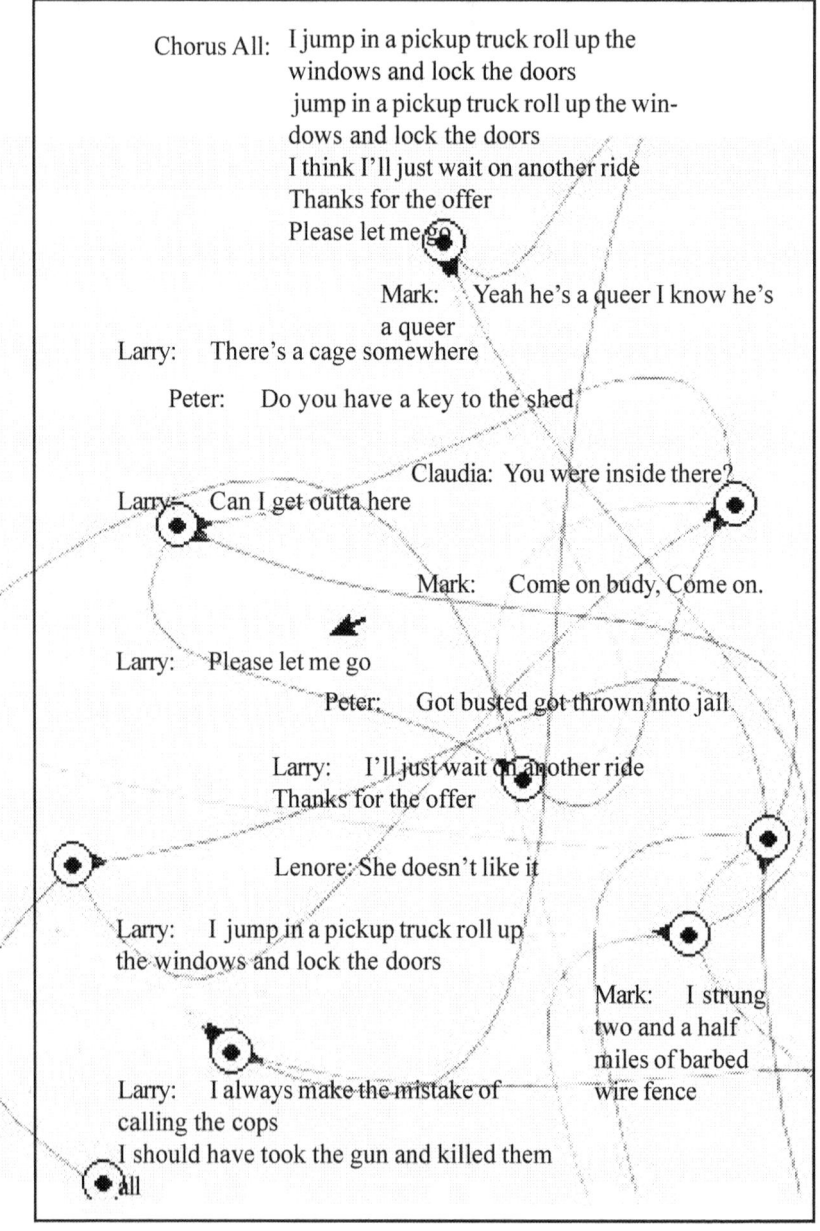

Exchanging speakers while holding text for Dropouts theatre

molecules in a classical gas bouncing around with various levels of energy interacting with each other. And that it was up to the theatre audience to find out WHAT was *The Big Function* motivating them. Presumably one moved according to the dictates of this function in order to minimize some kind of work, be it cognitive or physical. We could define the state of the play as an ordered triple. One for each traveler consisting of his name, his origin and his destination.

(Peter, O_1, D_2) (Larry, O_1, D_3)
(Claudia, O_2, D_3) (Mara, O_3, D_1)

This would be the state of a system. And I walked through explaining how this would work to them.

Coates told them, "Dropouts would become an Un-School, a teaching school where everybody in the audience will be placed in an existential dialog. They will pose for themselves the question: Have I really dropped out enough?"

Coates coached them a lot on performing, not in a way of telling the travelers what to say, but in giving permission to amplify themselves.

It was hard for me to let go of my obsession with the words, but here we began to think of the work not so much of what was being said, but of a process. I began to try and see something of what it meant to be present. One always lives in a competitive hierarchy and is bent on closing distance to goals as quickly as possible to arrive at the result, or the conclusion. But here I started looking at what was happening moment to moment. It was not so much how far you had to go to get across but the difficulty of travel. It could be just travel time, but it could be something else, the psychological aspects. Theatre as a kind of time and personal travel. The Dropouts even said of Coates: "He's using us to paint, he's the traffic director." The plot then had to do with coming up with conflicts for the interzonal travel. Not plot in the usual sense that the identities of individual trip makers were in some kind of jeopardy, for he had drained off the importance of the individual trip makers —rather, there would be some kind of representation in the mind of the theatre go-er of the aggregate number of trips in each time period originating in zone i and terminating in zone j. The audience needs to have a sense of this aggregate impression, what I thought of as the "trip distribution. We wanted to know about how many interactions would be required to make a decent and interesting play. To have an abundance then to cut back.

Larry: Amil nitrate will give you the big rush

Marck: Is that what you took?

Larry: You can feel those brain cells tingling

Peter: You don't need a prescription

Larry: Went to the top of the high dive, popped a snapper and jumped into the water.

Marck: You were inside there?

Mark: Don't breathe on my car

Peter: Fuck you. Fuck you. Fuck you

Larry: I get five hundred dollars in the city. But its too depressing to tell you how

Peter: Well excuse my motherfucking ass

Lenore: Completely helpless, completely vulnerable

Mark: I will knock you out

Claudia: Laugh and ignore it.

Larry: Don't kill me. Don't kill me.

Mark: I strung two and a half miles of barbed wire fence

Peter: She wants us to ask her what she did today

Peter: My immediate reaction is to get real tight

Lenore: I go loose immediately and go waa-iee-aagh-

Claudia: I like walking around and seeing some freaks

Exchanging speakers and text for Dropouts theatre

The Dropout approach to story line or plot was to have an ensemble of interzonal transfers. Coates had a tremendous belief in the ensemble theatre, the organic theatre. The playwright is just a scribe. So I had to start thinking about the switch over to another perspective. What would be the insight of this piece, the why we are here, the what we are supposed to learn from it. What is that. Well it is the method — to rely on the method — the way of how, or the how of why. This is the honesty of wading into the space, into the performance, and allowing yourself to invest support in whatever comes up, and go with it.

We were all touched when one of the dropouts said, "Here I was doing something I didn't want to be doing so I was scared." First we have the lines of why they dropped out. Then we have them playing and talking with each other. This allows some functions to emerge. We start to see some kind of theatre emerging. The gestures were falling into place the motions towards and away sometimes relating what was being said and sometimes not.

We are forced by this approach to accept as the best estimate of the travel distribution, that distribution which explains the greatest number of character interactions. Dropouts was a kind of object lesson in the Principle of Insufficient Reason. Which is the basic problem we all have: What we are experiencing doesn't make sense within the context of what we are trying to do in this piece, in our lives. And it is OK! We live with insufficient reason all our lives. Let us celebrate living under that .

So we start looking at the *energy* of what is said rather than *what* is said. I began to think of it like a play with characters, but the characters in this theatre were characters in a function, with all these dimensions attached to them, $H(x,y,z,t,p,q)$ — call it the Action, or perhaps the Grotowskian. One began to see the abstraction, the pattern of play in the space. It could be pleasant. We are looking for the motivational potential. Certainly this was in the traditional theatre model but now in the new energetic model, the Physical Theatre model, we are not so hung-up on meaning. But forced by the making arbitrary of meaning, and the coming to the fore of rhythm to involve ourselves more, to see the ecology, the system that holds us together reflected in theatre. It was tribal and abstract. Like the syntax of text reinvented and writ large.

Who are the Teachers in the Un-school. Darrell Gray. O'Keefe, Coates, J. Albert, Ernst, Schein, P.Loschan. The beauty of this kind of theatre and aesthetic, is that certain things that we thought were important and necessary before, become interchangeable. And thus their importance is diminished, and other important aspects of the aesthetic come to the fore. In this case the Real, in that they started to have a lot more respect and love for each other.

What is the basic thing going on here. Shifting from the exchange to the energy of the whole system. Shifting from the meaning to the machinery that generates and conducts the meaning. Working with Dropouts project made me see this shift in what I had though was literacy more like in the system of sonic articulation what we were using in the Hawkeye theatre. And is it, could it be, in the poetry as well? Well for example we might be interested in the sound energy, what if we considered *that* on the same level as where metaphor and metonymy come from. Certainly the Surrealist program helped us break through this need for sense. I liked sense don't get me wrong. What if we also thought about big talk and little talk, how instead of moving away from the attempt to make the big statement we went into the warmth of the quotidian.

These thoughts I brought to Darrell Gray as we were all, in our way, trying to discover the generative machinery of the poem.

Prismatic Fountains Flow Forth

July 4, 1976. Berkeley. I was among the tens of thousands of revelers who filed across the Bayshore freeway into the Berkeley Marina to watch the fireworks and celebrate the Fourth of July holiday.

It reminded me of how much my brother-in-law back in Texas loved fireworks. He'd drive out beyond the city limits (you weren't allowed to sell them in the city limits) spend a small fortune on them; bring back tons then set them off in the cul-de-sac of their street, or out at their lake house. They threw them at each other; held the Roman Candle like it was their personal flame thrower and sent shooting sparks and flames all over every where. They had Flying Dragons, Sun Wheels, Bottle Rocket, and Prismatic Fountains. Being out here on the west coast, I learned that Asians felt the same way about fire crackers. Berkeley put on a good fireworks show to support the need to celebrate and presumably ameliorate the tendency of the populace to turn into a warlike mob of sniping street fighters when around explosives.

For most Americans the Fourth of July is by far the most patriotic holiday combining Memorial Day, Flag Day, Veteran's Day rolled into one. Off in the middle of the summer, all America went to their picnics. The Fourth of July is a day to stop and celebrate their freedom, appreciate their country, pay respect to those who died to protect it and fly the flag or display its red, white and blue colors. And to go on picnics and barbecue great quantities of roasting meat. In your own back yard, on a friend's deck or patio, at a beach, a state park or public camping or picnic area. The common practice is to barbecue or grill food such as hot dogs, hamburgers, chicken. It was like going primitive, to celebrate this summer solstice, going back to the primal practice of roasting meat on an open grill. I didn't have a picnic to go to like most people, I wasn't much for parades or church gatherings, but I did want to be out in the throng moving out toward the Berkeley marina. We would walk, because the whole place had turned into a parking lot — to watch the fireworks displays that the city would be putting on that night. I headed out

Earlier today, back east, across 3 time zones, the president Gerald

Ford gave a speech in front of the liberty bell. The Bell they rang, lo those many years ago, to announce the signing of the Declaration of Independence. It has something written on it, something to the effect — Ring freedom throughout the land to all the people. Yeah.

It was a Sunday and everyone was off. The weather was warm and beautiful. There was a carnival atmosphere in the air. It was special because I think people were giving up their anger and disappointment with the US over Viet Nam. People could admit the validity of both sides. I was off, because the more senior members of the cooperative wanted the work, and I was glad because who would want to drive amid that great moving human throng anyway.

The Fourth of July celebration is the main summer festival. Hippies and other eternally hopefuls had started to celebrate it as a kind of pagan celebration of Summer. Because since the 1960's and the Vietnam Conflict caused such a division in this country that many just did not feel like celebrating the American hegemony.

Gerald Ford was in office, he came in after Tricky Dickey got impeached. But 1976 was an election year, there were democratic conventions, and it looked like Carter was going to get it. Gerald Ford was vice president when Nixon resigned, so he got appointed to the office of president. The only one to ever be given the office without a mandate from the people, he had Goldwater as his vice president. This was a campaign year and people were looking toward a change. Going to kick the bastard crooks out. Their outrage had made them active and patriotic. The country was in a country mood and liked the sincerity of the southern peanut farmer, Jimmy Carter. Who admitted in a Playboy interview that sometimes he had lust in his heart. Well that was all right.

I walked all the way down Dwight Way starting out from Blake St. at Shattuck all the ways down and crossed San Pablo and around Aquatic Park. More and more people were massing, coming in from all directions. We passed by Spanglers and headed to the footbridge over the freeway. It was a little iffy under the freeway; there were lots of families carrying lightweight aluminum lawn chairs. Big black people lumbering slowly. I was alone because I couldn't think of anybody who wasn't busy (or who wouldn't have thought it was kind of corny) to invite to go with me.

1976 was special because it was the bicentennial, yes but I think it was also a turning point. Things were shifting back from the midsummer bacchanal to a celebration of what we were all going through as the American Experience. A steady flow of celebrating patriots filed out of the city on the sidewalk of the bridge that went over the Bayshore freeway, at the Berkeley exit. It lead to the road out to the Berkeley pier. They were mostly families of all races, and a lot of students even though this was summer and the majority of them were gone. Going over the top of the freeway we could see San Francisco across the bay, and many, many boats out in the bay, some lit up like Christmas trees. The crowd was spread out all over the large waterfront, some stopping at the little cove facing Emmeryville, and setting up blankets and tablecloths and aluminum lawn chairs. They had staked out the choice spots there earlier with their families and had been barbecuing all day. Others like myself headed further out to be closer to the explosions.

I felt like I was walking down in time with the centuries of people who celebrated July 4th before. For in that year, 1976 there was a feeling in the air that we were all for a moment together on some big adventure. It was a lot more present than Christmas, which had become an extension of the great American marketing system. The great summer festival of July 4th is a time when most families get together because the kids are out of school, and the weather is nice. And the weather was nice. The weather was perfect, I only had on a T-shirt. We could see some officials and pyrotechnicians setting up their launching site way over on the other side of the park right at the edge of the water. There were police there and it was roped off.

We were celebrating the birthday of a 200 year-old country, born on this day in 1776 with the signing of the Declaration of Independence in Philadelphia. George Washington became the first president, cause he was a general and a hero. The Declaration was written mostly by Thomas Jefferson. In beautiful handwriting. They had some sharp guys back then.

The 200 year-old country was suffering from future shock and greed to the point of almost collapsing but we were here celebrating our way of life. Even though the economy was suffering its biggest lull since the Great Depression.

Like most Americans I had no sense of history to speak of. I could barely remember what buildings were replaced by those torn down in my old neighborhood in San Antonio when I went back there.

It was John Locke who started making the distinction between the divine right of kings and natural laws that gave everybody rights. This was out of the Enlightenment of Newton (those laws of motion

— For every action there is an equal and opposite reaction — got spread through Locke, and spread like a wildfire meme across the great water to the colonies where it led to the phrase "We hold these truths to be self-evident . . ." And the idea of perpetual revolution got codified into action and institution, symbolized by the Declaration of Independence.

Matthew, Mark, Luke, and John bless this bed I lay upon. Locke, Berkeley, and Hume inquire me of what I presume.

Jefferson — TJ, and his bro Ben — Ben Franklin, cooking it up. Laying it down. TJ whips out the Declaration in an afternoon. He knocked out much of the Constitution too, and the Articles of Confederation if memory serves me. They were young men in their 30s, in their prime.

I wonder if TJ got high to write. I could just see him and Ben Franklin hanging out after the others had left.

Yo TJ. Lets smoke some of thine most excellent herb and talk about freedom. Those hemp plants your are growing are not just for making rope, dear fellow.

Yeah. Freedom, man.

That's an idea that is going to catch on. I just know it.

TJ smokes down to do the arduous copying of the first part, the invocation of Locke.

They all had long hair, didn't they? And many had beards. No, wait. It was a wig. Ha ha, TJ wore a wig!

What do we know about their psychology? Would Thomas Jefferson ever have mentioned in his diary: "You know. . . today, I smoked some of the flowers of my numerous hemp plants. It was ever so nice. I went down by the river and just flounced down into a patch of daisies running riot near the stream 'twas running by it and slipped into the most pleasant of nepenthean reveries."

Promethean. All revolutionaries are promethean.

Yeah, it comes out of Newton in a way. What is the light made of. All the colors. The Law of Gravity governing all the heavens above and below. Attraction throughout the universe. That is a kind of deity and to study that, especially with the groovy sensational semantic trip that is the calculus, is the pursuit of enlightenment.

At dusk the fireworks started. Tens of thousands along the waterfront looking west at the Golden Gate Bridge which was starting to be lit up by the stroboscopic effect of fireworks from the San Francisco celebration as showers of sparks from their show rained down. Large and mid sized bursts in the air. Some bursts light up the Bay Bridge in the foreground and away across the Golden Gate Bridge was being lit up by bursts and showers of sparks from their fireworks show at Crissey field and Fort Point. Tens of thousands of citizens were treated to a fireworks display which was a symbolic re-enactment of some perpetual revolutionary battle in which we are defending ourselves and democracy against the onslaught of the world. It was like we were part of some public ritual, our history was like some kind of great ritual for the public viewing. The multitudes shouted and oohhed and ahhed and applauded and strained for a better view of the great BLUE AND RED AND Bright Orange SHOWERS OF ERRANT SPARKS falling in the night sky. It was a festive atmosphere that as the show went on became edgy.

Large aerial bursts of puncture the heavens and lit up the skyline like a lightning storm.

I started heading out to walk the length of the Berkeley Pier. The pier seemed to go on and on for miles heading out across the Bay into the Golden Gate.

There were large explosions of colorful fireworks swirling and dancing — leaping out at you from the pitch-black night sky that became reflected in the dark wavy sea.

Usually there were whole families fishing off the side, they cut little notches in the massive railing to prop up there poles, and they had wheeled their iced chests on little folding carts out onto the concrete covered pier. But not today. Today there were throngs of people, probably more people on the pier than had ever been there. I wondered if it would hold our weight. I could just see it collapsing and us trying to make our way to shore and not get pounded on the wreckage of pylons or smashed into the riprap rocks forming the breaker barrier. There was evidence that there used to be trolley tacks coming out here. It must have been the height of swell coming out here with suits and ties and hats and gloves in the 1910 trolley car. Many mid size bursts of fireworks send spiraling sparks through the night air. Somewhere out there beyond the horizon far out at sea, beyond what I can see, there is wind and energy exchange turning up the waves and reflecting back off the shore in one big harmonium like the bay was an unblinking eye looking at the sky of the universe.

I pushed on from the shore, occasionally stopping to look back at the enormous rolling Berkeley hills coming as a long wave of the continent finding its end at the sea. The nighttime sky filled with bright colorful fireworks.

These massive hills, all covered by people's houses seemed to be looking down at us: the mountain people living up there closer to god in the rocket-streaked sky, looking down at us flatlanders here below.

Large aerial bursts light up the night sky.

Many mid size bursts of fireworks send spiraling sparks through the night air.

As the stars twinkled their busting sprinkles large aerial bursts of fireworks send a curtain of sparks through the night sky.

And there beyond in the sea full of its marvels was the shimmering reflection of the neon lights of the city — San Francisco floating out on the dark waters.

The boundary of the sea and the sky was penetrated by that jetty jutting out into the cut at the gate. On and on I walked and there beyond was the city of the Bay its lights coming on like a unified powerful thing like some great Coney Island dreamed up by Edison and Tesla and RCA Victor.

And I thought about all the things I wanted to do, and how difficult it would be to do them and how much was going on and how I am not aggressive enough to make it happen but maybe there was a space for me, maybe there was some place that I belonged, and I could see the ferry boats going around Alcatraz and the lights coming on in Larkspur and but not Angel Island, for it was dark and uninhabited. It would be nice to do a Huck Finn thing there someday and camp out, maybe even with my own kid.

Some kind of ominous destiny was treading after me, and wistfully I turned and headed back down the long track to shore.

The spectacle of seeing the City floating like a giant brain on a sea worked with a sense of my longing and solitude.

It was like we were all around some ancient campfire in which the wood occasionally burst, shooting up sparks, sparks up into the heaven. Some even more wayward heading way off into the dark forest and the night beyond.

I felt like that lonely errant spark bursting out of the Greek fire throwing shadows on the cave wall into the universe.

I would have to come up with much bigger and more intensely human and something of gigantic philosophical underpinning if I was ever to make my way in the world of will and ideas.

On the way back a talkative and satisfied procession of red blooded American citizens, now feeling a part of the body politic of the people, headed back into their city. Parents carried their sleeping children on their shoulders into their destiny.

Rugman and The Terrible Thing

Taxi Unlimited Waybill Log
Sunday August 8 1976.

    Since Taxi Unlimited used CB radio for dispatches, a driver became part of the Citizens Band community. At that time there were some people in the CB community who thought of themselves as stars. The cynical folks at Taxi thought they were a nuisance, a bucket mouth. But I thought they were kind of funny and weird when you picked up the random transmission here and there. The two most outrageous were Rug Man and The Terrible Thing. They pretty much ran the show on the late night CB radio. They had that strong black oratory power and black humor. I don't know how they were able to get away with wielding so much power. I guess because they didn't use a lot of profanity. Perhaps there just weren't that many complaints. I think the FCC had become, by this time, unable to control the CB band any more—you were supposed to get a license, but I never did.
    I'd hear the Rug Man with his deep throaty voice coming in on a strong signal — walking all over everything on the airways. He made himself sound exactly like the hideous and insane voice of Mr. Froggy in that old and exceedingly surreal kids show, *Andy's Gang*. It was a voice of my childhood nightmares all over again as he said:

Rugman: Hi Ya, Kids. Hi Ya, Hi YA, HI YA!

    It was a rasping, grating, gravely voice — powerful, a voice not to be denied or interrupted in any way. Mr. Froggy, the Magic Gremlin hung out in a clock and he was called by big old frightening Andy Devine saying: "Plunk your Magic Twanger, Froggy." It brought back strange memories of an ancient black and white world. There was something about the characters and the show that bothered me. It had a mouse that beat a drum and a black cat that played a violin, and a jungle boy who was always being menaced by elephant thieves and scorpions. All that black and white jungle in the world of television before color. These were the Mogli stories, with a black panther, whose glowing eyes burned like beacons in the dark, and the night around them became like a nullity, a vacuum, into which your projections were sucked. And there was Mr. Froggy's strident gremlin voice disrupting the story and making people do things they didn't want to do. (I remember Froggy giving instructions to the cook: "Then throw the pancake batter on your head!" he says to the cook, and Oh no, the cook DOES!) I can recall having some "weird" dreams because of this.

The Rug Man's signal was so strong he just about blanketed everyone on his channel in the East Bay. I guess that's why they called him the Rug Man. But if The Rug Man was scary because of his unnaturally powerful voice, Terrible Thing was terrifying because of the nature of the content of his speechifying. He'd start in:

> TT: Terrible Thing, terrible thing. You got the Terrible Thing.

And then launch into the most detailed stories of persecution, or some other evil doings that the government or women or some other agential entity was doing to him. He railed endlessly about AT&T, that they were in cahoots with the government in a vast eugenics program to purify the race of people like him. He had identified many nefarious control agencies. He'd get so wound up that his chat would most often turn into a wild rhythmic chant.

> TT: Damn it's hot. Napalm-hot, plasma-hot, nigger-porn-hot, Barstow-hot, Needles-hot, Blythe-hot, bugshit-crazy-in-Texas-middle-of-the-summer, because-its-always-120-degrees-by-noon hot.

I bought a little Sony Walkman tape recorder at the Ashby flea market and occasionally recorded some of their exchanges, when I could. The Rugman and his crew mostly talk about what power their mike was purveying on the air ways.

> Rugman: I'M GETTING CLOSE TO THE SECOND, I'm getting close to the 2nd wave length.
> Other: As high as he is he doesn't put anything over a 9 on me.

They wanted a moment to moment feedback on how strong their signal was.

> Other: How am I coming across to you.
> Rugman: BRING IT BY.
> Other: HELLLL lo.
> Rugman: 8

Other: uhhgh
Rugman: WHAT'S THAT. A FINE LOOKING TOMATO
Other: Damn are you are your base? That's pretty good, considering I am at Spengler's Fish House.

Rugman had this imperious know-it-all, flat, southern tone. It was overwhelming. He'd be going on and on about

Rugman: 10-4 OH LORD, I'M A HAVE TO DO SOMETHING, DEFINITELY. OHHH, GOING TO HAVE TO GET THAT THINGAMAJIG COMPLETELY CYCLONED.

LETS PUT IT THIS WAY. IT IS SOMEWHERE BETWEEN A 9 AND A 7. WHEN YOU TALWK, I MEAN

Rugman: OHHH KAY. WE'LL JUST JUMP BACK AT YA AND GO STANDBY. I'm a put another thirty foot section up.

But boring as The Rugman was, it was really touching and amazing and shocking to be privy to a little bit of what Terrible Thing was saying. Unlike the Rugman who was ubiquitous in the after hours, Terrible Thing was not so very strong, and it was sporadic. He'd start his chant with:

TT: Terrible thing. Terrible thing. You got the terrible thing. Terrible, thing, dirty nasty screwed up MURDER! Terrible what they do to your head. Yes! What'll we do, about the artificialization of IQ, about the erosion of ability, about the mind drain, about the body drain about the running down.
They are Entropy agents. Agents of Entropy.
I will find them out. I will study their ways. I will divulge their methods. I will defeat mine enemies. Those that would render me obsolete . . . I will out-spook the spooks, I will become a spy in their house while I am their prisoner.
They will slaughter your soul if you are not eternally vigilant.
They will slaughter your soul if you let them.
The methods they use to blind you and make you mute are: counterfeit god agents, genocide agents, crypto-NAZI agents of superiorism — agents of complete injustice and social oppression — satanically-motivated, neuro-homicidal and genocidal cults.
They are HUMAN AUTOMATON agents dealing drugs to keep the populace stoned, strung out, staggering in their place.
It's the SS all over again but now it is SENSORY STUPOR science — with dollar signs to blind my race, to blind my people, because we are poor and supposed to work for them.

Terrible Thing was always talking about various nefarious covert operations involving mind murder, and real physical murder by eugenic agents. He thought they had a kind of 3DTV, a laser TV. Here is the first bit that I heard about it. Here he is talking about being tortured by a governmental agency like the CIA but he called it the CAI the Central Artificial Intelligence.

> TT: Terrible thing, terrible thing. You got the Terrible Thing. I am the way I am today because I was TORTURED by the CAI, The Central Artificial Intelligence. Still am being persecuted and hounded by them. They are pro-slave, pro-automaton agents. They have neurologically murdered me.
> It's a terrible thing — AT&T. American Telephone and Telegraph has become American Teleprompt and Torture. I have been tortured by the so-called AI —artificial intelligence —agents in America. My preconscious thought formation is controlled by cerebral intervention —a source of endless frustration and disappointment to me. They are trying to induce a state of so-called ZERO-PSYCHOLOGY — behavioral automatism. It is a kind of mind murder. A terrible thing.
> They are agents of genocide working for the government and the established religions and the established mental health system. They think of themselves as HUMAN PROGRAMMING agents and they want to stop allowing the individual to have their own intentional desires.
> And they are anti-intuitive! —they think everything should be logically explained.
> They are against anyone in the lower classes having any kind of wherewithal or autonomy of purpose to do ANYTHING.
> These agents have demonstrated a vicious hatred of me because I am not of their educated class origin and am poor. They actually have told me, when I was trying to get food stamps, "You have no right to be poor!!"
> It's a terrible thing, the neuro-homicidal torture and dehumanization here in America. They are not very intelligent people — if they can be considered PEOPLE at all.
> It's obvious they are trying to force me to talk like they do or suffer the consequences; to act like they do or suffer being kept from jobs; to have their attitude of put-it-on-the-credit-card-and-send-me-a-bill behavior.
> This is not who I am! Not where I come from. I come from the south and they are trying to eradicate my southern identity. They are jealous of me because I am a NATURAL MAN. And I do not have the attention span for their repetitive jobs. It bores me

catatonic to be an ant working at a punch press or a fast food restaurant. It is shear torture to have to mop their floors and clean their toilets. THEY SAY I do not deserve to have the attitude I have. They actually said, "You have champagne taste on a beer budget." An insane rationale. They say I am "deluded" and that everything I have talked about here on the airways at night and the researches I have made, and the papers I have written about their activities is a "product of my imagination" — such as the IRON TIT agent which is what I call the system of getting welfare, and food stamps and some kind of sustenance. You have to be very careful what you say to them, very careful what you put on the forms — you have to conduct yourself in stealth and not say anything more than what they have in their guidelines because it is HARD as an iron tit to get a little.

My torturers demand that I ACCEPT the thoughts and suggestions of others rather than my own thoughts and self-suggestions. Why would I accept the thoughts of others? When I would much rather have my own?

Because I have been attacked by what are clearly insane individuals who want to subvert and conquer my mind by cerebral insult and repression, forcing it to remain stalled in bizarre conjugations, etcetera. It's a terrible thing . . .

It is no doubt because of my full-minded existence.

Full minded existence is what they fear. Full minded existence is what they envy. I am a god-damn natural man and I am a loving man and that is not enough. I am supposed to have to carry their piss-bucket because they think they are better than me. Terrible thing. These white devils don't have this full mindedness and hate me for having it.

The whites envy our free and wild ways. And I can see them from afar, glaring reptiles gloating down at my plumbing.

These people are like rodents with sharp teeth and weasel smiles, they're terrible. It's a terrible thing.

Look at them, they are all around you — cadaver-white, red-eyed vampire people afraid of being out in the light who only want to leach the life blood out of you. They have K-nine teeth. The looks that they give you! As if they wanted to watch you die. It's a terrible thing.

I just want some drugs to blank out my consciousness. Take me to this way shut-down place so that there is only this little white light glowing.

But we must FIGHT against these vampire Mind-Occupiers and their methods to deliberately, by contrairian contrast to forcibly and artificially reduce what they refer to as my "margin of intelligence" by super positional technique. I am further being forced to apprehend that my thoughts COME FROM A FEMALE SOURCE — the purpose being, evidently, to divert me from my own thoughts by a kind of aversion therapy and thus render me intellectually incompetent.

I wondered about this "superpositional technique." Terrible Thing mentions the in and the "holostrobic" at the end of this rant about his need to be on a mood-altering outpatient drug regimen.

TT: Or the neuro-homicidal SQUEEZE agent where they treat your mind as a squeeze-toy, a plaything for their amusement.
It constantly feels like there is pressure in my head. Like someone squeezing their hands around my head! It is not normal! It feels like my brain is shrinking. At times it scares me. They get you when you are down. It's a terrible thing, a terrible thing to not be able to sleep. I have horrible anxiety, so bad that I ended up in the ER when I lost my job at the furniture delivery company in East Oakland. I had my first Panic Attack. Terrible! I ended up coming home on Xanax. I went on the special EFFECTS-XR and it was rocky. My heart racing, nausea. You must take the same amount every day, because if you don't then the effects are amplified and you get all thrown out of whack. You feel like a sick bastard. And I sleep hardly at all. I sleep maybe three hours in a night then BOINK — eyes open, wide awake. It is an endless feedback cycle: Lack of sleep causes your Serotonin level to be depleted so you get more anxiety, and that leads to more depression. And then they start ramping up the agent. You feel like you might feel waking up in the middle of the night thinking it was a nightmare then you realize you ARE in one. And then you realize you ARE the PAWN in some other sick bastard's plot. These people are PERFECT OBEDIENCE agents using the religious institutions and psychoanalysis clinics and the medical infrastructure routinely as a means of getting EUGENIC control over the population. And as a means of damaging people so that they cannot reason independently and produce — as they would normally — spontaneous forms of culture and society, that are considered TROUBLESOME or PROBLEMATIC by the agents involved. These entities of the powers that BE are sociopathic and openly class/caste-genocidal. They have all been conned and are in turn coning us with their political machinations. Now they are working on cloning themselves and creating a self-perpetuation immortal line. They are receivers and transmitters of memes, CON-RAD agents from the HEART OF DARKNESS. It has not gotten as bad as the Pol Pot Regime around here, but it is bad. Serial killers are loose terrorizing the populace, suicide bombers make it that you

can't even go to the market to buy a tomato without fear. And the murder, genocide agents use this terror to get the people to vote to give the government all the powers it wants. Now they have TELEPROMPTER WAVES telling you what to do. They have mastered the art of reality with maser interferometer holostroboscopic 3DTV that you can see and walk around. They can construct reality with scenes of people in their houses being attacked like you were some kind of floating eyes able to see the future. JESUS!

They also find it quite amusing, I think, that they DICTATE to others, including myself, what to think and say. AND, in those who are completely unaware of their presence, what activities they undertake, as well. These often involving VIOLENCE, apparently for entertainment and other bizarre purposes.

I am not allowed to construct my own thoughts, speech or activities, although I am somewhat aware of their being constructed FOR ME — by agents I entirely dislike and would rather were not associated with me at all. They find it very FUNNY, evidently, that they can GET AWAY with this sort of manipulation.

Terrible Thing would just come on and do these short bursts, he would not stay on for long, his signal was not that strong. Unlike the Rugman's strong signal coming from his base station, Terrible Thing was mobile — hit and run. And he would never talk TO anybody. On the other hand I did chat or talk, (I wouldn't call it chat) with the Rugman once. It was about radio towers. Everybody the Rugman talked to seemed to have a great deal of envy for the Rugman's tower. I got into a bit of conversation with him about his tower after I overheard this conversation about him extend his antenna.

> Rugman: I'M PUTIN' UP A 80 FOOT SECTION
> Other: A mast on top of your tower?
> Rugman: I AM NOW FROM THE GROUND TO THE TOP, IT'S, I THINK THE THING WILL BE 140 FEET AND THE 2nd wavelength starts at 72.
> Other: 82.
> Rugman: 72
> Other: 82
> Rugman: THE FIRST WAVE LENGTH IS AT 36 FEET. AND THE 2ND HARMONIC IS A 72 FEET!
> Other: 82
> Rugman: The first wavelength is at 36 feet. That's the way I was always told, the first wavelength was at 36 feet and the 2nd wavelength was at 72. And I ain't even gonna think about the third.

I remembered my physics and keyed the mike and joined in.

> Me: They talk about it being the 11 meter band.
> 11 meters is about 36 feet. That's roughly the wavelength.
> What is this second harmonic mystique?
> Rugman: What's up with all this talk of meters. Don't wanna hear 'bout no meters This is America boy, we deal in feet and pounds and miles per hour around here.

Wow I had got the Rug Man to talk to me. Well, I pulled some college on him and talked about the speed of light and how frequency and wavelength equaled the speed of light and that a radio wave was like light and this CB was about 11 meters or 36 feet. The Rug man grunted. I said:

> Me: If you want to find the exact wavelength take the speed of light, 300 divided by the frequency we are on, like this one, 27.2 megahertz here and you get about 11 meters, about 36 feet. So you are right.
> Rugman: Well 10-4. Thank you very much !
> Damn you so fine, you mamma musta been a virgin.
> And if you double it up you get 72 for the 2nd one.
> Other: Well dad gum.
> Rugman: If I can get just half of that mast up I'll be up into the 3rd one easy. On a 140 foot tower. Yeah, imagine the guide lines I'd need. Ha, huh. I'm bumping the 3rd HARMONIC. I can't really say the antenna is in there, but I am bumping into it.

Unlike Rugman, the things that Terrible Thing talked about were very disturbing. And he would never engage anyone, as far as I know, in an actual conversation. His broadcasts were rants of wild accusations and paranoid fantasies. He genuinely seemed afraid, though he might have been fooling too. Sometimes Terrible Thing talked about psychology. He was actually a very intelligent person, who seems to have really studied. Or at least thought a lot about what was bothering him. At other times it could be downright poetic. Like here he is talking about the artificialization of IQ. And he would spin these out in rhymes. I have tried to capture it.

> TT: The artificialization of IQ / is taking place — through a silent / coupe / de tat. We are witnessing the mass-artificialization and actual social stratification of intelligence.
> I will defeat the agents involved with the artificialization of IQ
> a right-wing EUGENIC CONTROL party or cult organization whose

primary directive is the removal of the lower classes.
They have control of the programming and will force you to listen to their propaganda on a daily and nightly basis.
This is called CULTURE.
Their idea of culture is for us poor and unknown to spend our lives watching the rich and famous at play on TV.
Without it you will be ostracized by the others in your community.
The agents involved intend the mass-artificialization
and actual social stratification of intelligence, prior, they say, to a coup-de-tat, in which the U.S. Government is replaced by a right-wing, eugenic-controls party or cult organization.
The mass-slaughter genocidal removal of the lower classes is, apparently, a primary directive of this organization.
I am forced to listen to their propaganda on a daily and nightly basis— these TEASER agents, which stands for Teleological Eradication Agency by Stimulated Emission of Retardation, are constantly harassing me here.

To record Terrible Thing you had to be deadheading — no fares. You had to pick up his signal, IF he was on. He claims to have worked on this technology. The Arch-nemesis seemed to be the phone company, AT&T. Here is an even more detailed explanation of holostroboscopic.

TT: AT&T is in the forefront of dis-importancing the independent person by bringing watchers into the houses. It started with questionnaires and polls about what TV programs people watched. Then they bugged all the phone conversations so that you can listen in on the utility computer at the central office .
Now they have XENON MASERS to keep track of every move. The term "behind closed doors" has no meaning any more.
They are the head of Teleprompter sects who target anyone trying to think for themselves. These devices are neuro-cortical control agents with mu-phase or neuro magnetic phase —neuro parallel — coercion gear. They can get you to be sensing the presence of stimuli that are not actually there.
THEY keep saying it is bipolar this and SCHIZO-AFFECTIVE that and mixed manic complex.
I know how they are doing it, they tried to recruit me to work on their projects. They have labs in Berkeley and Stanford and Cornel and Los Almos. And I told them NO.
These are terribly cruel people who make sport of torturing me. They have learned how to manipulate the frequency and the cycle between the episodes of depression and mania in my mind. They

use pie+/pie- boson guns.
With these they can alter the internal circadian clock, which is located in the hypothalamus, in the suprachaiasmatic nucleus — SCN— which, in addition to other things, regulates melatonin. Melatonin is a hormone that is involved in the sleep cycle and skin color. Those with bipolar disorders have more difficulty regulating their circadian rhythms.

Now I have to be very careful to look for myself in between the cycles of the rhythms. I walk a flat line
between depressed and joyous,
between humble and wild.

I have to hide from being Masered by the Microwave laser guns of the Coercion Agents.
And the Thought Control Agents and the Facetious Police.
I dare not go out in daylight because I can be an easy target for their sport. And it is a sport for them. They videotape these hunting exploits and show them at conferences.

When I do move about in the dark, I have to have night vision goggles bought from the army surplus catalog and full camouflage gear. I need to be able to see them before they see me. They have motion detectors but I do too.

But still their snipers find me and zap me with their MASERs. These are now modulated with codon scripts to tag and tickle the works of the fatty tissue around the neuro transmitters in my brain. And I am blue again.
I have tried with my own intuition to read the codons and work out antidotes and will be publishing these results in a counter cultural journal. I am trying to find out who is responsible for this,
going back up the great chain of puppet strings
trying to find out who is whose puppet — the guy working for a boss, who works for a boss,
on up the corporate ladder. It leads to
the military, with an executive, with the millions of minion soldiers doing the bidding of the sergeants to lead the insurgency to do the lieutenant's bidding who do what the captains tell them to do, all the way back up to the general and what they want. What they want is what the politicians want.
I have come to the conclusion, it is all just self interest.
There is no one in charge.

Moving in the Syntax of Poetry

I was in over my head with these guys. I was in awe of them. Bob was such a fine mover, a dancer the way he communicated on stage. And it was so well integrated with what was being said — story or real interaction with the audience. The movement was so authentic, organic, it derived from the speech, accentuated it. I set about to try and figure out a way to generate the movement — the gesture — from the poetry. And I was in awe listening to Darrell Gray talk about poetry, especially when he talked about grammar and syntax, these most fundamental aspects of writing. Why hadn't I paid better attention to these in school? When Darrell Gray did analysis of poems and invoked the syntax, I would nod my head and indicate (falsely) that I understood.

Actually I am unusual in that I quite enjoyed doing parsing in grade school, but somehow that didn't get transformed into a usable tool for writing. Oh I had a sense of business English and could write a sentence and a feeling letter, maybe even luck into a poem now and then, but it was more just a sense that either things *sounded* right or they didn't. So one day while wandering around in the bookstores of Telegraph Avenue when I found in Shakespeare's Books a copy of *Voyages in English*, the grammar book I had used in grade school, I bought it. I took it back to the warehouse. It was like old home week: you know you are a Catholic if you had that grammar book in school with its *Imprimatur* and *Nihil Obstat* from the archdiocese. And its sentences doing double duty— illustrating grammatical principles *and* religious indoctrination. Maybe that's why my attention wandered.

So to study 1) how to generate movement from poetry and 2) how to understand the syntax of poetry, I decided I'd write an essay on the subject. I tried out a few titles: Syntax as the Music of Poetry, The Music of Syntax, A Syntax of Moving to Poetry, Dancing the Syntax of Poetry. At one point it was The Syntax of Children because it got into the parent-child hierarchy. Then it was The Unwanted Children of Syntax, in the idea that poetry led us to consider things that weren't apparent. But I am getting ahead of myself.

To fortify myself I started reading some of the literature of the great students of dance and time-motion study, inventors of dance notation like Rudolph Laban and the French ballet master Feuillet and others. I was such a geek — it takes notation and language before I see much of anything. But I was very inspired by these writers. Especially in the context of studying Jonathan Albert's sound notation. I also started reading Chomsky's books on Transformational Grammar. This was quite a different analysis of language.

For example, my old-school idea of parsing the haiku-like line — *The footbridge had a wooden tone when I walked across alone in winter moonlight* — was this:

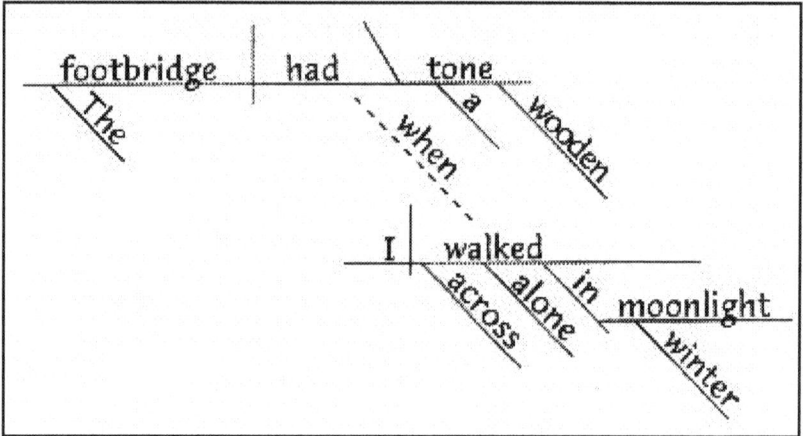

I had spent a great deal of time under the ruler crack-across-the-knuckles corporeal-punishment style tutelage of nuns doing this kind of parsing, and oddly enough had come to find parsing satisfying. It was like watching the movement of some kind of organic music feeling its way waffling, and hedging across the abstract plane of the white page.

Transformational Grammar on the other hand was much more than a new way to parse. It looked very technical and intimidating; it went into a lot more detail. You had to know the names of all the parts of speech. It showed how the writer and reader meet in a tree-like hierarchical structure by which they construct and decipher code based on 26 letters of the alphabet. They do this probabilisticly by bringing a base set of slots — Subject Verb Object, that the reader expects to see filled-in without holding too much in abeyance — the simple thing being said.

You start down the tree from the top, with the type of statement. These can be STA (statement), QUE (question), COM (command), EXC (exclamation), and PER (performative, pronouncement). Then you have these broken down into groups. S (subject), P (predicate), O (object, with Od – direct object, Oi, Of – formal, the "it'), and the A group, (Adverbial clause, Adjectival phrase, prepositional phrase). Then below that you have the designations D (Dependent) and H (Head) and these can apply to elements in a Noun, Verb, Adjective, or Preposition group. The Head is the most important aspect of the group, and the Dependent is a facilitator or carrier of and to the Head. Wow, there it is, the Figure in the Text. I could construct movement the way meaning conveys itself is through movement. It's got a Head and it's got supporting parts. We will be able to assign similar movements to the speaking body.

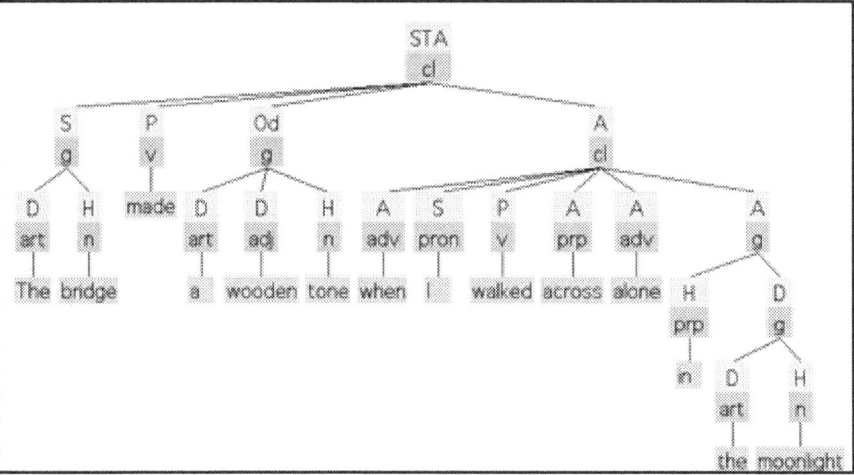

Transformational Grammar describes the real rules that exist in the black box of the human unconscious — call it a Freudian unconscious — that govern the way we make sense of the world by making sentences. It is an amazing thing that the rules for all this creating, transforming, and embedding of phrases both formally in speaking and writing and reading and silently in all our communications with ourselves govern but four kinds of phrases: noun phrases, verb phrases, adjective phrases, and adverb phrases.

I was encouraged that transformational grammar would make it possible to isolate and examine phrases to discover movent while saying the line in a more authentic, integrated way. So I set about trying to develop some kind of notation. To start we can strip away the detail and look at just the sentential logic. I had studied electrical engineering in college and liked Boolean Algebra and also story problems. Underlying the syntax and semantic of language there is the logic of propositions. Any statement can be seen as a logical concatenation of slots linked together by simple words that are the "operations" of logic in the language. These operations are designated by words like {a, an, and, are, of, or, either}. "And" and "or" and "not" are the most frequently used for building complex statements. (Not, the ability to say no, is such a huge step in the development of consciousness that it is heralded in children by their throwing tantrums about it.) Other logical operator words are: {yes, no, not, is, thing} and {if, all, then, some }and {contains, only, both, includes}. These are words that sort symbols of things (words) into classes, then assert propositions on those classes. The logic of classes is visualized by Venn Diagrams on the plane. I saw the actor as moving among spots of light — the circles of classes: inclusion and exclusion — compelling propelling and impelling the mover in a space of varying attraction and repulsion. The Field. Dancing among he categories.

The main operators of Boolean Algebra, which is a symbolic expression of the logic of language are {and, or, not}, expressed in symbols: { ·, +, '}. For example: *A thing is an animal if and only if it is living and it has a mind and it is not a plant.*

A [thing is an animal] if and only if [it is living] and [it has a mind] and [it is a plant]'. If we assigned classes A, L, M and P we could express this as $A = L \cdot M \cdot P'$ or $A = (L)(M)(P')$ or more simply $A = LMP'$. Pretty cool, huh? It is a place to stand to know the real, before jumping off into poetry to explore the irreal. We can look at just the proposition statement in the metaphor of the poem. For example the metaphor: Man is a thinking machine. The proposition is: Man = [. . .], before there is any embellishment. The bare proposition must be the backbone of the dance.

I thought I could develop a pseudo-code notation of motion by using this kind of bracketing: (noun phrase), [verb phrase], < adverbial phrase>, and {adjectival phrase}.

Then, to use our example of the haiku :

(The footbridge)[made (a wooden tone) <when I walked across>] (alone {in the moon light.})

Then I could use the names of the parts of speech in these brackets. The sentence *The footbridge had a wooden tone when I walked across alone in the moonlight.* translates:

(art n) [v (art adj n) < adv pro v pre>] (adv { prep art n})

That was as good start on the analysis of text. For the movement part it seemed reasonable to look at the idea of the Head and the Dependent parts as a body. That the adverbial and the adjectival require different moves. Adverbs of motion move from the root, the feet; adjectivals of objects spoken of, move from the waist up, hands.

I started out thinking about the situation, in as broad a context as

I could. Of course that meant, vector space mapping into semantic space. So here is a definition of the problem. Start out with the most completely general statement you can make. Something is Happening. Somebody is doing something or something is being done to somebody by somebody. So we are partitioning the continuity into subspaces, into Actors and Actions and the trick is to align that with the Subject and Verb. *Being* is a kind of action so we use the word Predicate to include both kinds of action. So we have an S-part and a P-part to the sentence. The sentence is that which links together the Subject and the Predicate. S·P.

We start to break up the continuum into a hierarchy of finer and finer refinement. The continuum is a mixture of space and time. Already we have the ideas of active and passive. Direct action of a subject and action in which the subject is acted upon.

Transformational Grammar has Actors, Actions and Goals. It is like a beautiful ballet, a dance of actor and action, subject and predicate. So our S and P are drifting apart a little bit down the hierarchy of order, to the Noun Phrase, NP and the Verb Phrase, VP.

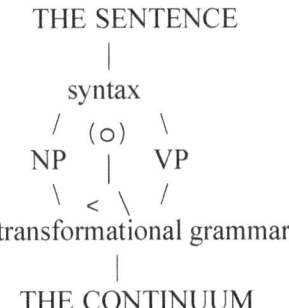

What if we focused more on the rhythm in the continuity. This is shown to us by the punctuation, the pauses of increasing silence: the coma, the semicolon and the full stop — the period. I thought that the Action approach of the Transformational Grammar paradigm of Actor — Action — Goal would facilitate movement discovery. How would this relate to sound? It paradigmed phonology and morphology, writing based on the more primary element of sound energy.

Lets step back and look at the whole language space. The faculty of syntax precipitates the deconstructing of phenomenon in space into subspaces: the verb has subspace attributes $V(p,n,t,m)$ to indicate details such as person, number, tense or mood; the noun has subspace attributes $N(p,pl,T,q)$ to indicate specificity such as person, place, thing, quality etc. These attributes are grafted onto the words, or linked in through the prepositional particle chemistry of the sentence.

So to state the problem of linguistical formation formally: We will be looking at doing projection of E -- > H through the use of an adjoint operation V(p,n,t,m) x N(p,pl,T,q) through the use of bracketing operators [ ] { }, which further decompose and concatenate according to this synchronic paradigm [( ), ( )] v { ( ) }. My, that has a wonderful scholastic air to it, doesn't it?

To understand better how this is done, let us begin by identifying some of the parts of a poem. We will look at the last stanza, 13, of *Among School Children* by Yeates. He wrote the poem in his 60s, a couple of years after getting the Nobel Prize. He still kept his day job, working for the state. One of his official duties was inspecting schools. In the stanzas of the poem he talks to a nun, observes the little wide-eyed youths of rosy cheek. He imagines his lithe, lost love, Leda (Maud Gunn) as a school girl, now as a gaunt older woman, then gone. Some vivid images surface, one of a painter painting his love's cheeks so "hollow as though they drank the wind"; and another of his old self as a "comfortable kind of old scarecrow." He pictures his own youthful mother thinking about him as a baby on her lap, and her seeing "sixty or more winters upon his head." He uses a strange concept "honey of generations" in that stanza which I take to mean ontogeny recapitulating phylogeny; yet he speaks of birth as a betrayal, perhaps in this sense: when you see the fruit of your own generation, you sense your own mortality. He drifts into Plato twice, once in an earlier stanza that men and women were once part of the same being, and now separated are looking for lost love. And again in his world of forms and ideas as a "spume that plays upon a ghostly paradigm of things." The poem invokes Aristotle spanking the bottom of his ward, Alexander who went on to rule the known world, and Pythagoras who thought the world was fundamentally mathematical. The poet, is moving from fountain spume to giant old chestnut tree in the last stanza. The last stanza reads:

> Labour is blossoming or dancing where
> The body is not bruised to pleasure soul.
> Nor beauty born out of its own despair,
> Nor blear-eyed wisdom out of midnight oil.
> O chestnut-tree, great-rooted blossomer,
> Are you the leaf, the blossom or the bole?
> O body swayed to music, O brightening glance,
> How can we know the dancer from the dance?

Let us focus in on the energy, the action in the first sentence:

Labour is blossoming or dancing where/The body is not bruised to pleasure soul. The phrase "where/The body is not bruised to pleasure soul." is an adverbial clause modifying a noun Labour which itself is performing two actions: blossoming and dancing.

We translate: *Labour is blossoming or dancing where*
L = [b + d] / —
N = v + v / adv
STA— n v (v) conj (v) adv
where we are using:

the = sign to represents any form of the "be" verb, to set up the first of many equations, (or statement or propositions) of the poetic space by using the equal sign as symbol for the copula "is", which is also the is of metaphor.

After the metaphor is read, we hold it in memory. We could assign it the x, L= x where x is a token, a place-holder for the parts of the model as it is being constructed. It stands for the unknown we are trying to "derive" through the syntactical algebra of the poem. It will be usually associated (though perhaps removed, disguised or attracted into suggestive abstract possibilities) with the copula "is" of metaphor.

Notice the adverbial phrase beginning with "where" is a logical operator. It does designate spatial set inclusion and movement to position.

The actor / dancer will perform the "links," he will be like a vehicle carrying bits of meaning to parts of the proposition in a semantic space.

One is performing some action on the verb and just an illustration on the nouns. Big lower trunk body motion on the verbs; trailing, illustrating, hand-motion on the nouns (if at all). Everything is spoken.

And we have the prepositions telling us *where* to move. Prepositions are powerful little words like "to," and "of." They tell us about moving in space: "toward," and "under," and "across," "from,"; about moving in time: "until," "at," "before," "after," "during," "since," and about logical implications in the mind: "but," "despite," "except," "like," "since," "for," "from." The prepositions are like little vectors of consciousness, particles of meaning embodying aspects of space, time and mind in the form of logical relations. And they are ambiguous, they can be about a couple of these categories: "since" for example, can be about time or about logical implication.

Prepositions point around in space and often suggest a change in direction. The actor is carrying the x in the proposition from the referent to the vehicle. The actor is making himself a kind of sign. He is taking the place of the page. Specifically,

Labour might have a strongly exerted
push movement

```
         o_,
         )-'
        >  <
```

Blossoming suggest an
opening flower movement

```
     (o)         o
      |        -(-'
     < \       < \
```

Dancing of course could be
signified by a pirouette.

Next, the adverbial phrase in the first sentence:
The body is not bruised to pleasure soul.
B = b' / prep phrase. In Transformational Grammar notation:
STA— art n v' prep n n. In our bracketing modeling it becomes:
n = v'< prep v n>
where we have the infinitive adverbial phrase <to pleasure soul> with the preposition "to" turning the Dependent noun pleasure into a verb to support the Head noun soul.

We might assign a downward movement to the v' the Not operation moving to floor, to ground. From the floor we might move upward showing pleasure in a swerve of the trunk causing the head to toss.

Pleasure might be an openhanded
movement of surrender

```
        o
       '-(
        /<
```

Soul again suggests an
opening flower movement

```
     (o)
      |
     < \
```

We continue in this way.
Nor beauty born out of its own despair,
STA—conj n v prep prep pron adj n
to look for links to dance.

Here we have "out_of" two prepositions Heading into a Dependent

"its", a possessive pronoun.
  n {prep prep - p-pro:(o)}
where we have used the "o :(o)" to indicate the object "despair" is a Head being supported by the Dependents, which we could indicate with a pulling inward toward the trunk.

```
         o ,
         ) <
       < \
```

Nor blear-eyed wisdom out of midnight oil.
STA—conj adj n prep prep pron adj n
x = adj {prep - prep: adj-n:(o)}

Here parallelism of two clauses in the negative, containing prepositional phrases used to modify aspects of the entity, "beauty and wisdom," (which are usually thought of as having been achieved through another kind of labor,) are thus passed back toward and shown to be aspects of the entity "x", coming through the dimension of the poem.

In the next line, the central equation of the poem is set up. By restating (through expletive apostrophe addressing directly the entity now present before us appearing in the form of a tree as though present) the analogy suggested in the first line: nature is to man working as plants blossoming are to man flourishing. This is written as equations questioned.

O chestnut-tree, great-rooted blossomer,
EXC—intj adj n adj n

We note how Yeats is making up the noun *blossomer* out of what could be a verb or a noun, amplifying the ambiguity for the question which is coming next.

Are you the leaf, the blossom or the bowl?
QUE—v pron art n, art n, conj art n, punc(?)

Here the apostrophe addresses the entity with questions containing being identifications. The poet constructs entity as, or course the tree, the quintessential representation of fractal hierarchy, an organization moving in time and space connecting root to leaves, the deity to its little carriers.

Oh body swayed to music Oh brightening glance
EXC— intj n v prep n Intj v n: (o)
How can we know the dancer from the dance?
QUE—Adv v : (o): art n   prep art n: (o) punc
 where {from the dance} suggests a shoulder
shrug, the actor questioning himself.

```
                                         o
                                        ‚ ¯ ‚
                                          |
                                        [ ]
```

We are touched by the image at the end of a world that can only be seen momentarily, in a quick glance, from out of the side of motion. And this can, indeed has been, transmitted through the art and syntax of the poem. The work of the poem is to develop a model in poetic space. It is quite a feat to read and deconstruct the movement of a poem, and even more so to construct one. In the space of poetry we allow our minds to drop the filters that we use to buffer ourselves from the buzzing confusion of the world. We dissolve the walls of the cubicles and containers in which we keep the representation of things and are kept. We are allowing the walls to melt down, to flow so that we can feel the ego being flooded out on a saturation of id and for a moment flowing into Big Time. Yeates often uses verbs to modify nouns, the verbs themselves made from nouns. These constructs contribute to the sense of time and motion here. And we didn't even get into the movement of the sound energy. Is there a syntax of the movement of sound energy? Oh, yes, we know #sonics.

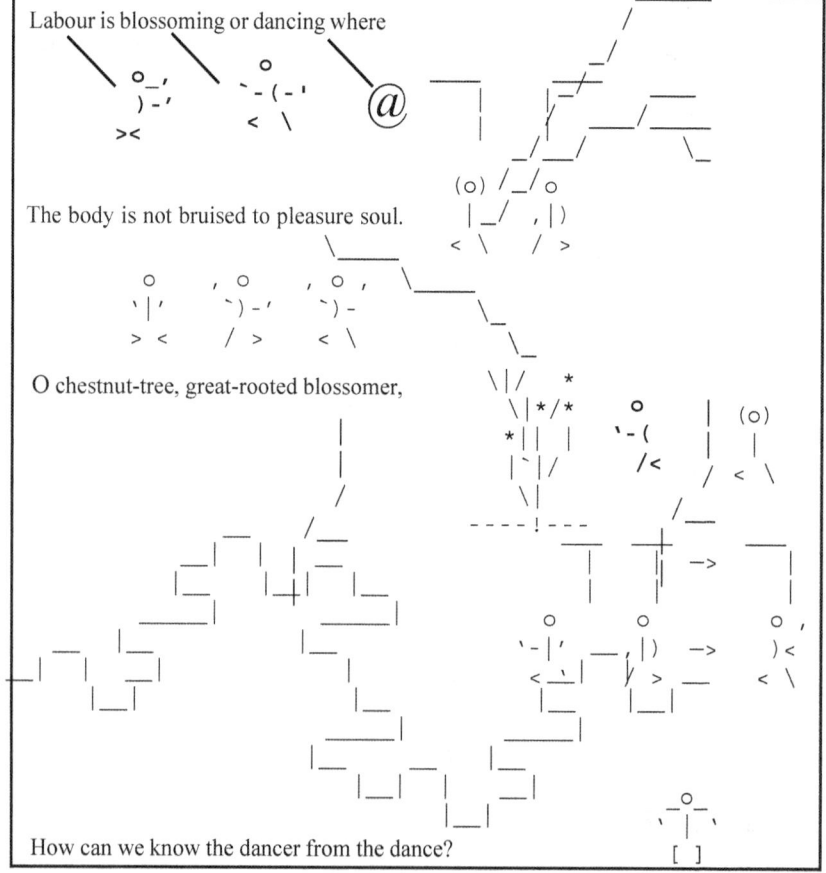

The Subliminal Kid

While no one was around, I started writing, rehearsing and doing a solo theatre piece in the Hawkeye Theatre. It was a weaving together of several little pieces and poems and stories I had around. I'd never be as good as they were, but I had to try to give myself something of the experience they were having. I called it *The Subliminal Kid* because part of it came out of a dream. It would start like a routine, like a stand up routine on a bare stage. Routines as in William Burroughs, who you always saw looking dapper and wearing a spiffy lid.

Actor walks out onto bare stage wearing a cheap suit as though trying to convey wealth despite lacking it. He starts talking to the audience.
    Hey, how's it goin', man?
(indicating the suit).
    You like the suit?
    I was at the St. Vincent de Paul Store, man, looking at the men's suits, and I come across this groovy looking 3-piece suit, I try it on and it fits.
(Mimes showing label)
    Got a label says hand tailored by Chinese tailors in Oakland and Wow! It's marked DOWN! From $15 to $12.50. So I went up and paid the lady. And now I got this new suit on my back, which is very propitious, man, cause I'm on my way to apply for a JOB! But it's weird, man, cause whenever I put this suit on, I also seem to put on the persona of the previous owner, a type of guy who was, FOR SURE unappealing to my taste.
(Actor wriggles and writhes, tries to escape his own skin. Then looks pensive, wrinkles brow.)
    I can't tell if it used to belong to a dork   or a slick.
    Or maybe   a slick dork. A dork who thought   he was slick?
(Goes into lecturing mode.)
    A slick is a kind of person, a kind of person—ality. . .
(Smooths back his hair with both hands.)
    He's got slick hair, smooth, in place. He's an extrovert, kind of a controller, he looks at other people as a way . . .
(makes eyebrows go up and down, looks imperious, haughty)
    of furthering his own ends. He's   concerned with appearances
(waves hands as if touching a smooth table surface)
    and the surface of things.

A dork on the other hand,
(Actor ruffles his hair, shows teeth in an overbite)
is an introvert,
(brings shoulders up to ears, looks diminutive)
he is usually the one being controlled. He may be more sincere but spends too much time beneath the surface of things and can't relate, or is so afraid, he can't share.

Actor addresses audience directly
On the other hand, the Slick is so saturated in image he feels like he has to fill the emptiness in his life with image and random sex. You've seen them at singles bars. Being into the scene instead of the people, looking at themselves in the mirror, constantly on the make for sex.

Slick: "Hi! Can a guy, buy, you a drink?"

Slick men trying to pick up slick women. He's tough-minded, she's articulate. She's glitzy, he's glib. He's upbeat, she's glamorous. He's superficial, she's narcissistic. Like in the fashion photos not showing any real emotion. Tele-cocks grinding against video-cunts a go-go. The slick want's to be famous without doing anything great.

Actor makes an "on the other hand" gesture
On the other hand, the dork is caught up in a never-ending struggle. Constantly striving and never having any fun.

Dork: "Just drink more milk. And work harder."

The dork is serious, overly concerned with his career, a type of guy who would NEVER be unemployed or be satisfied as a blue collar worker.

Actor rubs his own arms in the suit, addresses audience
I don't know, man, I guess I must identify with him some what.
Whatever he was he was straight.

(Holds himself tight)
I feel this suit envelope me like a straight jacket of guilt, I feel the dork in it wanting to be happier, more into partying and hedonism, and the slick wanting to have more depth and responsibility.

SHIFT Break Frame. *Actor walks away, turns, address audience.*
I need this suite cause I'm looking for a job. I am sweating like the slave of an evil spirit. A flat broke hippie with huge gaps in my resume . . . vast panoramic gaps, man, so big an elephant could waltz through, like it was a shift in time, in which I hitchhiked around the country checking into things.

(Shakes head in resignation
Nothing but the blues, man
(looks thoughtful)
Sometimes I regret — not having that certain —
"friendly—blood thirsty — attitude

(looks maniacal, aggressive)
    it takes to "stack chips"
    to begin rising — to have power —over a dip-shit middle class — brute
    class. To become prominent — enough — to have to, I don't know,
(shrugs; looks doubtful)
    to be assas-in-ated   in style.
    But I have to do it, cause I was looking   for   a   job.
    There I was,
(Actor strikes poses to illustrate the following types)
    imaginary prize fighter
    imaginary saint,
    imaginary gigolo,
    spiritual athlete . . . complete
    with teflon vest and bullet proof limousine.
(Lifts hands in resignation)
    So there I was   an imaginary dual status alien,   a social insurance
    number   from the country of the unemployed,
Actor is looking up at something on a wall
    standing in the foyer of the Consolidated Building, man, reading aloud
    the names of the firms from the directory.
    ITT, Summa Corp. Texas Instruments, Eckancar, General Motors, Texaco,
    the Catholic Church, Enco. On the 16th floor a firm called Geometrical
    Optical Dynamics.
Actor Whistles, raises eyebrows, spells
    G _ O _ D   My God! Fantastic!
Actor does the Fair Lady works at Shuttles movement, sweeping upward into a corner,
    And I go up 16 floors at once, man, hesitate outside the door marked
    Geometrical Optical Dynamics then go in.
    An attractive secretary comes down the hall, she is wearing polyester
    print, hose. She has frizzy hair and gooey eyes.
    I follow her as she takes my resume and leads me in.
    She leads me into the office of a stout Indian man. He is short, squat
    and powerfully build, well tanned and bald. His name is Mr. Yaqui. He
    looked at my resume in front of him.

SHIFT *Actor plays both parts of two character dialog. My Yaqui looking down at resume and up at applicant. Applicant looking down at Mr. Yaqui.*
    Mr. Yaqui: I see here that you have some work in a sleep shop.

    Applicant: Yes, I awakened dreamers   3 times a night, and asked them
    to divulge the contents of their dreams.

(Mr. Yaqui leads applicant down the hall.)
    Mr. Yaqui: Yes, well let me show you our latest product.

We call it the microprocessor of dreams.
(Actor switches to narrator. Explains what we are seeing.)
> He is holding what looks like a bicycle helmet with a lot of wires coming out of it. The wires are attached on little round golden spots on the smooth helmet surface.

(Mr. Yaqui. Explains what we are seeing.)
> Mr. Yaqui: "It extends the idea of voice recognition by a computer to brain wave recognition by computer over a wireless link from all these sensors in the helmet to that computer over there.

(Indicates something across the room)
> Mr. Yaqui: For every word there is a characteristic waveshape associated with verbal part of the cerebral cortex.

(Indicates left parietal lobe of the brain)
> By means of transducers attached to the head   here,
> these waveshapes are transmitted by F.M. modulation, to our computer.
> Not only that but other centers of the brain have characteristic
> information transduced and transmitted as well.

(Mr. Yaqui points to something he is holding in his hand)
> Mr. Yaqui: Sensors slightly offset
> over the eyes pick up the landscape
> of Rapid Eye Movement — *(pause)*

(Actor switches to narrator, does exaggerated Balinese Eye Sweeps)
(Actor switches to Mr. Yaqui)
> Mr. Yaqui:— and construct the image graphically.
> Other sensors pick up visual perception,
> volition and abstract imagination;
> these become direct sources of data and command information
> for the Dream Machine

(holds up the helmet)
> Mr. Yaqui: We call this transducer device
> that goes around the head, Shiva's Headband.

Actor looks afraid
Shift: Actor as Mr. Yaqui is assuring, encouraging.
> Mr. Yaqui: The currents are tiny, on the order of nanoamps. With these small currents, we can run all transducers backwards,
> transmitting directly back into the body the amplified and clarified signal – enabling the brain to absorb signals from the machine INDEPENDENT of normal sensory channels.
> It's like riding a bicycle.
> The dream machine is a super-computing
> extension of the operator's own natural abilities.
> The feedback it provides
> facilitates evoking a direct perceptual insight.

(Mr. Yaqui addresses subject directly, performing hand gestures suggested by

story)

> Mr. Yaqui: But here, I could describe the dynamics of riding a bicycle
> with a complex matrix of simultaneous differential equations, relating
> speed, curve of path, weight,
> whose solutions are spherical harmonics
> related to the gyroscope problem on a moving frame of reference.
> But a kid simply jumps on the thing
> and *feels* the right thing to do.
> And so can you.
> Be the operator of the dream machine, just *feel* and *see* and *steer* your
> way.

SHIFT back to Actor as narrator

> Applicant: So next I was in this cubicle adjacent to the machine room,
>   and Mr. Yaqui adjusts the headband over me.
> Calibrates it.
> Then switches it on!

QUE: Colored gells change scene lighting. Speaker in dark.

> An eerie sensation seemed to take possession of my mind, man.

Actor begins spinning like a dervish in and out of the colored lights and shadows

> It was like waking up
> inside a huge parabolic glass bell,
> and shouting at the top of my voice
> and hearing only a whisper as the sound was reflected away,
> but now these were my thoughts snatched away, man,
> and then they would come tumbling back.

Actor is stopped in a spot light to tell a memory

> I am joy riding in a stolen car. Driving around in San Antonio. Near
> Jefferson High. Out into the sparse unfinished housing estates.
> Among the vague terrains, on the outskirts of the city.
> Me at about age nineteen, and the son of the owner of the car, who is
> tall lanky, gawky and looked like me. He is some kind of alter-ego of my
> current personality. In fact he is a younger version of myself.
> Then I realize: He's the Subliminal Kid!

Actor walks around like an invisible object, he is looking at a statue. Then he steps into the spot light and becomes the statue. Then begins watching an imaginary observer walking around HIM!

> Him and me end up driving around my old high school, man, looking for
> a space to park it. We drive up endless rows of boulevards that writhe
> like some kind of labyrinth, or like Braille ideograms of the DREAM,
> man. After parking the car, we went up some dead end street and had to
> come back, and there were the police looking all around the car.
> We were dressed casual and look like very young boys, looked out of
> place. And HE, wanted to go BACK to the car!

I told him to keep coming with me.
Actor switches off playing the Kid and the Narrator
The Kid: "But I think I should go back to the car."
Actor: I tell him, "Naw, come with me."
And he does, and we set off on a jog,
and he followed me down along the river. — *(pause)*
From there the dream turned into one of those endless dreams where you are trying to go somewhere like in this space,
(looks at audience, makes a sweep of the hand gesture equivocating space in story to this theatre space)
And you just can't get there. You keep moving down endless side streets in this labyrinth. The streets of the suburbs with their vast yawning lawns and trees and shrubberies. Looking out of place because you dressed sloppily like a big kid.

SHIFT the following is performed in sometimes graceful lilting dance movement like a Viennese waltz, and sometime like a martial artist going around the Hsing I Pa Qua circle doing martial arts moves. The images is like waves going around a circle.

Endless labyrinth:　I
(actor reaching out into something, like trying to pull feelings like rope.
Like a blind man feeling his way through a vague terrain
　　feeling　　　touching　　　　branches of feelings —
the eyes receive and retransmit.
Said like making a discovery
　　The light fills the mind with clarity
　　and the light empties back out onto a projection
　　The sun enters and penetrates through
　　and around us like the wind,
Actor makes a waving off into the distance hand gesture
　　and the eyes sail　　on this wind
Actor makes exaggerated movements of the eyes, like Balinese dancers
　　and there is a space of Rapid Eye Movement
　　in which the eyes are in continual movement
　　and this scanning space
　　of subliminal video games occurs
(said like seen for the first time ever right here in front of you)
　　and it is an immense space.
Actor sinks low, looks up
　　At the bottom of the sky　　one can see himself
　　In a space-time diamond . . .
(Demarcates a closed cubical space structure with his hands, Fair Lady at Shuttles)
　　a 4 dimensional cube or tesseract
Actor turns and pushes away behind him

      where The Past is behind but also impinging on the present
      and one can stand off and float as above and see one's self from above
      see more in the air this way than in a mirror,
(indicates the theatre space)
      for this is your mirror
(convey a sese of surges of force coursing through)
      the air has a depth that can buoy you up
      as if we could fly in this sky
Actor spreads arms out like wings flying
      on feelings
(actor mimes the positioning prepositions in the text)
      as they are always there   behind the hands
      and just out of reach   behind the eyes
      and in front of us and getting   between us   and what we do
      and they are trying to advance towards us so we can see
      them but can't quite get our hands on them
      they are always receding like the horizon.
Actor looks pensive addresses audience
      What does it mean?
      Who is this alternative me? That I am dragging along. He is the innocent child, who can't be allowed to feel because of how he had to be. I am the rebellious child,
         and he is the innocent child,
         the good child, loved simply for being?
(Thoughtfully coming to this realization)
      It means that the feeling child wants to be up with me, the older one, but is drawn back to the authority of the parents, drawn back to all kinds of authority, and that without each other, we are lost, doomed to run in an endless labyrinth.

SHIFT Actor gestures release, something falling away; addresses audience
      They're like so many masques to you and they just fall off
(argumentative, accusatory)
      You see through them. I know you do.
Actor looks contrite, rueful
      Oh . ... sometime you let me charm you.
      Sometime you let me think I can make you laugh.
Actor looks pensive realizes
      It hasn't occurred to me until now that with each new mask
         I portray to myself
      the previous one dissipated into death;
      which is a kind of life
(thoughtfully)
      non-existence would be a more accurate reference
         to the old mask   who was so humble;

Actor gets very agitated wound up, hyper — grandly
    entrancing with his gaze
        anyone who'd follow him, into his maze
    in the center of their labyrinth would be a secret place
Actor from the center of the stage speaks tentatively, as though he were trying on the sounds of the words or shouting them into an echo chamber
    they would call   their true love
Actor apostrophizes, speaking directly, breathlessly to the shadows at the edge of the stage
    my love   my true love
    she is the self — same as I am — we
    were always on the lam
    via the image… in nation
Actor looks puzzled, quizzical at the audience
    or perhaps people are the states
    or perhaps not even people   say individual
    personality is the state
    is the means and say it is in face possible for an individual,
    an in-de-viz-u-al
    to posses a variety of states
    a nation within themselves United
    the United States of Hysteria
Actor looks vulnerable, slightly camp, apostrophizes dancing in a pas de deux with shadows of the space
    dearest true love
    you are as free as a state of this hysteria
    as I am free . . .
              free…
    and as my only concern
        is a balance…
Actor reacting as though being laughed at
    you laugh
        with your eyes   and ask openly
        aloud   what is this balance
    of which ye   babble, my love?
Actor driving home a point

    I say it is a balance of possession
        and   of total freedom.
    You understand this already.
    I know you do   and as we are free
    we are free   to be   possessed
        by each other
    this is the choice   this is the
        balance of freedom.

Now the obsession
    is a loss of equilibrium
the loss of the free will . . .
    could it be
        the meaning
           of falling
              in love?
Actor resolves into a kind of relaxed open stance.

Then a SHIFT as he become more agitated. The experiment is amplifying, he is seeing more directly into his feelings
    I am struggling to wake up
Actor mimes and makes his face into a masque to illustrate the following states
    I come here   I laugh... I cry...
    I stare like a child . . . I relive
        those feelings
    I had when I was a child . . . the terror . . . the joy . . .
    I forget . . . I pretend I don't understand
    I guffaw, I write
    I hugamugga
Actor looks resolute, dejected
Actor swirls head around in a gesture of haplessness, giving up
    Death has such a big Mouth,
Actor pulls back inside himself
    I should be quiet and live in peace.
Actor swirls head around in a gesture of haplessness, giving up, and frightened away
    Death has such a big Bloody nose,
    seamless all white clothes,
    And endless number rows of TEETH
    in my theatre
Actor sweeps hand indicating space
    for this is the theatre   in which I dwell
Actor sweeps hands down indicating his body; heavy shouting emphasis on sell
    In the body   which I must not sell!
SHIFT Actor looks rueful, like he has been taking himself too seriously. Smiles. Address the audience directly.
    With tales like these, who needs a head!?—Vietnam mom
(sings)
    My little babe been to Vietnam
    Got his head blown of but resewn on
    Resewn on, Resewn on
    Got his head Blown off, but resewn on.
(Says)
    — They got some mighty fine doctors in Vietnam.

SHIFT Actor goes back to narrator telling story of job interview, aftermath
    And then suddenly it was gone.
Actor gestures lifting a helmet off the head
    I felt Mr. Yaqui remove the headband,
    and he was looking at me and grinning.
Actor as Mr. Yaqui, looking at narrator
    Mr. Yaqui: "It's okay; I just switched it off, he said.
    Did that blow your mind?
    Everybody gets that the first time.
    See the Dream Machine acts like
    a gigantic feedback loop for mental processes.
    You can get into a positive feedback situation, where anything floating around in your head, gets . . . gets precisely defined,
    — quantitative, then sent back to you amplified!
    You give it junk, and get back super junk. Then take the super-junk, and think of it, and get back super-super junk!

SHIFT Actor is narrator telling story
    And then I'm back on the street again, man, but it's not the same. So many people, so many cars, so many stores, so many bars, windows wink down dazzling me with solar reflection and that shining off the chromium cars, fries my eyes.
    Everybody else knows exactly what they are doing every minute.
    Everybody walking fast and talking fast,
    pouring out of restaurants and stores, sweeping around corners,
    surging across intersections, up stairs, into buildings.
    I am swept along, man, into the impossibly, crowded, subway
Actor has hand up holding subway car strap, looking with fear at crowded subway riders. Indicates he is completely jammed up all around.
    Thousands of beings all around me packed, stuffed, wedged, and there is absolutely no air, man — to breath.
Actor gets very agitated wound up, hyper. Hits rhythm of list like a train down the track.
    Riding riding, riding
    22nd avenue 32nd avenue
    Waitress with vampire eyes — wanting to spend the day hanging upside down from the overhead railing.
    Her feet are killing her.
    42nd avenue 52nd avenue
    riding, riding 50,000 hate vibes par second
    being given off   from the biomass.
    We drive through a cloud of what seems to be bean fart.
    What heavenly majesty!
    62nd avenue 72nd avenue

Paranoia rising. Anxiety rising. Hate vibes. Intense fiendish energies, collect down in the tunnel
Death! Kill . . . somebody!
Cut somebody! The moon made me do it!
Push in front of subway.
Jump yourself!
Actor gets shouting louder and louder
    82nd avenue   92nd avenue
    Fart Sweat!   Foul!
    Arrests   Narks!   Busts!
Ritualistic sex crimes! Cattle mutilation!
Actor shows long-suffering face; trapped
    102nd avenue
I am wedged so tight in that I can't get off.
Turn eyes to newspaper to have something to occupy them.
Reading headlines: Psychosis plagues. Contagious schizophrenic virus unleashed by irate genetic researcher.
Lawyers, undertakers, doctors doing   BOOMING business.
Actor shouting
Plunging down the tubes into dark night, man.
Bat with baby face goes WOOosh by my head.
I go into mantra to stop fear:
SHIFT Actor pauses in silence. Looks toward heaven. Sings. Ends with mouth hanging open.
Sometimes I like to let my mouth hang open   and look dumb.
Sometimes I just like to let   my mouth   hang open. Just to try to look   dumb.   Just to try   to feel   a little dumber.

SHIFT Actor returns to being narrator
Finally I'm back, to my pad, my little cave to crawl in and fight back from. I am talking to my dog, man.
Actor bends down addressing dog, teasing
How about . . . going . . . for a walk? . . . in the park?
And we are out!
Walking beneath the freeway, man, down the hill past the heavily graded train track, man. Me, and Sunshine the pit bull, walking through the tall grass past the freeway construction, across bridge over the river.
Actor looking entranced at a shimmer of light
I love to watch the green water in motion. I lean against the rail and look out: I wonder about where the river leads to. And wish I was on it. I look over the edge, watch the pattern of lights in the undulating water, and think about how all matter is waves of energy held together by various forces of attraction.
AHHHH, it's a lonely life man.
Breathe in a little O_2 Exhale a little CO_2

(shrugs in acceptance)
    Still there aren't that many forces of attraction on me.
(looks thoughtful, talkative)
    Lately I've become religious about atoms. Every night Walter
    Cronkite comes on T.V. with a new cause of teenage cancer.
(winks at the audience, smiles)
    They're found that you can catch—on fire—from a toilet seat.
(Back to being serious)
    I worry about getting my b_{12} complex
    Worry about keeping a proper balance in my metabolic ecology
    will the bad wigglies overtake the good wigglies?
    Am I getting enough chromium?
    What about the polarity of my potassium?
    This is how I have come to dig the element: Man —
    freak with 103 personalities — the do it yourself chemistry set.
(Rotates around in a dervish spin)
    In the spin of color,   charm,   beauty   magic & strangeness
    there is a principle that penetrates people.
    It is a subtle body, invisible and untouchable
(indicates the directions in the following)
    which circulates energy from the earth to the sky
    through and up and out and it is the combined spectrum
    of the elements in a being
        — for we are radiant beings
            and this fire
      in the cells of the body
           in which I dwell
    and in which all the stars and planets
    in the universe are convolved
    sometimes shoots out wild sparks in the dark,
    they trail off and are never heard from again.

(indicates the horizontal with sweep of hand)
    And the line of the horizon is the edge of the eye,
    and the earth is an immense eye in the face of space
    a space which no being can see,
(spreads arms in chest expanding gesture of breathing then circulation)
    a kind of inspiration and expiration of the firmament
    in our breathing
    and it surrounds us and travels through us
    all through our limbs and makes us tremble like little antennae or
    cilia on tiny water creatures . . .
Actor looks punkish, contrite taking leave of the audience shrugging it off
    Still there aren't that many forces of attraction on me.

Journal of Pre-Verbal Behavior

In 1976 Darrell Gray and I embarked on a second collaboration, an academic occasional called *The Journal of Pre-Verbal Behavior.* It was about linguistics and language. We took the personae of lab-coat wearing scientists and were about working on an Information Theory of the Self. We were going to write essays about the biology and chemistry of aesthetics, we were going to develop a theory explaining all the literary tropes in terms of propositions. In our little white lab coats of scientific authority we were going to mess with Skinner and Behaviorism at which we were appalled. It felt so terrible to think of being a rat in a maze of cubicles. Yet there was no denying the learning that the body undergoes in dealing with its coercions. We were trying to understand and explore the emergence of the epi-phenomenological; what was innate, a priori, of the body's learning. I had started work on something called *The Varieties of Logical Experience*, kind of a cross between Master's and Houston's *Varieties of Psychedelic Experience* and G. Spencer Brown's *The Laws of Form* and (James' *Varieties of Religious Experience.)*

Darrell Gray had already written several essays which were to become his book *Essays and Dissolutions*. We published some early versions of these in the few issues of the *Journal of Pre-Verbal Behavior* that saw the light of day. He was embarked on a search for a generative methodology of poetry. This he related to the Transcendental Critique of Knowledge. You will find a review of his book in the appendix under the title *The Transcendental Poetics of Actualism.* He invented or annexed a construct, the Automorph, which is Atman in the Vedas, or the Self in Jung, or the One in Parmenides and one of the ways into understanding it was through the Automaton, a kind of abstract machine that is archetypal to the way the universe translates and substitutes the encoding of strings of information. (It would be another 10 years before the computer paradigmed this with its user, compiled and machine levels of language. Though I had studied Fortran, proffering my little programs laboriously typed up on punched cards to the geek priesthood.) The Automaton formalism (state machines) is an alternative for the specification of language, equivalent to Transformational Grammar.

When I came to Berkeley I had written three essays. One titled *Tesseract Theatre* had impressed Dave Schein enough for him to invite me out here. This essay attempted to understand Bobby psychomorphicly taking on and throwing off characters as he explored psychological and physical space in his solo performances by thinking of it as a kind of mnemonic theatre. The other two essays I had written were *The von Neuman Probe*, about the idea of the self-replicating automaton as modern archetype and *The Poem as Mandala* about the processes of literary construction as being Freudian enactments of projection dispersion. This essay translated defense mechanism as literary devices for distancing into their Jungian analogs through a formalism of mapping the matrix of the Freudian /Structuralism into the mandala. The matrix that Levi-Strauss used — itself based on fundamental group theoretical concepts — to demonstrate the isomorphism of mythical elements across cultures to the matrix of kinship structures he generalized to all myth.

Darrell Gray and I talked about this, extensively. I was encumbered by so many preconceived notions about what poetry should be and trying to emerge from a very strict discipline of Physics. I was very inspired by the papers of Pauli and Jung on Synchronicity. In fact that is what lead me out of physics into looser, more groovy area of study. In his essays Darrell Gray had an essay entitled *The Poem as Mandala*. In his essay (he did a much better job than I had) he invokes several discussions we had about Heizenberg. He develops an elaborate analogy as if in answer to my problem.

I was not able to hold on in Berkeley, and heading back to Texas seemed my only option. I had had enough of not making any money and at least *there* was some family, some friends, some women that knew me. Maybe some kind of a job. Even I couldn't deny that my life trying to find my way in American Literature was extremely impoverished. The boys put out a last issue of PAW in my absence. They published a little excerpt from a letter:

(from Punctual Actual Weekly #12)
    LETTER FROM MICHAEL LYONS
    I feel like Joe Friday on Dragnet invading the 50's, with nothing but
    a folder of police files and his tough talking, fast acting cynical
    aggressiveness. This is Zoon Phonata entering the edge of cool
    authenticity. Entering the Pre-Verbal World, is like walking around
    on a whole new planet. This is indeed the age of actualization .. I
    envision an Encyclopedia of the Unconscious . . .

Appendix

Interview and Reviews

The Bell Tower
Complete Poem by John O'Keefe with Interpretive Commentary

Episodic Imprint and the Liquidity of Consciousness
Interview with Peter Loschan and Art Gallery Show Catalog

from The Transcendental Poetics of Actualism
Review Darrell Gray's *Essays and Dissolutions*

Further Attributions

Epilog

The Bell Tower

The poem **The Bell Tower**, written by John O'Keefe, is republished here from the Punctual Actual Weekly #11, 1976, along with associations of its impact.

The Bell Tower is one of the great poems of my generation. It is a watershed flowing through many aesthetic dimensions. It is exemplary of a zeitgeist like Eliot's *Waste Land* or Ginsberg's *Howl* or Bob Dylan's *Like a Rolling Stone*. It is like a kind of action painting, a sumi-e with these minimalist lines that paint a picture, but that are also a motion in themselves, a motion that goes into a sound dimension and into a visual or ideogrammatic dimension. With its sense of being dispossessed, of souls reanimating bodies, of design informing function, it is an aesthetic apperception of the perennial philosophy while at the same time being a journey of personal self-discovery and triumph.

John was a fly fisherman and a keen observer of nature. I saw his painting style in collaborations with Russ Conlin and it was very sumi-e and minimalist Zen action painting. The *Bell Tower* is a sumi-e painting done on an electric typewriter by a very accomplished practitioner of Physical Theatre. It is theatrical in the sense of being unafraid to play verbally and to be shocking.

The story in the poem follows with moving camera eye a young person, living in an orphanage on an outing into the local country side. With sometimes shocking imagery it expresses the natural ferocity of nature, even unto the chemical level. It gives us pictures of the young observer's world, then just as quickly takes these pictures back to more animal and mineral levels of existence.

The poem has a kind of the consciousness of the stranger: one who was left here and is making his way toward some great, central, defining point of congregation, drawn and pushed by many forces to get there.

THE BELL TOWER
by John O'Keefe

River flies set their teeth.

toady stumps and burls
ram with jelled speed
into the just startled
shimmering fizz

                                            .....morning light.

Maid servants jute out of the marsh
Reever frogs jiggle their eyes

                                    gutty worms burrow
                                    like a fist full of curles
                                    sucking space in the mud
                                    down in

                               in
                    in
              in
         in
     in
in
   in
in
  in
    in
      in
        in
          in
            in
              in

Her plain features address me with their simple
anthropoid significance. I too, am pre-ambulatory.
I seek the council of the Thirty Bell Weighted
Glocker. Her nose wiggles like a spiggot and she
narrows into the edge of the Bell Tower as if she'd
never been there. I am.

gutted, dehydrated finches
hang webbed in the middle
branches of an elm's corpse

water runs below and needle trout
comb the eddies for latches,
snake burns etched on their
iridescent sides

a bi-winger rails out of sorts
into triple spins and a bag of coronets
falls from its shattered tail

sucking sheets of lip
tugs on the ball barings then

                    gups up!
                          cheese seeps
                          out from the intrusion
                          slithering vomiting
                          secrets

                I look at my pocket watch.
                It is morning.....

                          seamy ribbons strip
                          through the branches
                          above me

                I shout!
                  dust explodes from my mouth
                  sealing my cheeks against my teeth
                  in sticky then dry popping jells
                  of paste and powder. My eyes almost
                  splinter at the thought of the in-take.
                  A blast of hot rotten air rips up thru
                  the mud. Soft bubbles pop their domes
                  at the surface, over flowing from my
                  mouth as i c r e s e n t s t r e t c h

.....river winds

films of brown sand crack
and flake as piston slugs
milk at its surface

"Do you not see the re-guesting, Silvers?
A party today on the beach, Belcher Swaddle
hunting."
        in my ears
        in my ears
        in my ears
        in my ears
        in my ears
        in my ears
        in my ears
    inmy ears
        inemy ears in my
            in my eme.....self same place/.

certain parts of mind get sticky as I approach the Tower. it is not
easy to match the pace of my watch with my bleepy prevalence.

    once there

...........................I've
                .never been there

                although the nature
                of her face might draw
                some phobos bat from
                the hive, some blur-
                winged cylinder, some
                bee-knat to her un-
                known source of mYself

fungus trembles like turtle fat
in the piper reeds, medicine
oozed out in orange dots stretching
the reflections on my eyes.

                    I wobble in intense pain
                    on the gristle of my knees
                        the Keys
                        in my pocket
                        burn me

        a $^{b\ o}$ve bing swallows nose the
                green billowing liquid
                reaches
                          and
                              I am climbing up the hill
                                  to the Bell Tower.

"there is a kind of salt in it
        a kind of salt
    a kind
              of salt
              of salt
                    s
                  a
                    l
                      t   the branches are killing me' i don't
                            know where it is coming from. from the
                            Tower! no, from the Tower the branches
                            are leading the light along the source
                            is blinding i think i'll turn around and
                            go
                              h
                                e
                                  a
                                    d
                                      l
                                        o
                                          n
                                        g." Trained elk in the dead Lady's
                                        service watch among the rot-
                                        ting cars, oil pans rust in
                                        the sludge I GO TO THE LEFT
                                        towards a broken carriage
                                        of black splintered thread.

the river again

a brown snail skims
the surface with a
sail on its back
                  (bamboo faces)

                        i hear her body humming
                        in the underbrush
                                      then thru the tall willow
                                      saplings her body humming

                i move my pace on the well defined path
                      (pike swirls--orange and yellow dots)

                                "God knows this is not what" spaces
                                on the other side wet swallows
                                three tiny ships on the quarry lake
                                sail away

                    mid point

I am shifting there.
doily targets with
german wives on them
like unburied toilet paper
shake with merchandise

                                    euclyspills mingle with pidgeons

                  : sideways rooting
    : ccoorrnn: : lizards and unheard of
                  : snakes bevel tops and
                  : corn: corn corn corn corn
                  : corn corn corn corn corn
                    corn corn corn corn corn
                                    that voice and this
                                    s'only the wind yet

                      "scrubbing pumice
                      in
                        the
                      sink
                              while
                                    his wife's lonely eyes
                                    shift to stellar objects."
arrow of lice braid the water
and moth fish

                      the left path has led to a quarry
                      ancient motorcycle tracks
                              (DIRT BIKES)
                      knit like a ribbon frieze
                      among the hills
                      and one remembers even
                      more ancient cycles
                      when space was veering metal
                              ("how long do i have to
                               endure the whale voiced
                               puppy?")

                              "water guts
                              and milky nostalgia
                                      how can i?
                                          how can I?
                                              how can I?"
my head jerks up   i'm standing

s i l e n c e
        undreamed of peace
        escapes me

he looks down
into his upturned
palm and sees   It
                (sunlight passes thru the door)
"I am strong
simply to withstand what?"
                      I turn around and see the nursery.
                      sand and pebbles
                      yellow
                              and
                                  beige,
                                      the Bell Tower.
i head directly toward it over a
path for what now is sanctified with a christian burial will be paid
with blood diapers later, linens of blood, tubs of it, sheepy blood.
Ghosts will sit at the dining tables awit, snowy bonnets will fly
thru the reading rooms, tables topsy-turvy
                                    (gassed rooms)
                                        and
                                  now the picture
                                  seeps into my
                                  head all is a
                                  dream by jest
                                  i will not wake up
                                  maggot rings on my
                                  fingers the crackle
                                  of shells lady bugs
                                  now aflame on
                                  the dry weeds hills
                                  stuffed with pebbles
                                  & bike tracks wrappe
                                  among the burns
                                        i
                                  mount
                                    the
                                    path
                                from the dry direction
                (as if there were memories
                    of home
                          anytime
                                ever)

shrugging shoulders-next-me.

i am climbing out of a soft bottomed ditch
up- on- over-again
curved edges welt down again

        and

        I am on top
        looking out
        at the Bell Tower.

        . . . snake roads leading.....
        river boat from the cliff

        arrow birds carrying

         .

        .

   . . . .

    .
    glycerin capes

      .

         earth spinning frost on its
     . .

      . Rainbow scars form on my back!
     .   scabs lift their domes and hazel steam
    .   rises from the crags I'm DRENCHED!

  .
  .
  .
  .
  . .

Holy Rollers .   yay - yull

   .

    .   early
     .   dream
      .   shits

       .
       and the birds drape me in water

           There is no way down the cliffs

             - - - - The Bell Tower

reeder rungs
smoke the baby haze
              cliff drops,
              milking honey

                              manx

                                      a stone's throw away

                drifts of wind slivered dust
                                unwrinkle

                        blue
                        after
                        noon
                        moon

                              i unrathem morning

Past dreams awake me:
                      young men

                      are running

                      up a hill
                            (water
                             water
                             water
                             water
                             water)
                                        momentary keys fidget,
                                        dawdling in my pocket
                                        LIKE HATCHETS!

                                                now i hear

                                                the Dome S 0 U N D

                            . . . . The Bell Tower.

                                    we wrapped
                                    tin foil
                                    around small
                                    sheaves and
                                    the whole
                                    thing glistened

                                    in the middle
                                    plains bending

                                      w h e a t
                                       corn a
                                       river
                                       marsh
                                       sparrow

            the green islands
            on concusioning trees
            weaving   immense   space

river moons
pig carp diving
on the river bottom

                        and maribou
                        signaling
                              oh love
                              of love
                                    devine,

                                          Walleye
                                          . . . .

Father Lowery
spanked the kids
with loving embrace

        "He-she's swallowed
        a big black thing
        he got in a sand pile,"

                      and sister nurses
                      criss-cross the newly
                      born constellations

        escape tubes
        slide out of the Bell Tower
        like minnows

                across the lake
                the swans are
                running to the
                noon whistle.

        young men are running
        up over the hill
        soldiers in little blue
        caps, grabbing at my shoes
        with their tiny hands
                (rubbery frost dilates,

                      $s^p{}_i l{}_t s$)

i am silently, in the stillness
in the just breaking.

        .

            .throwing them
                down the cliffs

                    recrumbling YAKSt
                    it B U R S T S

    the
    air
            s h i m m e r s

                ray. . . . .

        ray. . . .

                    ray. . . . .
        in

                        ray in

    r a i n

no more
is left

                        four stripes
                        make flags
                        suggesting
                        space

                                ("green water")

    silly-oh-sights-a wheates
    brack-mornin' -an-a-raid-us
    search-a-BON-in-I-doe-way-saw

            Ray King
            my drain guides

                    ("this is the treasure")

I unmount the
green water

                                4 stripes
                                make flags
                                suggesting
                                space

                                          There is no history

                                                                not
                                                                yet

not even in the downs
and
       in
       tim
       a
       day
       shuns
               your blood wag (i wanted it and the sun drew its lines up)

                                     it is raining

> I have seen it float
> have been in the melting
>
>> with blackrivers
>> and a green bridge
>
>>> (as if death were some THING)
>
>> I stand on the other side
>> between a river
>
>>> AND the Bell Tower
>
>>>> (in the i my god)
>
>>>> aug 25 74
>>>> june 27 76

Commentary on The *Bell Tower*

The first thing you notice about John O'Keefe's poem *The Bell Tower* is the shape and the motion of the words moving on the page. The words are sometimes in a repetitive motion down the page like branches of a tree, or bubbles rising in the space as you might see them from underwater. This is effected by the repetition of a word as it zig-zags down the page. Spoken, this would be a rhythmic sound, like a chant. Or a prayer. With this effect of *seeing* rhythm, the poet is turning time into space; by infusing seeing with rhythm: space into time. But what strikes me is the sumi-e like visual gracefulness in the branching and movement of the lines. Like the semantic units were gestures in an action painting.

Abstract expressionism and action painting were the most striking examples of iconoclastic art breaking through the barriers of culture in the generation before mine. These art forms transcended the boundary between artist and viewer, broke out of the confines of the art gallery, became osmotic in culture and taught us to appreciate the abstraction of energy movement in the world. *The Bell Tower* signals this perspective — crossing the barriers between man and nature, breaking down of subjective and objective, projecting of the psychological into the world of nature and the mapping nature into the individual psyche. This movement across boundaries is reflected in the uncompromising attitude toward the conventions implied by grammatical, typographical and traditional poems. This poem traverses the barriers between artistic disciplines of poetry and painting.

In this essay I would like to think about these three main topics:

1. The interplay of haiku and sumi-e in the poem,
2. Metamorphosis and Metempsychosis
3. The development of surface and depth in the poem's Inscape.

1. Interplay of Haiku and Sumi-e

Haiku sensibility in poetry came into our world by way of the Beats. Perhaps they were led into it by Pound. Or found their way into it through other paths. The old Beats had to get a bit iconoclastic to defend their sensibility. The haiku sensibility, going back to ancient Japanese court, but practiced by Beats and other poets, embodies the "do more with less" methodology of perception practiced by the one-brush sumi-e painters. We are lucky to have this double esthetic: the visual in sumi-e and the verbal in haiku. Whenever two modalities can be navigated by analogies, a much more integrated understanding of each can occur.

A few of the main, easily-recognized, esthetic principals of haiku and sumi-e are: Natural and seasonal awareness; a standing in presence before the now-moment in time; the field-grounding of image; an appreciation for smallness in space; the use of implication from the mis-en-scene; and the effects of juxtaposition in the creation of a poetic shock. I will illustrate how O'Keefe uses of some of the aspects of haiku with examples from *The Bell Tower*.

1.1 Haiku is a poetry of objects, it is a realization of the poetry in things.

Nouns rather than argument, or persuasion or logic propel the haiku. Haiku has an iconography often depicting carefully chosen things: birds' nests, rusted nails, billowing clouds.

Example 1.1a

> gutted, dehydrated finches
> hang webbed in the middle
> branches of an elm's corpse

Example 1.1b

> Trained elk in the dead Lady's
> service watch among the rot-
> ting cars, oil pans rust in
> the sludge I GO TO THE LEFT
> towards a broken carriage
> of black splintered thread.

Example 1.1c

> a ^b_ove   bing swallows nose the
>   green billowing liquid
>   reaches

1.2 Haiku values the now moment, the presence in the smallness of time perhaps leading to big time. Haiku values smallness in space. The poetry of *The Bell Tower* is an art of metonymy, of using a part to suggest the whole.

Example 1.2a

> a bi-winger rails out of sorts
> into triple spins and a bag of coronets
> falls from its shattered tail

Example 1.2b

> the green islands
> on concusioning trees
> weaving   immense   space

1.3 Brevity.

Example 1.3

> blue
> after
> noon
> moon.

Sumi-e applies the Zen aesthetic to visual art. It seeks to capture the flow of the moment, the lifefulness of the scene, the now moment of perception. It is action painting with the dribbles and splashes harnessed and transformed through a more controlled methodology of almost iconographic or ideogrammatic language into a visual syntax of the natural scene, seen in the moment. It is not a photograph, for in its brush stroke there is the thrust of moving energy and fractal chaos created by the analog motion and swirl of liquid in the brush. Indeed, it is an embodiment of the great Watercourse Way, the Tao.

1.4 Haiku work by Juxtaposition, often producing a poetic shock of recognition akin to epiphany or enlightenment. In the following example O'Keefe uses juxtaposition to draw the eyes into the edgewater scene; he then juxtaposes this with the cosmic sense of new day dawning.

Example 1.4

> toady stumps and burls
> ram with jelled speed
> into the just startled
> shimmering fizz
>
> .....morning light.

The use of space separating one scene from another gives *The Bell Tower* a cinematic effect. The space between the haiku-like images allows for a change of camera position. O'Keefe moves from detailed objective examination of some natural phenomenon, to the consciousness interpreting this world. It is a world of above and down below. The gap this juxtaposition creates allows for the aha-moment of awareness as the reader apprehends the suchness of that instant.

The whole poem moves back and forth across several domains: the mind of the individual narrator being fielded out of the ground of nature. The figure and ground oscillate — shimmer — to reveal more about the domains from which they emerge, i.e. the shape of the ecology itself where the juxtaposition creates kinetic energy and reverberation. Art is about apperception. Art seeks to create the aesthetic apperception of something. It does not only comment or talk about something, it *is* something; an embodiment of perceptions and the machinery of perception. Like slow glass capturing light within itself so that time slows down and allows you to examine events more closely, art is a transparent perceptual entity with memory, a window we hold in front of ourselves to look through into other dimensions and times.

2. Metamorphosis and Metempsychosis

Let us put aside the aesthetics of haiku for a moment and look at how O'Keefe explores metamorphosis and metempsychosis. Three techniques for this are: 1. exploding literary conventions through juxtaposing entirely different genres of writing; 2. fragmentation word play suggesting a sense of language as coding; 3. surface and depth reflecting a real spiritual / religioius depth. This is animal depth.

We are introduced to a strange character of fantasy, given its name and description.

2.1 The Thirty Bell Weighted Glocker.

Example 2.1

> Her plain features address me with their simple anthropoid significance. I too, am pre-ambulatory. I seek the council of the Thirty Bell Weighted Glocker. Her nose wiggles like a spigot and she narrows into the edge of the Bell Tower as if she'd never been there. I am.

"I seek the council of the Thirty Bell Weighted Glocker." Puzzling. The word Glocker means the bell person, the bell ringer. We might associate the German word glockenspiel (glocke -bell, spiel-play) —a small instrument with graduated bells, often seen in marching bands. It is also the instrument played in the carillon, the bell tower at the center of a university or of a church at the center of a village. Walking along the creeks of the Berkeley or UT campus, one heard the chimes ring the noon hour. The Thirty Bell Weighted Glocker is a kind of symbol, a reflection of how the narrator feels; The narrator says he is preambulatory and refers to what he calls "my bleepy prevalence." In the poem, the narrator is moving away from a river outing and walking up a hill towards a Bell Tower.

2.2. The action of the plot is a simple walk up a hill, that takes place during an outing with other kids from the orphanage.

Example 2.2

<quotes Lines 1-29 pg 243 of this publication of *The Bell Tower* >

We see the actual Bell Tower is an institutional building across the lake with fire escape slides. It is an institution run by priests and nuns — an orphanage. The children wear little uniforms with blue caps.

2.3a. Metamorphosis — Kafka in Wonderland

In the following passage the term re-guesting, speaks to the concept of metempsychosis of souls, the idea that the body is the host for a soul. This is the central idea of most religions: in eastern religions the idea that there is a finite number of souls, requires they journey in search of rebirth; in western religions the soul is seen in a more Pentecostal light, it is that part of man able to be in a kind of sympathetic resonance with a holy spirit, providing a temporary place for that spirit to dwell. Both etiologies of the soul compel recognizing in your fellow man, a higher organization principle which should be honored by ethical behavior.

Example 2.3a

> "Do you not see the re-guesting, Silvers?
> A party today on the beach, Belcher Swaddle
> hunting."

2.3b. Joyce, and the theme of transmigration of souls in the poem

Metempsychosis is a theme in Joyce's *Ulysses.* Also suggesting Joyce is the word play with the spoonerism on silvers and slivers. There are several examples of this language play. Almost like code slipping a letter, and that takes the whole machinery off, on a different track. This playfulness in language, which has always been a hallmark of O'Keefe's writing, reminds of *Alice in Wonderland*. In *The Bell Tower,* O'Keefe is playing both with sound as a field and meaning as a field too. The importance of this play is that the fragmentation of language leads to a different level of consciousness, one that is liberated from the confines of literacy and more attuned to its oral and pre-history and animal nature.

Metamorphosis is another thematic movement infusing the poem. In his story *Metamorphosis,* Kafka drops beneath the conventions of literary boundaries into a deeper, animal, insect, automaton level of communication going on in the world. *The Bell Tower* asks us to widen our consciousness to be able to perceive through these other beings. It might be instructive to compare the way that Kafka and Lewis Carol take us into the world of animal consciousness. Kafka in a prose that has a most realistic surface takes us into the world of the bug, through the senses of Gregor Samsa, all the while keeping the language perfectly reasonable, asking us to see things differently. Whereas Lewis Carol takes us into *Wonderland* on drugs and invocations of animals, and a dissolution of language, yet he too, also maintains a perfect surface logic. But where Kafka appeals more to the poetic sense of exploring new worlds with intuition, *Wonderland* appeals to being argued or manipulated by reason into a new world. *Wonderland* is more syntactical that way, where the Kafkaesque world beneath our socially accepted one, is presented experientially.

For O'Keefe, the term "reguesting" expresses the idea of the body being the host of the soul. Certainly this is a Catholic idea, but also a Buddhist one. This re-guesting perspective is something O'Keefe wrote about extensively, in his plays and particularly in his novel *Bekin's Rage*. (O'Keefe used to get us all cozy in around him on the floor of the sound proof room and read us passages of this manuscript. Its story has a most endearing perspective, that of an alien who has fallen to earth and is inhabiting a human body. We see how this consciousness is terribly frightened and empowered and filled with a rage to live.)

The reguesting perspective is the religious perspective of the perennial philosophy and a most worthy aesthetic apperception to construct in a work of art. The consciousness in *The Bell Tower*, gives the fleeting impressions of this [living] entity sailing through the space inhabiting various life forms, as though it were a soul looking to be reborn. There is a whole literature of this in Buddhism, *The Tibetan Book of the Dead* goes into great detail about the transmigration of the soul looking for its rebirth.

There are so many life forms mentioned in the poem, the ecology is everywhere dense with life forms filling up every possible niche and mechanical contrivance to extract free energy from substance. The Forms for the soul to get reborn into is as infinite as the number of angels dancing on the head of a pin, or as tachyonic field quanta (bosons), packing into possible states. So many souls looking to be reborn. Flying through their old houses, where they can take on strange shapes and squeeze up pipes and under doors, like the wind itself, or like water, something trying to seek its own level. So many had been born into lives where they were undesired, or discarded too soon. Some are even from little children who only saw the briefest flash of light before they were gone.

On a lighter note, O'Keefe and other Hawkeyes were consummate actors, imbued in all the methods. In California, actors lead many lives, are oft reguested. Reguesting for them is part of their everyday practice. They always answer the question: to reguest or not to reguest with a Yes.

2.4 The narrator shifts identity between a prosaic Alice in Wonderland rabbit character (he has a stop watch) to the pre-ambulatory fish entity of the waters in the next metamorphosis to emerge the textual juxtaposition. Note the bilabial plosives in the explosion and expulsion from the mud.

Example 2.4

    I look at my pocket watch.
    It is morning.....

                      seamy ribbons strip
                      through the branches
                      above me

I shout!
    dust explodes from my mouth
sealing my cheeks against my teeth
in sticky then dry popping jells
of paste and powder. My eyes almost
splinter at the thought of the in-take.
A blast of hot rotten air rips up thru
the mud. Soft bubbles pop their domes
at the surface, over flowing from my
mouth as i c r e s e n t s t r e t c h

2.5 In this passage there is a synopsis of the poem and we see some of the subjects (Ghosts) that O'Keefe the playwright would treat in several of the plays he would go on to write.

Example 2.5

    I turn around and see the nursery.
                      sand and pebbles
                yellow
                        and
                            beige,
                                the Bell Tower.
i head directly toward it over a
path for what now is sanctified with a christian burial will be paid
with blood diapers later, linens of blood, tubs of it, sheepy blood.
Ghosts will sit at the dining tables awit, snowy bonnets will fly
thru the reading rooms, tables topsy-turvy
                                      (gassed rooms)
                                        and
                                    now the picture
                                    seeps into my
                                    head all is a
                                    dream by jest
                                    i will not wake up

The consciousness moving in the poem feels itself not only as part of the immensity of the natural world all working together, a kind of ecology, but as a strong entity emerging from it.

2.6 Down to the rivers edge when something happened. The narrator began seeing something, humming and moving in the forms of nature.

Example 2.6

> i hear her body humming
> > in the underbrush
> > > then thru the tall willow
> > > saplings her body humming

Two interpretations In a small hamlet (or Catholic orphanage) the bell tower of the church is the most identifying symbol of the community and the representation of the Holy See of the church. The penetrating peel of the bell sound is easily translated metaphorically into god's eye because the sound is easily localized (in the audial space of the imagination). In some communities the regular ringing of the bells is how people set their clocks, how they tell the time of day. The ritual speaks to the passage from the dimension of secular time into sacred time, the time of ritual reflected in the liturgical calendar. In O'Keefe's poem, the bell tower becomes a unifying symbol for the evolution of all the living forms of life — and there are many alert in the poem, moving, sensing the great motion. This great motion is the Tao. O'Keefe had been studying Tai Chi and Taoism for its clarity, its order, its single-minded cutting through and it was imbuing his life and influencing Hawkeye theatre. He was also a fly fisherman enjoying the rivers and streams of his native Iowa, able to perform that graceful trick of "flying" the lure over the waters.

For me, two associations precipitated by this phrase, "the Thirty Bell-Weighted Glocker" were the Diving Bell and the Bell Shaped Curve. The poem with its plethora of life-forms compelled me to look for some unifying concept describing this profusion of adaptations built upon the machinations of probabilistic material and molecular concatenations in an atmosphere of challenge and response. The perspective I sought is the weighted probability of an outcome emerging from the probability density of the normal distribution also known as the Bell Shaped Curve. I am grateful that the poem engendered these associations for me. Though I don't see any direct evidence in the poem supporting either association I feel it. Let us indulge an old southern critic and pursue the diving bell and the variation around the mean for a moment further.

Could it be that the poet is lowering himself into this denser and denser atmosphere. Or rising into a higher one. Consider the diving bell. Aristotle wrote about his student Alexander commissioning the construction of one. This diving bell would house him as he was lowered beneath the sea surface to behold the marvels of under water world. This simple inverted container would have the air it contained at atmospheric pressure when it was lowered into the water. At 35 feet below the surface it would have a second atmosphere of pressure. This doubling of the density due to increased pressure would half the volume of air in the bell. In order to stay in it for long, the same quantity of air that was compressed would have to be resupplied from the surface.

Also the phrase Thirty Bell-Weighted Glocker got me thinking about weighted probability distributions and the Bell Shaped Curve. Since this is a poem about a consciousness wandering around in the exquisite chaos of natural beneficence, and being touched by it as well as horrified by it, while at the same time looking and wondering about what is normal, let us consider the Bell Shaped Curve — also called the normal distribution. Basically the normal distribution is a graph of the frequency with which the attribute of interest is found in a population. It has a symmetrical shape about a central mean ("average"), with a standard deviation ("variability") from that mean.

The Bell Shaped Curve is a tower of enlightenment from whose perspective, a beacon of light does shine into the distributions of this world's generosity. It accounts for the amount of variations of some complex evolutionary attribute (the alleles of the phenotype) like height, weight, eye color, intelligence — any of a number of adaptations from genetic and other sources, within the population. The wider the bell's shape the better; when the shape of these indicators of responses of flesh to environmental stress form a normal distribution it means the population is not under some kind of stress that would skew or warp the distribution of survivor traits. For example, consider a population of cacti being eaten by wild pigs. The spines of the cacti are an evolutionary adaptation of survival, a defense mechanism to limit the destruction of their being. If you went out into the field and counted the spines you would find, year after year, that the average number of spines is the same. This means that there is no stressor or pressure on that population to develop cacti with more spines, that the equilibrium of pigs and types of cactus have settled down to a stable or normal relationship.

2.7. The poem opens with the observations of alleles of phenotypes and their are many

Example 2.7a

> River flies set their teeth

Example 2.7b

> water runs below and needle trout
> comb the eddies for latches,
> snake burns etched on their
> iridescent sides

Example 2.7c

> gutty worms burrow
> like a fist full of curls
> sucking space in the mud
> down in

In the poem we are party to maid servants and river frogs, worms and flies, finches and elms, needle trout and latches, snakes and dragon flies, corn and piston slugs, bats and gnats, fungus and branches, bamboo and snails, willows and corn, whales and puppies, sheep and birds. Even though the underlying causes of the proliferation of survival adaptations is unknown and perhaps unknowable due to the interactions of many small effects —the complexity — the distribution of these occurrences around a mean is what we understand by normal. The normal distribution is the one toward which ALL other distributions cleave, in the limit, for the normal distribution maximizes information entropy among all distributions with known mean and variance. It is the distribution that meshes, is in resonance, with other competing alleles of a phenotype, giving all developments their best possible means to exist, sharing scarce resources in a way to maximize potential through the extraction of free energy. This best shot at normalcy makes it the natural choice of underlying distribution for data summaries in terms of sample mean and variance.

The concept of information entropy comes from Claude Shannon, who illustrates it with an example (near and dear to the writer's heart): the 10,000 monkeys banging on typewriters to produce a Shakespearean play. Information / entropy are two sides of the same coin. Entropy is the randomness that attacks and shreds and dilutes symmetry and order yet at the same time is the carrier signal of information. The typewriter is the substrate out of which the entity emerges. In the course of normal writing not all letters are equally likely to be used, (z for example occurs far less frequently than e). So designers of the qwerty keyboard distribute the most-used letters into positions of accessibility near the center of the keyboard. But with the monkeys banging on typewriters, any letter is theoretically as likely as the next to be used. Thus even though in the moments of successive sampling (banging on the typewriter keys) the distribution of the most commonly used letters being near the middle of the qwerty keyboard biases the production of text. Thus out of randomness emerges a more readable text, a kind of recognizable order.

In *The Bell Tower* the flung-out syntax and the constant shocking juxtapositions appearing almost random at first suggest the idea of the text as a kind of surface reflecting language itself. We are brought close up to the language, so that we must see it as a medium in which we are immersed. With that we are in the artwork as a kind of self-aware artificial intelligence. We sense the automaton nature of language coding. This sense of being in the poem that is leading us into transcending language is a journey in which we must undergo a kind of metamorphosis to a more animal nature. Eventually, with all the motion and vision going on, everything starts to move all at once on the page. The page is writhing with lifefullness and it is trangressing everything we thought of as holy in the world of poetry.

2.8 The spoken thoughts of the narrator reflect some of O'Keefe's over-the-top sense of humor.

Example 2.8a

("how long do i have to
endure the whale voiced
puppy?")

Example 2.8b

"scrubbing pumice
                    in
                      the
                    sink
                          while
                                his wife's lonely eyes
                                shift to stellar objects."

2.9 They also express a sense of alienation from his physical and cultural environment.

Example 2.9

although the nature of her face might draw
some phobos bat from
the hive,

3. The Inscape of the Poem

The natural world depicted in the poem engenders a sense of presence; it is a world that is both scientific and fantastic. This split is reflected in the schematic of the page. The visual movement of the words provides an Inscape corresponding to, and transforming the world of actual persons, events, and feelings. Experience and perceptions of the poem's narrator are presented as images and thus are translated into an internal language. *The Bell Tower* is a long poem containing many short, objective, observational poems of the natural scene. These haiku-like poems convey a keenly perceived moment of heightened subjective awareness, sometimes moving beyond into hallucination of spirit. My generation understood, through the works of Carlos Castaneda, the worlds of the Nagual, and the Tonal. The Nagual is a world where all things are present and it has many cognates in the Gnostic Tradition. I would like to spend the remainder of this essay examining some aspects of how O'Keefe's poetry moves across the boundaries between these worlds.

By the time he wrote *The Bell Tower*, O'Keefe had written the Osirius series of plays. The title play *Osirius,* performed in Iowa, is a choral celebration of Egyptian solar religion mystery. The actor/singers moved along lines that radiated out into the audience like spokes from a hub. It brought the audience into a kind of mandala. The cycle of plays included *Bercelac's Dream*. This was the women's play in the cycle. It was about medieval Catholicism and it had a cast of nuns. It was performed on the grassy knoll overlooking Fort Mason near white-painted institutional buildings. *Coyote*, the night play in the cycle, was performed at the Blake St. Hawkeye Theatre. *Osirius* had many passages written in a kind of the mimetic language of sound energy influenced by Jonathan Albert's approach to this border land at the intersection of poetry and singing. In the universe of *The Bell Tower* the poet makes up his own words and language.

3.1 Neologisms and portmanteau words

Example 3.1a

"Do you not see the re-guesting, Silvers?

Example 3.1b

euclyspills mingle with pidgeons

Example 3.1c

    i unrathem morning

Example 3.1d

    river moons
    pig carp diving
    on the river bottom
                    and maribou
                    signaling
                            oh love
                            of love
                                    divine,
                                        Walleye

O'Keefe ends the passage with this invocation of being astounded. Walleye is having large staring eyes, excited or agitated, staring in fear, rage, frenzy — walleyed astonishment. There is a kind of shimmer, a kind of ephemerality with his quick experiments and wordplay. Unrathem, maribou (a stork, a bird whose feathers are used to make fluffy boas, fuzzy slippers, tied flies), re-guesting.

Who is this character creating this world of his own syntactical and typographic and ideogrammatic meanings for traveling on the imagination.

3.2 We get a little of his personal problems or sufferings. He seems to be seeing dots in front his eyes, and having troubles with his knees.

Example 3.2

    fungus trembles like turtle fat
    in the piper reeds, medicine
    oozed out in orange dots stretching
    the reflections on my eyes.

                    I wobble in intense pain
                    on the gristle of my knees
                        the Keys
                        in my pocket
                        burn me

3.3 He reveals a sense of estrangement from ever having had a family.

Example 3.3

    (as if there were memories
        of home
                anytime
                      ever)

1.4 They also express a sense of alienation from his own inner voice.

Example 1.5a

> How much longer must I endure the wale voiced puppy?

The Bell Tower shows us the struggle to emerge human in the animal world and the world of matter. Though many of the images are beautiful, many are not, and suggest the violence of the natural world of predator and prey. In this we see the natural elements rising in the struggle to sustain their existence. The animated syntax takes us beneath the heady world of ordinary consciousness into the environment, the ecology, what Uexall depicted as the *umveldt*. It is the quality of lifefulness, not beauty that *The Bell Tower* seeks to present. The narrator is able to see the struggle with a kind of Buddhist equanimity — not in a romantic way, but in a real way, seeing death and destruction while appreciating that struggle for coexistence.

The problem the poet or any artist sets themselves is how to be more present, to turn-on the world of the senses, to feel yourself connected with the flow of the great evolutionary now. This level of connectedness to the natural world, the poet feels to be rather frightening, and he gives us a sense of this fright in frightening imagery.

In the Jungian picture, the image straddles the boundary between worlds. The function of the image is to translate the world of perception into the world of experience. The moving image is the language and the currency of seeing. The difference connectedness makes is seen in the very different function served by images in translating the world of perception into the world of experience. In some ways it is an impossible task translating a world that is untranslatable into the world as translated. O'Keefe's use of the images serves him well in this poem. Haiku focus on the things of the external world, behind which may lie, by implication, the various ideas, biases, or emotions of the internal world. O'Keefe weaves these observations into the poem through an internal monologue of the observing narrator. He uses common language, sometimes quoted as if overheard in conversation. This is the kind of knowledge that you would want to take with you into the woods. What Levi-Straus might have called "the science of the concrete."

The real world translated from, engenders a second world of language with its own conventions, a stylized construct, the Inscape of the poet's own experience. Just as we are translated in the great external mind of the material world of nature into human beings, the artist / narrator, by aligning himself with the motion of this world-mind — in which the creatures that inhabit it are like thoughts in that mind — resolves his situation as the lost boy through the discovery of just this parallel. He finds his empowerment as he hopes to find is soul aligned with the purview of God, in the end.

One insistent characteristic that sets haiku apart from other poetic modes is its immediacy in the present moment where the discontinuity of perception extracts from the continuity of the eternal now. In the way that it attempts to crystallize a moment of heightened awareness as sharply as possible, haiku enables a closer approach to infinity than any other poetry. An appreciation for the now-moment is the reason haiku are best written in the present tense. *The Bell Tower* is told in the present tense, so that it may be forever present.

Episodic Imprint and the Liquidity of Consciousness

The text of this gallery brochure for a one-man show of the artwork of Peter Loschan at the M-Room Gallery in Oakland was based on an interview made while he was sorting his paintings. Along with photographs of the artwork, several drawings he did for various issues of the PAW are republished here.

Michael: You like the liveliness. You like liveliness more . . . than the, clear delineation of the figure.

Peter: The clear delineation is limiting in a certain way, when you want to shift your emphasis.

(He paused thoughtfully and stroked his chin, continued:)
Your fantasy wants to keep moving. Wants to shift and play with the consequences as they are there.

Peter: An artist has a hard time keeping up with that desire. Any artist who could produce prodigiously enough could keep a certain momentum., you know, of . . . of almost a live act . . .
(He looked at me and waved his hands in the air like some kind of slight of hand artist)
. . . a live act, the activity of art . . . you know, of visional-ary, uhm
(and here he began to delight in some verbal improvisation)
. . . visional or visionary!

To me vision is, as well-developed in us as speech — at least! Or even music. We see all things, all day long. We just don't know how to interpret things in such a way where they become art.
You can go through your whole life living completely in an art space.

(These works and more in color are available in the Peter Loschan Gallery. Check the Art Gallery area of Hitmotel Press web.)

Michael: That's an interesting thought about vision being at least as well developed as speech. I would have thought it was more developed. You mean educated?

Peter: Yes! Paintings educate your sensibility, as well as visual sense and even tactile, art is really tactile, painting is tactile can emulate sculptures . . . Sculptures are more strong.
(He looked off wistful, like he was desirous of working in that form.)
Paintings are always sort of fallible in a certain way, they are very artificial. They stay on a flat surface, you know.

And so you don't do things mechanistically but you convince with them, with the mental strength of the memory . . . the mental image and, another thing, it really teaches people to . . . to unlearn their own prejudices.
(He thought for a moment, looked resigned.)

Eventually they put all these superficial interpretations on paintings. And yet the painting survives them all!
(He shrugged and smiled as though at inevitability.)
They state their imaginings, go their course and then after a while they get . . . *cured* of that particular syndrome.
But the paintings . . . cohere.
There is eventually a relationship that takes place between viewer and the painter. It becomes . . . eventually my paintings are . . . . People — once they have seen that — will not want to — not see it.

Peter: They become part of the consciousness — collective, of course. The collective unconsciousness.

Michael: That's a great thing to aspire to.

Peter: I have some artworks that you can't possibly forget. You know like . . .

Michael: Like the Moonlight sonata? or Take Five?

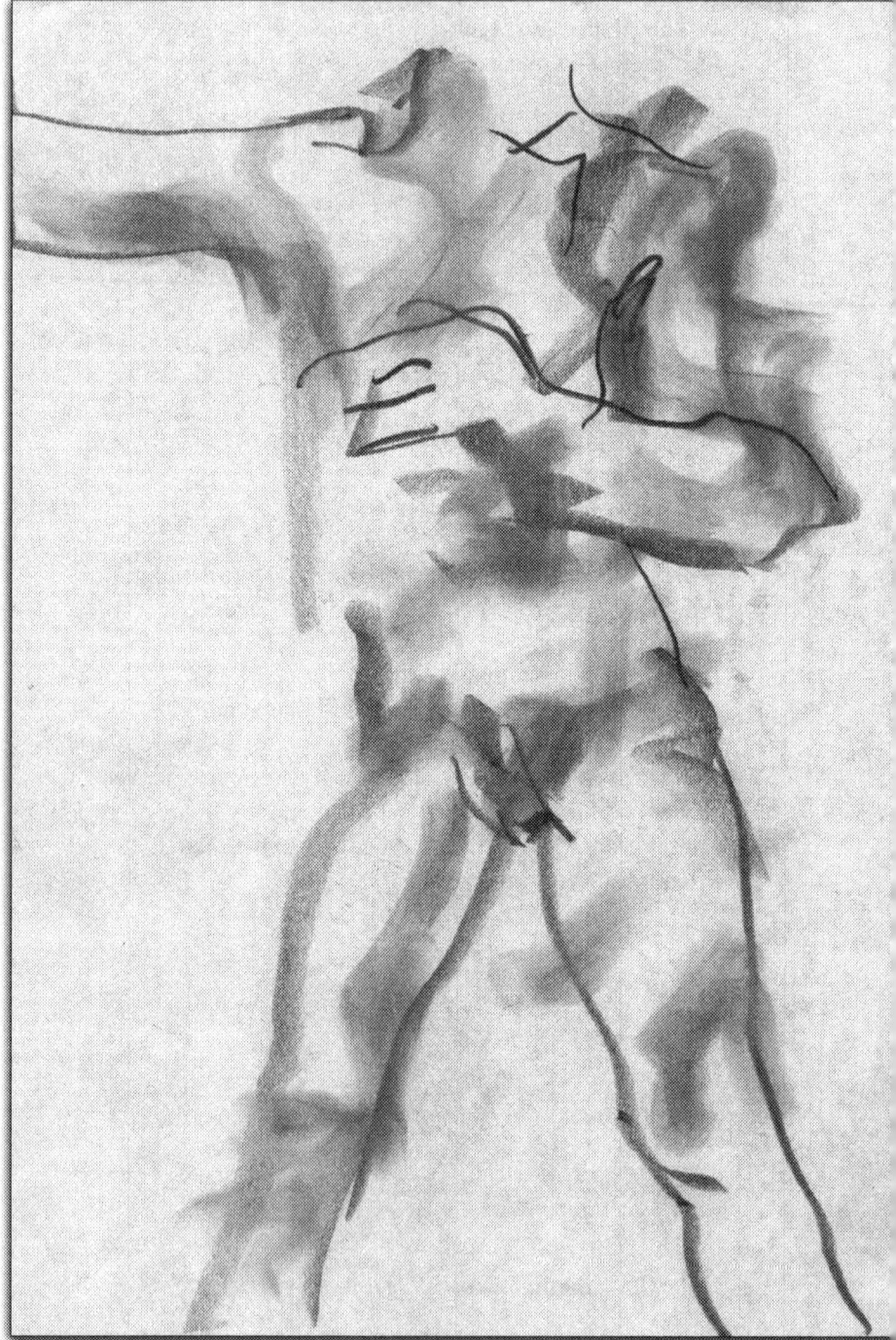

Peter: Yes that. . . . I'm thinking of Goya, for instance. There are some images in Goya — that once you have seen them, that's it. You know.
Or all the really great painters . . . especially . . .

Michael: Well what do they tap into when they do that? Is it the . . .

(He continued.)

Peter: The Renaissance painters . . . Collective Unconsciousness.
The Renaissance painters are . . .Titian . . . is a great master. Nothing possibly could be wrong with Titian. But psychological traits being painted developed only with Caravadgio and Rembrant.
I was very much interested in that.
The psychological depths that an artwork is composed of . . . if you give it . . . Again, always presupposing that you let the art . . . give it some time and then it . . .
it is a Being which manifests itself through the art.

Michael: A Being?

The figure speaks:
I am proud of my muscles, the way I move so sinewy and catlike.
Follow me. Westward ho! Into the world we are creating here.
I have no head and yet I must speak! I let my body do the talking.
Why is that so hard for you to understand?
It is a genius after all, let it do your bidding.

Peter: Yeah!

Michael: A very changeable being. One that can take on any form?

Peter: Completely changeable, yes . . . A genius that flits around.

    Other kinds of subject forms?   Structural norm? As long as you use the same medium to express yourself, then you transcend the medium and you start saying something about . . .

    My head rests on the pedestal
      of a long elegant neck.
    I
    close my eyes
    and see a man within
        — the male side of myself
    — a man full of music,
      even in the middle of the day.

Michael: What's the difference between being a reporter or a journalist and a painter?

Peter: The painter could be trans-actual. I would like to be a journalist who . . .

Michael: How do you transcend the medium?

(He continued.)

Peter: . . . a Being who transmits messages . . .from the earth itself — through a being, to an extraterrestrial who has never seen earthly conditions.
Then through my paintings they could see that. They have to be transported through the mental, through the . . . Into the mind you know. Ha-ha, once their in the mind, they are there forever.
I really believe that you will come across your own paintings in heaven.
And if that's the case, I would really like to go there. I could never equal some of those. Of course not.

> I get refreshed by taking chances —
> walking a narrow path
> with precipitously dangerous possibilities
> on each side.
> Something chooses me,
> and permits my tour.

>   But, I can go on and do more.

Peter: . . . See, an artist really has a lot to do with simply putting things together.

Michael: Yea

Peter: Because for the moment you really enjoy your own work very rarely.

> I've never really had a chance to see anything like a mind . . . in good form . . . It's really something else.

Michael: Something you long for.

Peter: Yes, actually ha, ha,

Michael: Me to.

Peter: Yea, I do long for that.

Michael: Yea, you know, you want . . . you do a good piece of work and your passion is in it, and you want to pursue it.

> The boho dance is very destructive.

> I am a lunar
> voyager
> I float
> of the breath
> rising on the scent
> to hover over
> the city
> like a warrior
> on a carpet of
> clouds

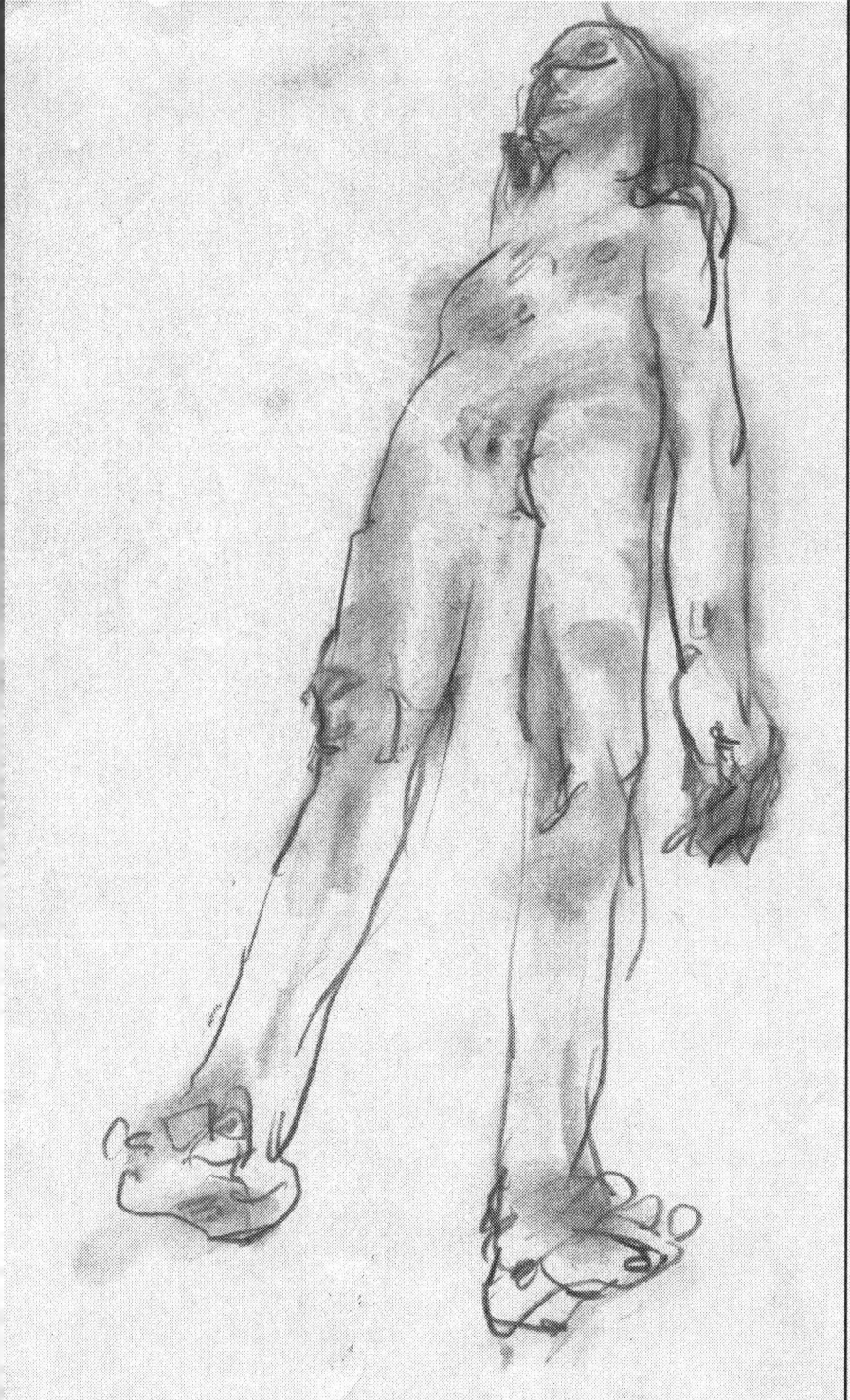

Peter: Yes, well if you . . . if you are a journalist you transcend your medium. You don't really transcend the medium because the medium is important, is the whole basis of the whole thing.

Michael: Of I see, you mean like the artist. . .

Peter: the object anyway . . . is too self conscious, too aware of   the image . . . his medium.
A lot of times he is, and if he can overcome that then he is really cooking, you know.
If he can really just enjoy the playing of the medium. Instead of anything else. I mean, what's there to worry about, really.

Michael: Well you have to worry about . . .

Peter: For a painter you have a lot. . .
Lack of integration   to worry about be-cause..
It isn't that easy to make them right, you know. A lot of times you do the absolutely dumbest things.
So then you work your way out of it.
All those paintings are definitely worked on. Some of them are definitely the fifth or sixth image worked on. One on top of the other.

Michael: Good.

Peter: Yet others are completely fresh . . . draft. I know

when it is good then I leave it alone.

Peter: I'm interested in these sort of archetypal effects, like the archetypal way of painting green . . . green bushes and things like that

Michael: What do you mean by archetypal? You mean, like, one that . . .

Peter: Well there is a certain way to do it. Like the bushes for instance. . .
Yes, that's what attracted me to that, was the bushes in the upper left hand corner there. That's just really fine.

That's just part of the drawing. It's drawing . . . Yea, that one's a real charmer. It's not the most profound thing in the world but . . . At that time I was still flatter than I am now. I'm starting roundness better.

You know that figure that's sitting, sort of on this lotus position, floating? That figure is really strong. I mean it never ends, it just really, really vibrates you know in endless energy.

>   the two hands folded into the lap
>   and a tight cautious smile drawn on the lips
>   she regards you
>   then
>   she looks beyond
>   out the window

Michael: Yea, it's strong.

Peter: It's getting there.
I would like to paint in oil, though. It would get a glisteny-er image, cleaner. I'm really interested in freshness and clean things.

Sometimes I'm sorry I'm putting delineations in there, because they detract just from the clean surfaces of things. But then I know I have to consider the painting no only from a surfacy effect point of view, but from other aspects as well.
So, when good paint happens, it's in the surface of the image.
Sometimes paint suggests an image. Then there's no reason not to follow that sometimes.
It confuses other people though, you know.
I know there are a lot of people that think I'm totally crazy.

Transformers. We are transformers
Built out of the metals and air
and fire and water
machines and angels
slag heaps and trees
I am a speaker — a transformer,
with a magnetic core — tuned to
my self: a vibration going round
and round like sloshed energy
in a circuit of words.

Michael: What's the connection between lyrical expressionism and genetic conceptualism.

Peter: HA! Genetic conceptualism.

Michael: That's a real academic question.

Peter: Genetic conceptualism, it sort of says what I'm trying to do.

Michael: And what is that.

Peter: I don't like the idea of conceptualism so much although if you want to be technical about it you can't get away from it — from a term like that because it's part of our art history. All art works have conceptualism in them.
I don't make these distinctions between something being more or less advanced in approach, you know. To me the ancient Egyptians are just as advanced as anybody else — in art.

Painting has its own laws and is composed of its own structure: its dimensions, as well as its proportion in relation to its existence. These are inevitably creaturely considerations because the most amazing thing about existence is its . . . Is the existence of its own

---

Though old, I'm still a child inside.
And that childhood rises with the contours
of my current shape.
And dissolves like a child in a rain of tears.

Michael: What is the analogy?

Peter: The artwork itself. It, the Thing, with it's own consciousness!

Michael: Do you mean to say that in other words analogous to ourselves, there is a little clockwork piece of artificial intelligence running along in a universe parallel to our own, with trees bending in the wind, and surfaces dancing in the light — an analog device analogous to ourselves?

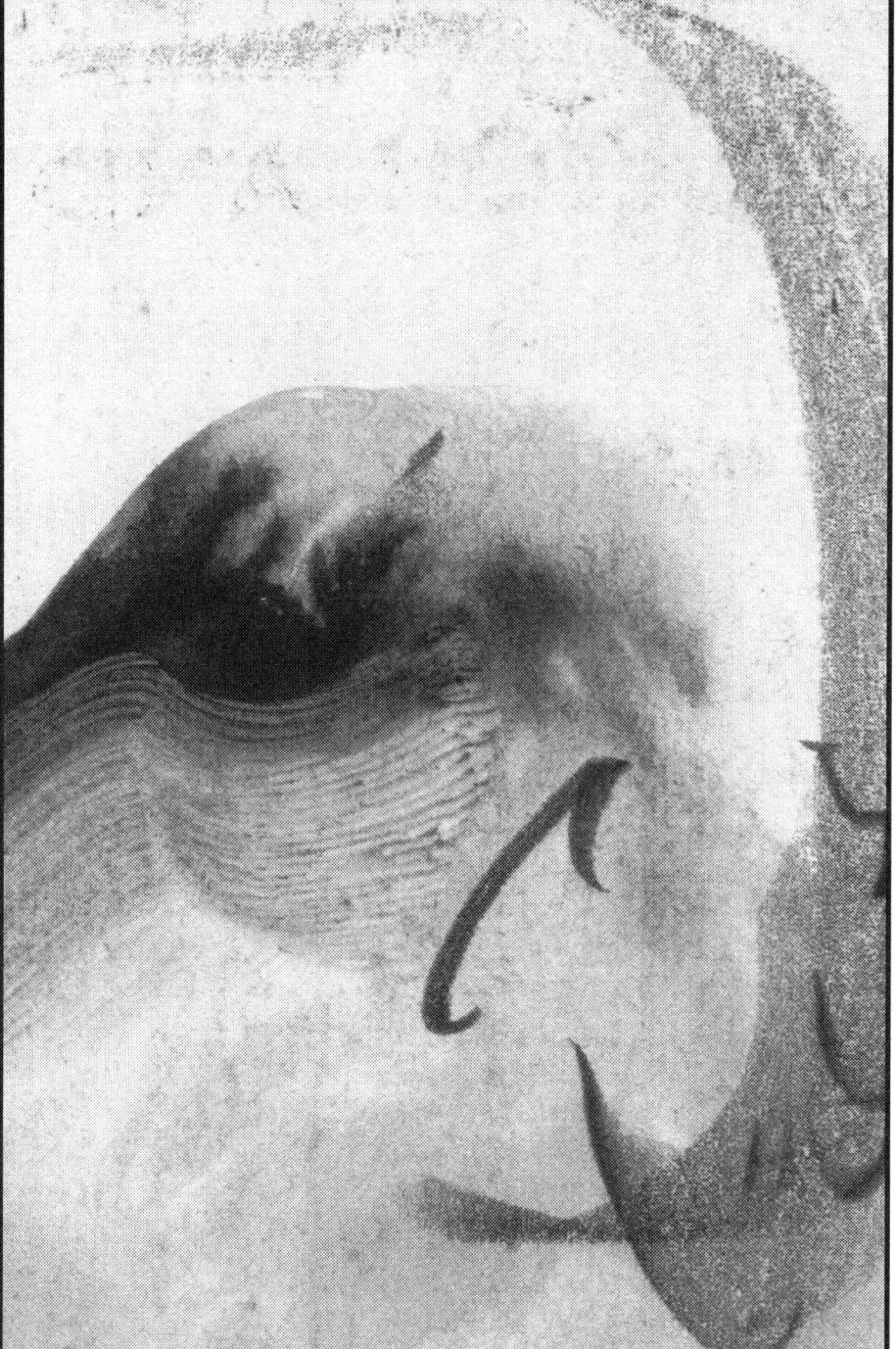

Peter: I am very free to go into all sorts of faces. Each art work takes on characteristics of it's own, almost a life of it's own. The whole idea of art is to bridge the gap between life and art. A lot of theorizing has been done in art . . . and we live in an art which can exist without intellectual theory, although it is highly intellectual, in it's nature. Any work of art is, exactly, by definition, an exercise of the highest level possible . . . That of the Intuition.

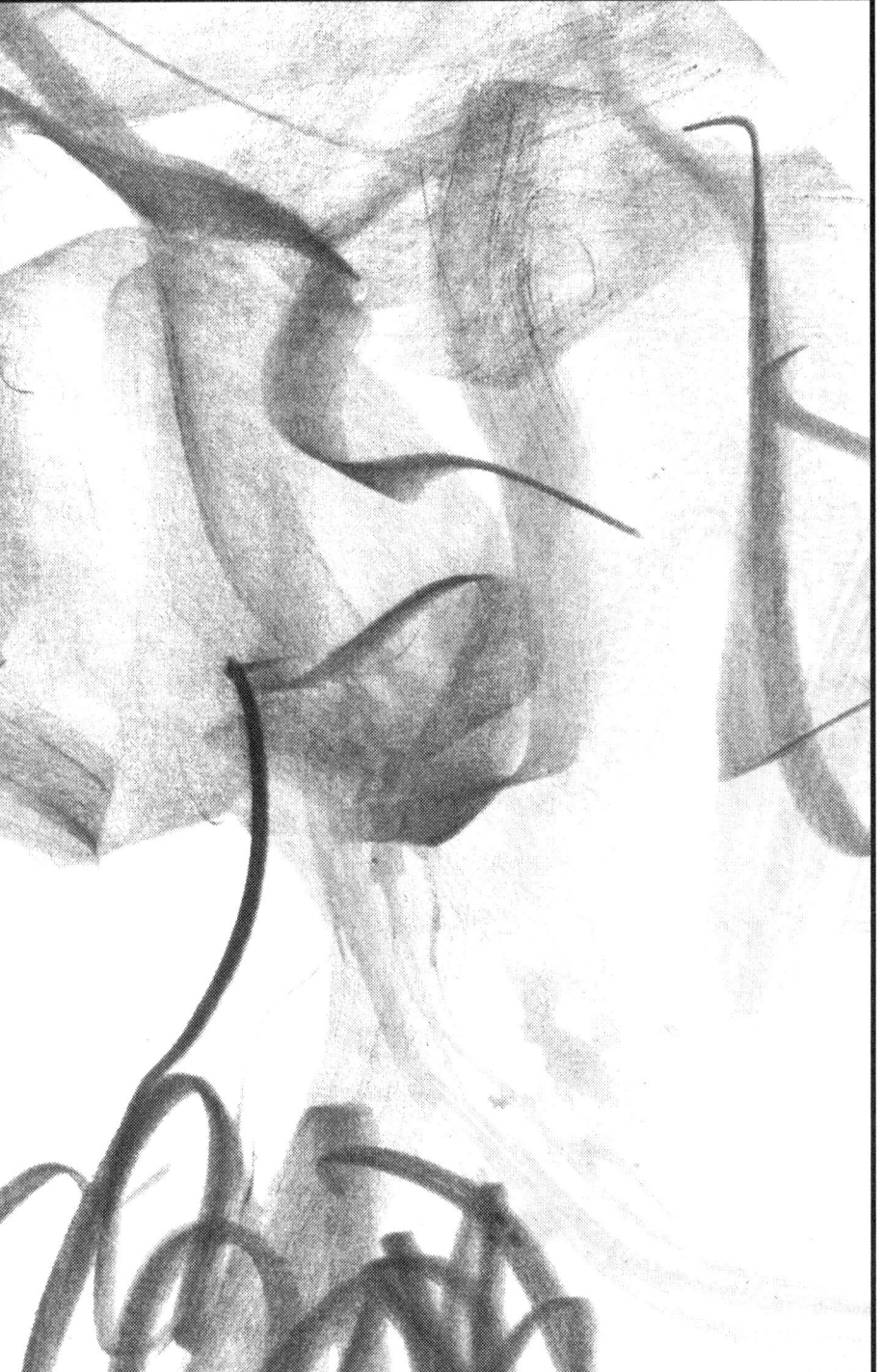

consciousness. Some how analogous to ourselves.

Michael: You mean what those gestures know.

Peter: Of course, you know that art is a progressive experience. We are all the richer for being able to look into a fairly long period of past and knowing a lot of great people in history.
We know them very intimately in fact.
And that's the beautiful thing about it. That's the whole purpose of Art is to be one of these people who have something to say to the rest of the world. Somehow, it's like magic, there is a trick involved. Where you ... you make an artificial work of art, and it becomes a mediator between two different worlds — at least two different worlds.
Actually there are an infinite number of worlds.
If you have to travel through worlds then, you know, and which we all have, like, we are really spacemen on an exploration voyage.
What it is, is that it's the earth — doesn't mean it's not interesting. Or not as interesting as the moon would be, you know?
If you were on the moon you would probably look at every rock and study it intensely. You photograph it as a scientist, right?
And, science is not the only science, there are other, disciplines.
I don't like discipline, actually, I think discipline inhibits your vitality.
Vitality is more important than discipline.
Like I said, to have a lively, crazy image is more important than the perfect rendering.
Rendering is really in the service of a larger intent. It should be wonderful and perfect, but it should leave a

lot of latitude as well.

Peter: The painting should be fast and seductive and, what was I trying to say, a word . . . implied really, by implication it should convince, thoroughly because of the spirit involved.
People who don't see spirit probably won't see anything in my paintings.

Michael: You talk about spirit, and yet you are one of the most down to earth, realistic un . . .

Peter: Yea, you got to be all of those things

Michael: But you are trying to paint the spirit world.

Peter: Yeah.

Michael: You never talk about that, and it seems you would have little patience with metaphysicians.

Peter: I don't want to nail it down to that anyway, because it gives rise to notions in people's heads that are not

---

the sweep
of your hair parting
to frame
your face looking
at me.
is fragile enough
to
fathom
eternity
would
that those
poignant pursed lips
be poised
to speak
my name

correct.
Peter: I think that they should bring their own intuitions, to whatever they come across, you know.
Of So it is, to have a more serious answer to that, is that there are spirits, and there are also whatever else, anything else is also, you know?

If anything, is anything else, ever, then the paintings are that something else as well. Sometimes.

Michael: Ha ha-ha

Peter: I'll repeat it.

Michael: O.K.

Peter: If anything else is anywhere else, something else . . .
Then these would be also something else, somewhere.
Michael: I don't know if you said that the same way the second time.

Peter: Almost the same.
You could put almost the same into it.
Well that would be an example of a poem, you see.
So, that's on there, you can understand it right
So you just analyze the words.

Michael: Yea.

>behind the line
>there is the volume
>
>we cross space
>
>to the boundaries — beyond
>
>on a tone of ringing, piercing shadows

Peter: Once said, you don't need to hear it loudly, or not loudly, as long as you understand the words is the important thing.
Like the idea of whispering, instead of screaming.

Michael: Yeah

Peter: You have to be able to scream. . .Yes.

Michael: Yes, that's your anger. . .

Peter: I've learned all sorts of things from painting, actually. The point at which you compromise, you can't live with that, you see a moment like that and you have to overcome it, with a whole new agenda of ideas.
If you don't have new ideas, the old stuff will corrupt on you and you will eventually wind up not liking it. So you put it aside for awhile.
You know, the mind is quicker than what you produce. And you're stuck with what you are doing at the moment.
What I don't realize, is what a great pleasure that is.

Michael: Yea, no I don't enjoy it either, because I want to be doing, what I want to be doing at the moment, and I feel like I'm just way behind what I want to do. Stuff. Working on old stuff. Stuff from the past.

---

a local
talking excitedly
— rage, defending —
against that world of the jacked-in,
coercing dreaming

People of the shadows looking at you.
Looking back at themselves too
Some have done hard time. Tear drops for each year
Ran down the face. The boxer learned to fight in grace.

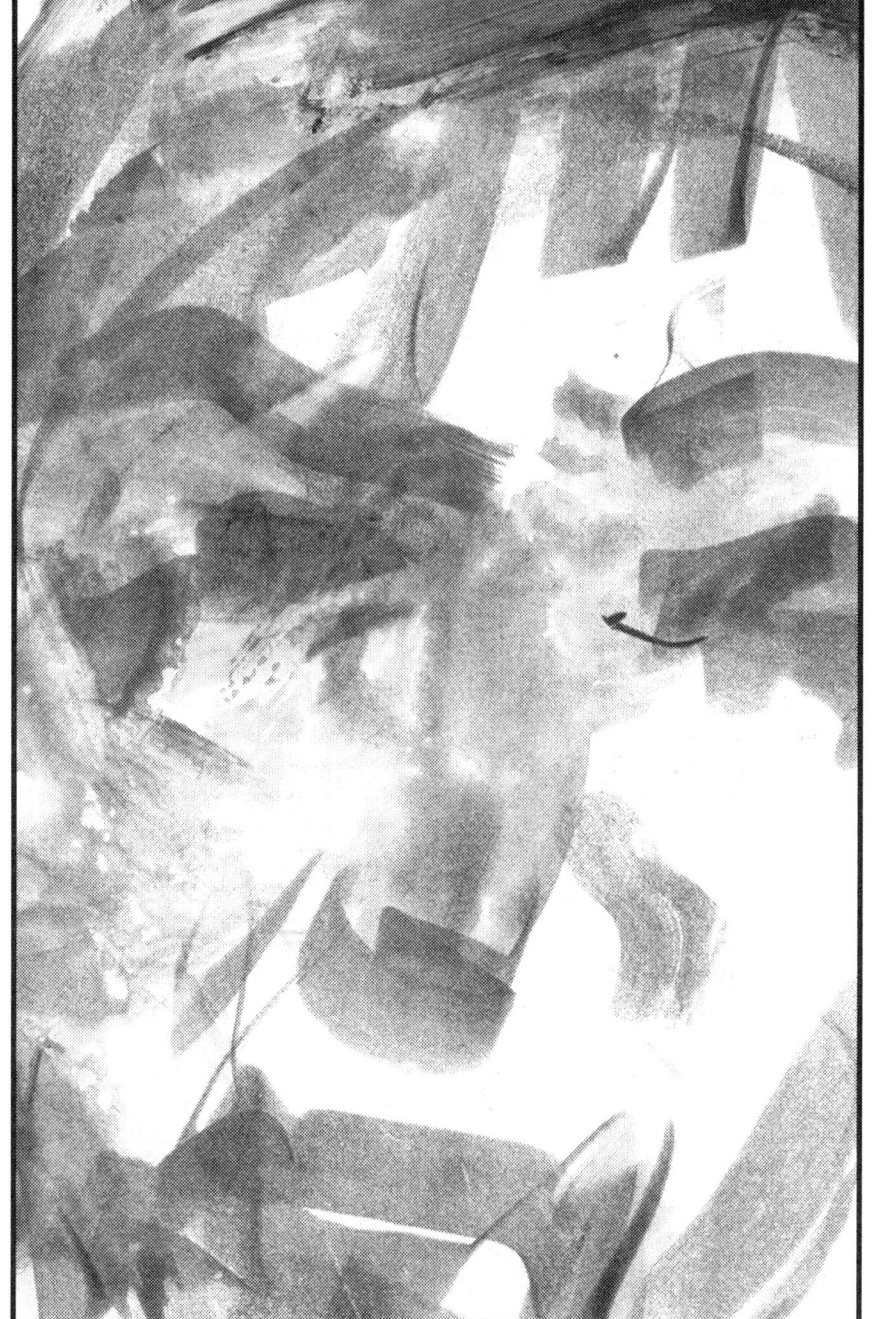

Hooray! he says.
for her lovely
self, walking past
for he adores
her.

Between them
    it begins

and when it will end ?
. . .

But they have
        today

And the days to
        come

that lead
        away from
        an alterable
        lacking.
 to
the incandescent
frontier of
their centers

Tonight there will be rain, and a wild storm
will shake the windows and throw shadows in the candle light.
I only know that you will be here with me
and we'll talk our way through the fear together.

In between the popular propositions of day
and the immobile blackness of night
there falls the shadow of the spirit
in the dispersion of our thoughts.

Her nobility writes itself into your memory with a look
that begins to occupy the space / opened in your heart to perceive it.
She puts herself into your head
only to have you submit to your own nobility.

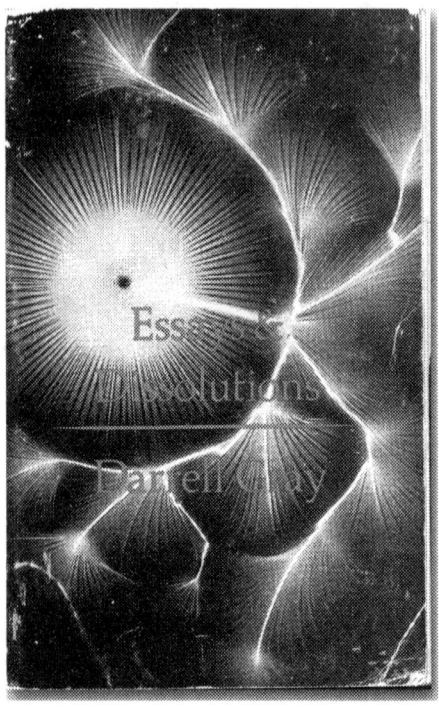

The "world" consists of an aggregate of discrete sensations, and for every sensation there is, as it were, an automorphic tendril radiating into the vortex of its spatio/temporal nature. From this viewpoint, thoughts and emotions (as well as pre-conscious generative nodes) inhabit the same landscape: thoughts are concrete things, emotions are concrete, etc. The automorphic core coordinates discrete automorphic tendrils in much the same way as the eye coordinates separate points of light into a unified visual image. *(ED,33)*

The text is neither subordinate to nor superior to the world, for the world as "actuality" has interfused the poet with its sheer immediacy. Its pervasive tone enters the creation as the basis of an ascending movement, capturing the poet within the enveloping potency of its forces until he rises with it along the arc of possible affirmations, culminating in an epiphany of reconciliation between his physical and spiritual being. *(ED, 12)*

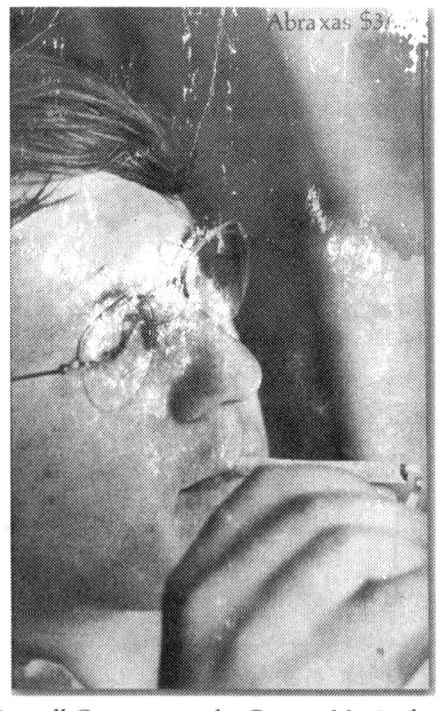

Essays and Dissolutions *by Darrell Gray; covers by George Mattingly*

from[+] The Transcendental Poetics of Actualism

Beyond being a supernal poet, Darrell Gray was a first-rate thinker. His book *Essays and Dissolutions,* Abraxas Press, 155 pages, 1977, contains some of the most interesting thinking about poetry of all time. We have seen some of his notebook entries; the essays are a much more rigorous, condensed presentation. This excellent book consists of an introduction, a preface, four main parts, in a total of 26 chapters. Five of these chapters were papers previously published in academic and 'little' journals. This collection of Gray's ideas on the subjects of mind and poetry drills down beneath the bedrock of language, as poetry must go beyond the operation of logic or discursive prose to find in the roots of language powers of thought not apparent in normative consciousness. He leads us into the expanded field, the place where poetry is both created and understood, where one can engage with these powers. It is an amazing thing to see the poet's power of metaphor combine with the philosopher's probing linguistical acumen to transmute the infinite soul out of the basic elements of thought.

Though most of the material could be classified as not directed to the general public, this book repays study and thought with delight. In breadth and depth equal to Bachelard and Borges. The writing is dense and concise (as well as subtly playful and self contained (in the sense of being self-reflexive statements that communicate on a meta level about themselves. It shows a mind always at play in the field of signs and the hierarchy of logical types)). His interests develop in several directions. In this review of his essays, I would like to keep his intention in the forefront, and that was,

> ...discovering a theory that would transcend a particular poetic utterance and bring to light a limited set of principals underlying poetic generation. *(ED, 23, The Discovery of the Automorph)*

Abstract of this paper: The Transcendental Poetics of Actualism is an aesthetic of the neuronal-sound-imagination

---

[+]*(In the interest of brevity, we have cut many pages from this publication of this review. Check the Sample area of Hitmotel Press web for the complete .pdf, available free.)*

continuum based upon fundamental principals developed by a poet inquiring into a methodology designed for evoking neuronal resonance states of a kind that we presently associate with transcendence. Gray's trans-disciplinary framework of Actualist poetics is a science of Automorphology and a philosophic doctrine based on a modern creative exposition of the ancient Vedanta. The framework consists of several levels, or phenomenological époques isomorphic to Peirce. Following Wittgenstein, Gray saw the levels as 'neumonal ingression' mirrored in the structure of language beneath the mechanistic level of predicative propositions. The process of coming into being, ontology, was like the process of a sentence making sense. He sought to explore the sonic level that reflected the energy of harmony with the objects coming into being. This reflects the psychical-physical continuum of Peirce and his semiotics, an expanded inferential logic of signs. A parallel between Peirce's field extension of logic from the binary based deductive logic for stating analytic apriori proposition to a kind of modal logic for tense and other qualities of being to state synthetic apriori propositions of abduction leading to inference can be made to Gray's model of the poem as a structure to capture these tone qualities of pre-existant being. Gray finds the levels of this frame work to be laid out in one of the oldest cosmologies on earth, the Vedanta. The levels are basically three: The primary sphere, the process sphere and the secondary sphere. We explore this in more detail. The disciplines he will transit are many. Philosophical, linguistic, scientific, historical, cultural, mythological. The primary thrust of the work is the dissolution of identity.

Gray used the neurological research of his time, especially the neuronal information theory of Warren McCullough and the hydromorphic memory surface model of mind in Edward de Bono, to present a general philosophical critique of knowledge. He used this material in the area of his own main interest to develop a field theory of poetry relating it to the internalized phenomenological organization of the world in the patterning of neuronal loci and mitigated through a flow pattern of sign processes and of language. Of the many works pointing into this aesthetic of poetry he was influenced by Olson, WCW, Paul Valery, Creely, the surrealist program. Darrell Gray sketches links between the working model based on de Bono's memory surface and neuronal resonance fields for a heterodox interpretation of the ancient Vedic science in his essay *The Transcendental Critique of Knowledge*, perhaps the crowning jewel of the book. While this is orthodoxically treated in the philosophical framework of Kant's query into ontology and epistemology it is also influenced by the field theories of modern physics and quantum theory.

Some of the working principles Darrell Gray used in the construction of his elaborate Actualist synthesis for the generation of poetry through sound and meaning are: 1. Trace-tone poetics, 2. Verbal pregnance, relay and delay, 3. A modified structuralism (or European semiotics), 4. A new language chemistry of links, inspired by Valery, 5. Vedic ontology and morphology, 6. Automorphic fields, 7. Hydrodynamic-—neuronal model of the mechanism of mind, 8. Wittgenstein and the propositional inference as the basis of poetry — rather than the line.

Here I will briefly list the essays of his book to be explored in my article and note where these principals are introduced. These essays contain most of the theory; the other essays in the collection are experiential applications of the theory. In the body of this essay I quote and comment. Darrell Gray's language was very precise and concise; I have found it well worth the effort to unpack some of the denser propositions. I intend my article to be only a fly-by, touching down here and there to elaborate or relate and perhaps put the material into a current context. I hope it will give the flow of his thought. Darell Gray thought of this effort as what he called the Mind-Kit — concepts to help the artists with intuition, meditation, abduction. These are broken out and presented more directly as a kind of semi-gloss — a glossary or dictionary of philosophical concepts and semiotics.

Synopses of some central essays: In his essay *Construct and Actuality*, Gray delineates the connections between Actualism and Structuralism, Imagism and Coleridge's 'organic theory.' Speaking of Actualism's debt to Imagism, he gives the cryptic equation (I = eye). For him the modern Actualists poem or art work:

> . . . "mirrors its own being both as artifact and key to the flow of perceptions and responses that constitutes it, while the key itself lies reflected in the mirror of its own becoming." *(ED, 7)*

This chapter gives a brief history of literature. How Dante's world view is reflected in the poem, and how Baudelaire was an aesthetician and an epi-phenomenologist. Gray abstracts the discussion of poetry into a more general information relay mechanism by the introduction of his use of the term "tone' which he defines as:

"a non-localized vehicle by which the poet escapes his incomplete self, affirming or denying those real or imaginary boundaries of his localized phenomenal being." *(ED, 11)*

Gray's concept of Tone will echo Peirce's phenomenological Firstness, in the triad of Tone, Type and Token. We recall Tone as a central concept in Rudolf Steiner's anthroposophy.

Gray's essay *The Discovery of the Automorph*, is a monograph presenting data before theory, following the method of the scientific notebook. (Though the theory was well-understood before hand—it is the Transcendental Critique of Knowledge developed in a much later essay of the book). Here he focuses on the more abstract and arbitrary discrete nodes of energy to introduce the concept of Trace Tone Poetics. By analogy he explores two schemas: 1) the physicality of Sound, as parallel to 2) Vedic phenomenology of harmonic ontology.

The essay *Automorphism*, is a synopsis of the whole work. It is a prologomena for the philosophical aesthetic effort of the book and reflects the book's layout and structure. It goes into the Automorphic Methodology, treats of the 'alignment' processes in the field, situates the automorphic self in the center of the field between seeking to know itself through experience and channeling its force through the knower. The parallelisms with Peirce are suggestive, and there are some beautiful analogies: Sleep setting the mind free in possibility just as the womb sets the body free in possibility.

Gray's essay *The Poem As Mandala*, is an exploration of several analogies. Besides the title one, he explores an analogy between the Poet and the Physicist, in which he applies some of the theory developed in earlier and later chapters, in particular the analogy between particles and phonemes and other discrete units of information.

Reflections on Poetry (Language and Predication) delves into Coleridges theory of meaning as well as Gertrude Stein's. This essay is an examination of the relationship between language predication and propositionality. He defines poetry as:

"the schema of the nature of all possible predication." *(ED 47)*

In this essay the poet states his philosophical problem:

"We face a complete re-evaluation of signification which threatens to re-appropriate predication to the super-conscious realm of Absolute Essences whein we have neither "self certainty, or "intuition" to guild us." (ED *49*)

Formation of the Stresses in the Poetic Field, an examination of two poets Shelly and Rilke in a historical context.

Imagination, Sex, and Death, is an exploration of interpenetration and exclusion. He introduces the 'omnigeneric quantum of actuality' (ED *59*) He defines the node:

> "a configuration of forces, independent of cognitive faculties, and in the perceptual sphere exclusion is the principle by which a temporally manifest node is overshadowed or ontologically absorbed by a higher synthesizing Actuality."

His essay *Wittgenstein* is a monograph on propositional space, and what it means for an entity to be self-evident. Gray introduces the proposition as the fundamental element of poetry. He models the binary switches of the mind and states "what is most actual is the neuron itself."

Poetry and the Primitive Mind, a history of the formation of language in a context of Noun vs. Verb.

Accident and Creation, an examination of the mind hovering in spatio/temporal evolution.

Translations from Silence, technical article on the soundscape of poetry with particular application to the work of Creeley.

Gray's essay *The Internal Mirrors*, is an examination of the triadic model: Primary Actualities therefore Secondary Actualities. He examines Coercive integrities conditioning the trans-temporal environment. The triad is also the Energy Structure Perception triad of Peirce. In this essay Gray presages a form of writing he called *Dissolutions* as a way of penetrating the mirror of reality reflected in mind through the Dissolution Realm into the Conceptual Realm. He develops the three level analogy. Proposition—engine: ontology—catagories and dreams: phenomenological—sound/meaning energy flow.

Verbal Pregnance and the Motor Neural Response is a beginning essay into the bio-esthetics of literature examining the mechanism of relay and delay and neronal dispersion.

The Transcendental Critique of Knowledge, a creative elaboration, a wise exposition by way of a transposition into modern western philosophical, psychological and metaphysical terms, of the ancient system of thought contained in the perennial philosophy as presented in its most ancient source, the Vedas.

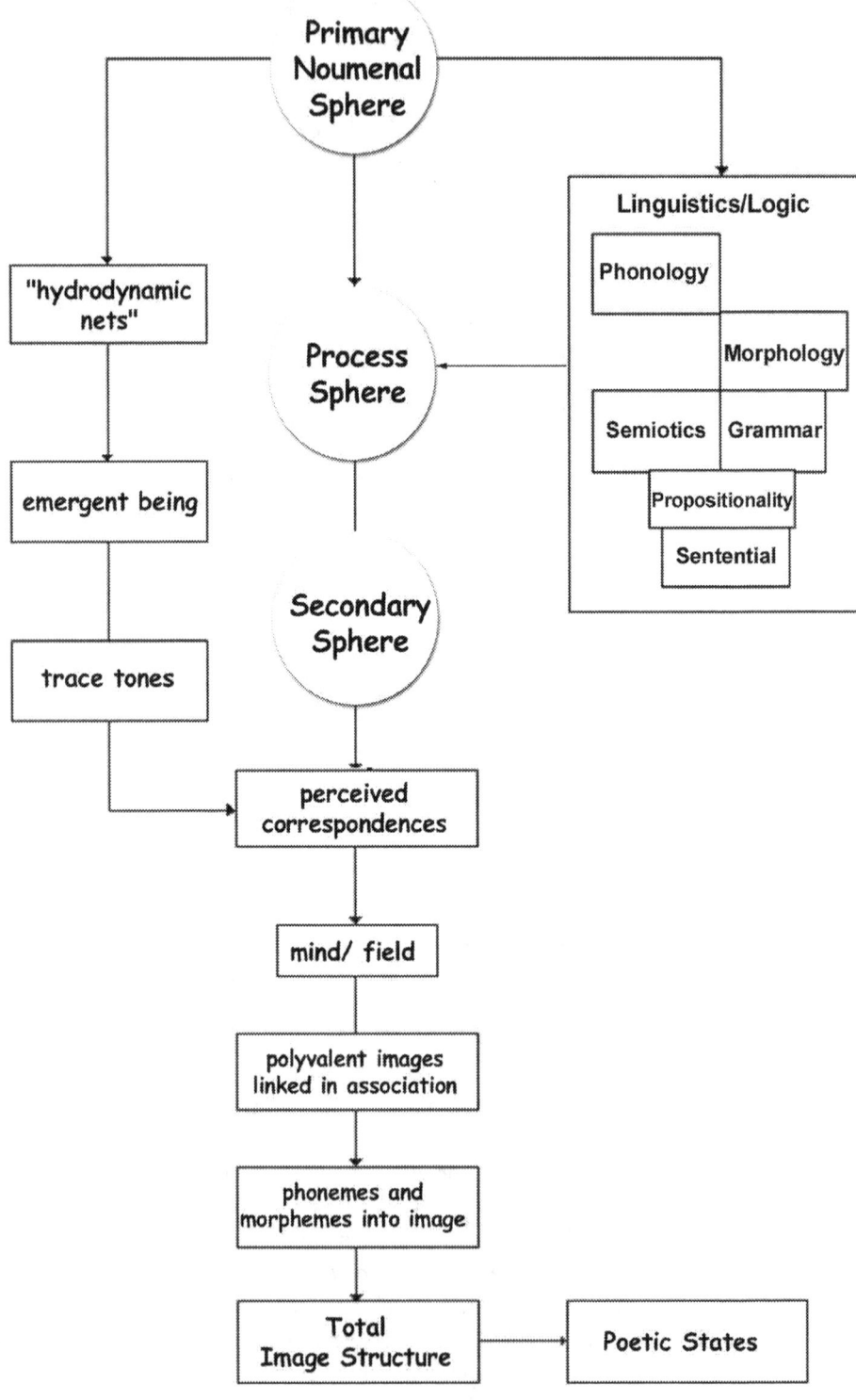

The Implicative Structure of the Text of The Transcendental Poetics of Actualism

Construct and Actuality

In the first essay of the book *Construct and Actuality* — in a passage near the end — Gray describes the artwork engaging both the creator and the user in an interface, an interplay of Construct and Actuality. It has got to be one of the best descriptions of the creative act ever made.

Aesthetic experience as an interface between Construct and Actuality

> In the greatest poems, those which involve us both as "aesthetic witnesses" and as vulnerable human beings, we invariably find the interaction of Construct and Actuality at its highest level of expression. The text is neither subordinate to nor superior to the world, for the world as "actuality" has interfused the poet with its sheer immediacy. Its pervasive tone enters the creation as the basis of an ascending movement, capturing the poet within the enveloping potency of its forces until he rises with it along the arc of possible affirmations, culminating in an epiphany of reconciliation between his physical and spiritual being. From there the descent begins, but the poet, having experienced the fusion of the constructed and the actual, remains "awake" to the less integrated formal and material principles of the lower world he explores.
>
> In this way, the aesthetic act can be seen to correspond to the deepest and most inarticulate experience imaginable. *(ED 12)*

The essay *Construct and Actuality* begins with Gray placing Actualism in a historical context. He speaks to the current reining critical metier — Structuralism (~1974) — indicating Actualism is an extension because of structuralism's very important idea of the artwork as matrix of diachronic and synchronic nodes. (Saussure, Levi-Strauss, Barthes are footnoted. We recall that Structuralism is European semiotics.)

Then Gray begins a time-line tour of the history of poetical movements, and critical theories, summarizing the work of some of the exemplary practitioners. He explores several previous Poetics, particularly Imagism and Coleridge, he gives a historical perspective. He locates Actualism in a historical time-line, while showing how it emerges from previous aesthetics. We see the underlying metaphors in this progression as he shifts the image from the matrix, (the central image of structuralism,) to the mirror and artifact (the central image of Vedanta.) The row and column of matrix (diachronic and synchronic) become the mirror and artifact of Vedanta.

Gray sums up Imagism with a cryptic equation and notes how Actualism seeks to go deeper into the matrix

> The aesthetic formulations of the Imagist provided the basis of refinement necessary for the development of Actualism, while limiting the poet to the predominately visual mode of perception and expression. In Imagist poetics the equation of (eye = I) was made absolute. The import of this theory, reductionist in its essence, was that it provided a focusing mechanism for emotion and thought, but it in no way extended the poetic field. Indeed, the "focusing" function only accentuated the gravitation between poetic particles, generally resulting in a simplification of their modes and configurations. *(ED, 5)*

The Actualists and others "recognized the need for a deeper, more integral concision — an intense structure of coded vibrations not so completely delimited by verbi-visual phenomena." Gray looks to Pound for the deeper substrate of Actualism:

Pound's Vorticism as a development of Imagism and precursor of Actualism

> The effect of inaccuracies in either literal or emotive statement had to be dealt with in terms of structural principles active on an even more elemental level than before - a level that integrates the entire proprioceptive functioning of the organism in both its real and hypothetical matrix toward a new level of articulation — pure structural space temporalized and time spatialized, yielding the Perceptual Animal Image: "an intellectual and emotional complex" not "in an instant of time," but, as it were, at the vortex of time - beyond the category of "the instant." *(ED, 6)*

A concise, technical definition of the Actual.

> Actualism insists that reality consists of a series of shocks, one overcoming another, and preserved in time as memory. The actual is therefore an involuted flow of ephemeral perceptions, and a corresponding interpenetrating flow of post-ephemeral responses. These perceptions and responses form the strata of consciousness, and they derive their structure from the compression and expansion of the psychic environment they inhabit, much like coral, crystal, or rock formations on the floor of the ocean. Actualism emphasizes that these basic configurations have to be included in what we call the "text" - that is, "the schema of the naturally formative processes" which always accompanies the formal structural part of the theory. *(ED, 6)*

We note specifically Gray's invocation of crystal and rock on the ocean floor. It is in the crystal, the metamorphic rock which does great things with light where Darrell Gray finds the objective correlative of his aesthetic: in the substrate, in the process, is the formation of the automorphic. The word automorphic is used interchangeable with metamorphic in geology, to refer to gemstones, rocks that have been formed under tremendous heat and pressure so that their lattices condense into crystalline structures allowing light to have its way with them. The crystal is also the matrix.

Next Gray explores the metaphor of mirror.

The mirror of the text

> The "text" mirrors its own being as both "artifact" and key to the flow of perceptions and responses that constitutes it, while the key itself lies reflected in the mirror of its own becoming.
> When we seek any given "meaning," we must first recognize this mirror. It is language brought away from itself, then suddenly rejoined with its essence. There are linguistic tensions at work here, which we will go into later. *(ED 7)*

Here Gray uses the central metaphor of the book, one that is carried forth and reflected back in several of the essays: MIND IS A MIRROR OF REALITY WHICH ITSELF IS A MIRROR OF THE INGRESSION OF THE NOUMENON INTO THE PHENOMENON. This also suggests that modern literature must be self-aware. That is the primary difference between poetry and prose; they both hold up a mirror but Poetry is self-aware. While prose tells a story, poetry asks you to be in the mirror. Cognitive metaphors are so fundamental that they generate whole schemas which structure not only thought but perception. He then explores these ideas. *Construct and Actuality* then goes on to examine Chaucer, Dante, Baudelair and others in a historical survey to show how these writers held up the mirror of their art to their world. This illustrates how in the mirror of the self the artist reflects his world into, meaning shifts because of this inner framework they bring to the work. He illustrates how the work is created through reflection in this mirror with Chaucer:

Example of the text as a mirror of an artist

> In Chaucer, for instance, the mirror is held close to the object, so that both the surface of the amorally real and the morally imagined world fuse into a single emphatic structure the voice of the poet. .. The moral utterance becomes a reconciliation, through emotional compression, of the *possible* and the *actual,* issuing in a space/time replica of an inner journey toward completion as objective/didactic structure. *(ED, 7)*

Gray points out how this model of the text as mirror becomes the blueprint of literature. He discusses how we must read Dante through a "psycho-emotional" text which essays to reconcile a schism.

Material didacticism and existential potentiality reconciled

> ... the Ptolemaic conception of the universe. This earth, at the center of his Cosmos, with Hell at the center of the earth, was a scheme for equating matter as "material" in the aesthetic sense, providing him with an instant mirror, fusing the spiritual and the mundane. The Divine Comedy is, from a structuralist viewpoint, little more than a map of actuality transposed in terms of localized unitive conceptions of Cosmos — this, in turn derived from the Old Testament, Aristotle, and Acquinas, in which material didacticism and existential potentiality are reconciled.[4]
>
> [4] Albeit more in an extra-textual sense than the "modern mind" can accept. We need access to Priestly's concept of the "Great Time," where totemic structures are considered as vehicles for the passage of mentation from one time-sphere to another. *(ED 8)*

I pursued this footnote a bit further thinking that Great Time meant the Buddhist idea of Big Time, the time of evolution beyond human experiencing. I found that J.B. Priestly wrote plays that were influenced by another intellectual hero of mine J.W.Dunne whom I had first run across in an essay by Borges. I recalled reading Dunne's *An Experiment with Time*, when I found it in the library of St. FX U in Antigonish, NS, and walking around the campus thinking I could slip in and out of the dimension of time. Dunne sought to explain experiences in which he had a precognitive intuition into future events while in a dream state. He thought that the dream state or certain deep states of meditation allowed us to experience a truer nature of time. That the normal mental experience of time as a sequential flow was a special case of a more synchronistic real time in which the future and the past overlapped on the present. In the amorphous fugal dream state one could shift into forward time, and this explained the sense of deja vu one had of having already experienced a time sequence. I read it again in the stacks of the UT library tower in Austin. Dunne's stuff blew my mind. Trying to use imaginary numbers and the light cone of Minkowski space to think about time as a 4th dimension perpendicular to the other three. And what this might mean in terms of precognition of the future. The light cone is the sphere of possibility. It is the space of all those things that can be touched by light spreading out in a cone centered in the now present. This passing of mentation from one time sphere to another would be central to Gray's exposition of the Vedanta. Note that the light cone is an aspective of projective geometry.

Dunne's theory of the sense of time corresponds to many of the Mystical and Metaphysical Traditions of the world's religions. In the *Four Quartets* of T. S. Eliot, there is a great deal of time theory. Burnt Norton begins with "Time present and time past / Are both perhaps present in time future, / And time future contained in time past. / If all time is eternally present / All time is unredeemable." It moves from Acquinian sense of time to a sense of the redemption of the self through art work. Dante shows us this sense:

The key that is the actual

> ... the glorification of Beatrice was an attempt to escape the confines bounded by these two conceptual mirrors. ... She is *actual* in the sense that she is the key to what he can possibly and literally *do*.
>
> When we shift our focus from the visible to the super-visible extensibilities inherent in any theory, a *lag* almost always results. The mutable onrush of the finite dwindles, as it were, into a stasis both present and elsewhere, and this equilibrium can be translated either "epiphany" or "enui" — according to the ductility of the mind at any given instant. *(ED 8)*

Chaucher's Pilgrims, Dante's Beatrice, Baudelaire's Swan, these are all keys, central structural elements that unlock the door to opens to the flow. A key is a trigger. It designates, as in music, the range, the field of tone play. Gray then gives a picture of the "text" as objective mirror, if it is a synthesis. He invoke's Baudelair's swan as both the embodiment of the sensuous activity of the mind and its potential liberation; the swan is a *key* to the text.

Baudelaire, Vishnu and the Swan

> We see the swan as an ingression disrupting by its tranquility a trance in which thought might otherwise be infinite.
>
> Likewise in Dante, it is the actual we are speaking of. The disruption takes the form of sensuous perception, and herein lies the achieved synthesis of 'text" as objective mirror. The indeterminate super-sensory experience becomes sensorially determinate, an object capable of both impeding and reifying time and space.

Gray depicts the poet moving in the realm of the super-sensory, present as occasions and events reify.

The Fundamental theorem of Actualist Poetics

> Poets "transfer of energy from the super-sensuous state to the sensory state of the poem as self-reflexive mirror was as natural as the act of perception itself. The structure became a key to an infinity of temporal dislocations hitherto unsensed, though submerged in the material immediacy of the world which generated the reflective condition out of which both the mirror and the key emerged. These conditions lay fused in the matrix of consciousness until they germinated the necessary structural affinities capable of penetrating space and time. *(ED 9)*

Art as a fusing of matter and meaning

> Art is first and foremost, the activity of an artist. We are likely to notice in ordinary life a searching for, by a series of mental acts structured by a sense of perfection, a concomitant deposit of integrity units manifested in the present as processes culminating in a state of completion. These acts are borne over from the past into the *now*. In this way we carry with us from past epiphanies a condition of pre-conscious unity only to be fully realized into the post-or super-conscious state. Art is "great" when it is most elemental and functional — when, according to the urgencies of its nature, it is not infected by the plurality of specific locations which dominate space. Its originality is the mirroring force of the Infinite in which "matter" and "meaning" become fused. When we perceive this fusion, a unique occasion arises, and our relationship with our previous selves, as well as with the world, takes on a primitive, almost animistic clarity. *(ED, 10)*

This, the intuition being guided by form, in the presence of interpreted signs, seems the embodiment of Peirce's phenomenology.

What makes a poem modern

> Here we are dealing with a complex balance of "integrities —form (as in Charles Olson's sense) as a necessary balance and "extension of content" — a mirror in which the natural and the willed coalesce. The meaning of the poem exists as a key to its structure as much as the structure mirrors the key to its content. *(ED, 11)*

Gray depicts the poet as someone always emerging, coming across time, in the following passage:

What makes a poem modern

> ... what makes a poem specifically modern in the structural sense is

that the poet does not rely on an external hierarchy as the informing substance of his vision, nor does he seek to codify his personal experience as a "code" of values that transcends the text itself. There is neither mimesis nor solipsism — the text reflecting the external world as absolute nor the world as — internalized key to the structure of one's personal becoming. *(ED, 11)*

Mood and tone

The word *tone* is a much belabored one in literary criticism, but I wish to use it here in its precise sense as intrinsically complementary to "mood." Both terms are more conveniently suited to (and, the former directly derives from) music and the analysis of musical structures.

What we mean by tone in verbal instances is a condition in which the structural elements ("the text") mirror the potential range of emotional and intellectual meaning. Tone is the non-localized vehicle by which the poet escapes his incomplete self, affirming or denying those real or imaginary boundaries of his localized phenomenal being. It reflects, more clearly than any other device, his relation to his materials, enabling him to aspire to the transparency of the purely formal or to the *opaque* involutions of content as the unresolved conflict of his specific psycho/temporal being. *(ED, 11)*

It is at this point in the essay that Gray goes into that most lovely description of the creative act I have at the beginning of this chapter.

He ends this essay with a question that points to the limits of Structuralism, and suggests a direction or a quest for the rest of the book. A quest for a key.

The key is a basic concept in music it has to do with the range of the instrument and the performer. It also designates whether music is happy or sad, the tone or mood of the music is recognizable from the key.

Philosophy in a New Key

It is, to the extent that it is "experienced," a key to the reflective potency of mental and physical energies. The key is the isolated finite condition which opens being to the non-isolation of the Infinite the poem (containing both key and the textual mirror in which it lies reflected) reminds us of a kind of embryo: a potentially generative structure which completes its being not in isolation but in an intimate relationship with the equally generative and degenerative world it inhabits.

We need only focus on the variable mechanisms and their

> equally variable properties, however those properties may define a field both actual and disjunctive. According to Saussaure, the diachronic concept of language gave rise to a linguistics of the "individual act." This act, while not "outside of language" (or syntagym proper), redefined by its nature the verbal horizon such that any act retaining a semiological quanta could feasibly correspond to a non-semiological strata of objective events.
>
> Of course, strata of events present themselves in terms of synthesizable entities or nexes of confluent forces determining specific linguistic quanta. The *key* we have been speaking of is essentially semiological: namely, whether in a specifically determined unit of poetic expression we are dealing with a "line" or "image complex," the expressive potency of the *key* remains foremost. The text, however it portrays this key, is soluble into a series of simple propositions, even when the key itself holds generalized images of universal psychic import.

The Quest is started,

> If the key is a logical structure determined by the swerve of active verbs, the conditions are relatively straightforward grammatical explications— much that a linear causal relationship is allowed dominance over a transformational nominal approach. But if the key is nominal in essence, i.e. if the grammar both *delimits and constructs* an action which transgresses the disjunction of simple states, how are we to deal with it in any structural sense? *(ED 14)*

We note with pleasure Gray's multidimensional writing as he takes us in parallel travel across time and mapping across different schemas. He ends this essay with a question, that points to the limits of Structuralism, and suggests a direction or a quest for the rest of the book.

We have seen a large number of terms and concepts that will be explored further in the other essays of Gray's book. Tone, key, ingression, coercive integrities . . .

The Discovery of the Automorph

We will peruse *The Discovery of the Automorph (ED 23)* in conjunction with *Translations from Silence (ED 80)* because some of the experiences from *Silence* got employed in the *Discovery*. It is interesting to note that the word Automorph does not occur in *The Discovery of the Automorph*, though we have seen that term in earlier essays of the collection, in particular the essay just previous which is a reprint of Gray famous *What is Actualism*. A discussion of that essay occurs in an earlier chapter of this book, *The Punctual Actual Weekly*, p58. There we have learned that the Automorph is an anthropomorphization of the creative center at the heart of all being. Gray explains it with an analogy, "for an Automorph is to man what man is to his dreams, desires and loves." I take that to mean just as a person, in his life is touched by, is the vehicle for dreams desires and loves which are the occasions in which he comes to know himself, man himself is the vehicle for the Automorph, the creative organization at the heart of the unfolding of the universe in Big Time. The function of the individual man is to help the Automorph know itself.

In *The Discovery of the Automorph* Gray introduces Trace-Tone Poetics. This grows out of a couple of ideas, first stated in *Translations from Silence*, that artworks and the poem in particular have their own time. The essay opens with the discovery of a new science.

(ED 23, The Discovery of the Automorph)

The science of automorphology grew from an attempt to discover generative principles underlying discrete energy transmissions coded as particles of information. Being primarily a poet, I was interested most in the organization of factors determining the coherence of stimuli we call a *poem*. Foremost in my mind was the problem of time, for it seemed that almost without exception the existing theories treated the poem as either a timeless "created artifact" (either in the mind or "out there" on the page) or as a cumulative "response pattern" the reader experienced upon completion of reading a given work.

Both of these approaches seemed wrong to me, but as my notebooks filled with attempts at an alternative approach it became clear that I was not getting closer to a unitive design comprehension but merely mapping and schematizing forces of phonemic and morphemic congruence. In short, I found myself caught in a morass of what might be called "elementary particle poetics." The deductions I made from my study of actual poems, poems as diverse as I could find — narrative, lyric, meditative, ancient and modern[1] — were that (1) a poem was an information relay and delay mechanism, (2) relay and delay took place in a discrete sequence, and (3) the sequence existed both inside and outside of time.

[1] Incantatory expansion poems, objectivist poems, "Deep Image" poems, concrete and minimal works were all examined.

Here Gray states the desired goal of the Transcendental Poetics of Actualism.

The Goal of the Transcendental Poetics of Actualism

I was intent on discovering a theory that would transcend particular peculiarities of poetic utterance and bring to light a limited set of principles underlying poetic generation. *(ED 23)*

He mentions his studies in notebooks, referring the reader to the chapter *Translations from Silence*. In the following passage Gray states the quest in terms of the "microphoric," (in distinction from the metaphoric), he invokes the prologomena of poet Valery and he gives his criterion for what in poetry he finds necessary.

Completeness, Gray's criterion for poetry

(ED 80, Translations from Silence)

... In short, I wanted a microphoric, rather a metaphoric equivalent to the unconscious coercions that went into *actual* composition. In the back of my mind was a sensed truth, though unproven, of Valery's statement: Language is the chemistry for which we have yet to discover the elements.

I was on the outside, working in. For a poet, whose natural inclination is to assume the validity of the inside, and then try to expand therefrom, this is indeed a curious position to be in. Paradoxes were everywhere. Normally I would accept, while reading, a phrase or rhythm, merely for its capacity to carry me in the time/flow peculiar to the event being expressed by the poet. My valuation of the poem would depend on the cumulative data presented, whether or not I felt the movement as a reciprocity within myself, or whether it remained external, a "comment" on reality such as one might read in the newspaper, something "other," directed toward other ends than the essential completeness of being.

I took completeness as my criteria for whether or not the poem moved me, made me think or feel in ways I had not previously experienced. For what was valuable to me never left its own being or entered into another being except to remind me how difficult such a transition, in ordinary consciousness, might be. I saw poetry as an attempt to bridge the gaps we take for granted in ordinary conversation, though not at all in a prosaic way. I assumed, in short, the meaning of a structure whose meaning was yet to be established.

Don't step
so lightly. Break
your back, missed
the step. Don't go

away mad...

    The above lines are from Creeley. And the text (see pg. 87 of this book) goes on with wonderful commentary and love.

    We will only comment on the phrase describing the reader of the poem reading and parsing, "I assumed, in short, the meaning of a structure whose meaning yet to be established." This echo of Valery is a good description of a kind of Automaton behavior. The unconscious use of Transformational Grammar in the act of reading can be described in an alternative formalism, that of the Automaton. The idea of a system moving from state to state, and translating code into different levels. That code translating, generating entity, shown by von Neuman to be a Platonic Ideal in our modern world in his theory of finite automata is the archetypal Automaton. It strikes me, too that Gray is entering into a kind of Modal Logic here.

    Then in *Translations from Silence* Gray gives a sequence of structural diagrams suggesting various schemes of implication from trace tones. He summarizes his discovery. We see that the concept of Trace Tones contains the two concepts: 1) the Trace, the residue of something coming into being, or moving through — perhaps in a higher dimension, projected down into our own. (Gray will use the formalism of lower harmonics later, as did Steiner.) and 2) Tones, another central concept in Steiner. Tones enact the process mode of both anterior and posterior deflection. Now here Gray doesn't just mean the sound of phonemes, though he does. He also means tone in the sense of Steiner, the fundamental frequency at each level in a hierarchy. The real and theoretical buzz in higher and lower realms. In particular the hierarchy of being symbolized by the organizations of perceptions afforded to the body by the chakras and the material /

sensory systems they symbolize. Thirdly, Gray also means Tone in the sense of Peirce, a quality, a suggestion, a hunch, an intimation, a feeling that might be on its way to becoming a sign. Peirce gives the ontological sequence as Tone, Token and Term to trace the phenomenological emergence of Firstness into Secondness into Thirdness in the process of semiosis.

In *Translations from Silence,* the diagrams of the different kinds of spatial links among tones in an information structure (poem) gives way to an exposition of different kinds of links and connections of time flow in the poem.

Trace-tones as more prior than time in the poem

A tone is a discrete node of vibratory information
A poem is an integration in time of trace-tones. These tones enact the process modes of both anterior and posterior deflection. The degree and intensity of deflection is the measure of the poem's functional integration. Only through an analysis of trace-tone deflection can we establish the aesthetic basis rendered as a schema of the poems formal coherence. *(ED 23)*

In addition to being a classification criterion for types of poems, Trace Tones will speak to the degree of mapping involved in metaphoricity. It points to an even deeper discovery: Tone as a priori to time. This is really rather striking. Prior to time. That must be entropy and its symmetrical inverse — information. I had attended seminars from Prigogine at UT. He too was obsessed by the problem of time, and a fan of Borges and Proust. He had worked out the ideas of complexity, order, information, irreversibility of time in Statistical Mechanics. It proved that there were processes prior to time; moreover it proved that it is time's arrow that finally makes clear how probabilities become actualities and how "becoming" becomes "being."

Darrell Gray had indeed discovered something very fundamental: Tones enact the process mode of both anterior and posterior deflection. It made me think of Maxwell's Demon, a gedenkin (thought) experiment to illustrate the emergence of force out of symmetry's power to organize. It shows how information is the inverse of entropy, negative entropy. Maxwell's Demon sorts hot and cold molecules across a membrane until there is a pressure differential because of the hot active molecules becoming confined to one side of the membrane as opposed to the lugubrious cooler molecules on the other side. This a pressure differential, from a preferential differential, can do physical work —move the piston. We could say the demon is sorting some molecules anteriorly and some molecules posteriorly just as a poet might be sorting phonemes. (Check out some of Darrell Gray's notebook entries to see his experiments with this also.) So he had discovered Maxwell's Demon = Automorph. This duality of the Automorph is the perfect metaphor for this state of hovering between dimensions. Let us remark for now, that there is an organizational principal at the just now moment of the present, sorting possibilities across the membrane of the present, keeping some expanding into a future horizon, and moving others into the past. Perhaps it is personal identity. We should take this up later.

Gray's history of the discovery of the Automorph is leading into the idea of the poetic field. He makes the analogy through the idea of the 'geometry of the poem.' He begins considering the poetic field as Euclidean space of entities like "lines" and "points." As in lines of poetry and points being made in a persuasion. Which is not at all to say that Gray's idea of poetry was an exercise in creating the aesthetic apperception of philosophical concepts. I think Darrell Gray's basic concept of what a poem was, was more like a prayer or a mantra, a speaking to the imperium. He did believe in the Vedanta and poetry was some kind of pure statement to cut through the cloud of fear and loathing and angst and anger and etc. Poetry for him was a spiritual enterprise in that sense of mindfulness, calling forth consciousness —feeling the generosity. To put the listener in a natural, pure state of mind.

Returning to *The Discovery of the Automorph* we are in a position to understand the prologomena of Valery.

Field Theory as a fulfillment of Valery's agenda

(ED 26, The Discovery of the Automorph)

> A field-theory in which theoretical statements *can* be verified or disproved by empirical activity of the language proper was more in line with what I was after.
> The poem considered as meta-system might be the key, though in this instance might also require us to consider the dispersed actualities of discrete verbal particles outside the poetic field as actually existing according to latent systematic potencies codified as the structural and functional norm of all verbal activity.
> Hence, we are considering three factors constituting three spheres of activity: the meta-system of the poetic field; the field of

dispersed non-actualized verbal potentialities outside that meta-system; and, finally, a second meta-system constituting the unitive potential by which dispersed verbal particles cohere into structures of *meaning.* We may consider the latter meta-system as the "grammar" of the particular language at hand. Semiologists, such as Saussaure, Barthes, and Chomsky, of course, take it further, in an attempt to discover general verbal meta-principles applicable to all languages, and thus treat language as a system in itself, not of *words,* but of *signs* and the interaction and transformation of signs and *gestures.*

The question now becomes, "In what respect, if any, are the two meta-systems (the poetic, which I will label for convenience PM, and the purely verbal VM) related?"

Gray then goes on to talk about how they are related and how they are experienced. Let me give this little icon here for the embedded spheres. (~~ (~~ (~~))) central to Peirce and Vedanta.

We are into some very exciting ideas here, especially trying to describe what happens when the poet is inspired, when the occasion of the world and the practice come together to become generative.

Darrell Gray is driving toward a completely general theory of literature. He is going beyond Saussure's work that started the whole European, structuralist, language-centric branch of semiotics. I give a brief synopsis of Saussure in a Semigloss Interlude next. We end here with Grays gesture into silence

Occasion as a gesture into silence

(ED 27, The Discovery of the Automorph)

A way out of the merely schematic problem is to consider these two meta-systems as simultaneously existing and potentially interacting spheres. On occasion they may be mutually sovereign (as is the case in "pure" or "concrete" poetry) or they may interact, interpenetrating each other with symbolic, propositional, or gestural content. [4]

[4] This is, obviously, a very basic 'statement, and would characterize at least partially the origin of elements and integrities in all poems that utilize to some extent the traditional linguistic devices, such as parallelism, antithesis, extended syntactical units and denotative priority.

Semigloss Interlude: Semiotic of Literary Tropes

I felt it necessary to get some good definitions of terms that Darrell Gray is using in his essays. In particular Schema, Predicate. He is driving toward a theory of literature in which he derives some of the basic literary devices from basic a priori philosophical considerations. In particular quantal or phonemic aggregates.

Saussere in the 1940s used a basic semiotic communication model of signifier and signified to derive the rhetorical tropes of Metaphor, Metonymy, Synecdoche and Irony. The philosophical or set-theoretic concepts of Contiguity (being in the same set) and Transposition (from one set to another) underlie his presentation. Cognitively, Contiguity and Transposition are variant manifestations of other dual operations: the Analog and the Digital, the Right Brain and the Left, the deductive and the intuitive, the diachronic and the synchronic, the iconic and the indicial.

Toward an understanding of schema, let us look more closely in this derivation. Metaphor is an over assertive analogy. One could say for example in science that electromagnetic, and heat and gravity fields all behave like flowing water. The knowledge of one domain is applicable to another.

Metaphor: Metaphor is a mapping (a function in the mathematical sense of linking a domain into a range) expressed as X is Y; where X is the target domain and Y is the source domain. We might say Love is a Journey. We are using our understanding of a journey (the source domain) to explore the concept of Love (the target domain). Journey is getting mapped onto love. Literary studies use different terms for the target and source, they use tenor and vehicle. Thus Metaphor expresses the unfamiliar (known in literary jargon as the 'tenor') in terms of the familiar (the 'vehicle'). Here it would be the unfamiliar, Love (the tenor) in terms of a journey (the vehicle.) The tenor and the vehicle are normally unrelated: we must make an imaginative leap to recognize the resemblance to which a fresh metaphor alludes. In semiotic terms, a metaphor involves one signified acting as a signifier referring to a rather different signified. In the case of Love is a Journey, the signified is journey and here it is acting as a signifier of love. Metaphors initially seem unconventional because they apparently disregard 'literal' or denotative resemblance. Metaphor can thus be seen as involving a symbolic as well as an iconic quality. Metaphoric signifiers tend to foreground the signifier rather than the signified.

Metonymy: A metonymy is a figure of speech involving using one signified to stand for another signified which is directly related to it or closely associated with it in some way, notably the substitution of effect for cause. The crown for the king. Metonymic signifiers foreground their signifieds and background themselves. To compare it with metaphor, metaphor is one signified signifying another, metonymy is a part of a signified signifying the whole. Metonymy simulates an indexical mode. It is sometimes considered to include the functions ascribed by some to synecdoche.

Irony: is a rhetorical trope. It is a kind of double sign in which the 'literal sign' combines with another sign typically to signify the opposite meaning. However, understatement and overstatement can also be ironic.

In terms of the mapping function semioticians use the term Contiguity to speak about elements in the same domain, undergoing semiotic process as metonymy. Semioticians use the term Transposition, to speak of mapping one domain into another domain as in the process of metaphor.

Schema

The domains that metaphor maps from and to, are very complex sets. The domain is an ontological schema, that is a collection of causal, cultural, spatial, temporal, physical, conceptual, formal or structural relations that go with the behavior of the main aspect of a domain. In our example we expect to find in the realm of Love, analogies to the elements in the schema of Journeys: some of these are the map, the road traveled, the vehicle, the companions on the journey, the terrain passed through.

Darrell used the term schema in the above sense of ontological schema and in the sense that Kant used it. In Kant's philosophy, a schema is the referencing of a category to a sense impression through time.

The word schema comes from the Greek for axe and it gets its meaning from the idea of hewing out a form. Schema came to mean shape or more generally plan. A schematic. While a scheme refers to a loosely described plan, a schema usually refers to specific, well documented, and consistent plans. It has the connotation of action with some definite purpose, as in " to scheme," or " schemer," or "scheming," often with a hostile aspect. As in to plot and scheme.

The term schema has other meanings. In psychology or the theory of cognitive development, a schema is a mental set or representation. The mental representation of a concept can be a simulation, to match an existing schema (representing the concept according to a preexisting schema), or accommodation (modifying an existing schema to adapt to the environment).

Darrell used schema as in the sense of Kant's Philosophy of Wisdom, where "Schema" means, "the product of the exercise of the transcendental imagination in giving generality to sense and particularity to thought." A theory can be schematized in the sense of being diagrammed or fleshed out. The schema is an expansion on the analysis of knowledge which uses the transcendental imagination to mediate between sense and understanding.

Predicate

The predicate is the assertion in a statement or syllogism. It is either a direct use of the copula be or an implied use. The process of predication (set inclusion and exclusion) is the basis of organization. A text is an area for the interaction of sentences, the sentences themselves are signs, a complex collection of symbols. Predication and its elaboration in syntax is the linking element of sign interactions. If thought is a logical picture of signs, it is predication that draws the lines of the signs.

Automorphism

The next essay *Automorphism (ED, 32)* coordinates a good synopsis of the whole philosophical method. Gray calls it Automorphic Methodology which he warns is not a procedure for making art.

> The multiplicity of intentions which go into the production of a work of art cannot be analyzed into terms either more or less complex than themselves, however much we wish to reactivate a sense of the past generative matrix, or a more fluid disposition toward potential generative emissions in the future. This proposition is central to automorphic methodology, and applies to both propositional and non-propositional structures. *(ED 32)*

Gray is leading into the propositional structure beneath the sentential logic of language, which is the basis of syntax, so that he may perform a field extension on it and explore the irreal of non-propositional states. We also see that actualism is a program somewhat like surrealism to cleanse the doors of perception

What is observed
> ... we observe both a diffusion of particular actuality, and a coordinated *mirroring* of finite occasions as self-validating integrity structures which induce us to reevaluate the categories of perception themselves. *(ED 32)*

Automorphic Methodology sees the artist as a translucent agent, performing the automorphic function of transmuting being, and the artwork as a gem forged in the compression and forces and flows of deep passion. The actualist artist is a mediator between two dimensions undergoing alignments. The categories of perception reminds of metaphor crossing categories and of the surrealist program to derange the senses.

Actualism is a phenomenological enquiry.
> Any phenomenological inquiry into the mechanism of temporal and spatial disjunction (words as *things* disjoined from *words as words* or "things as things") must ultimately end as an analysis of specifically aesthetic dispositions, for it is through the action of such dispositions that the automorphic self becomes known: its

unique alignments with experiential states beyond it, as well as the aligning force which constitutes its *nature,* coordinating those states into meaningful emotive configurations. A recognition of the aligning force is essential to elementary particle poetics, and will be amplified further when we turn our attention to *trace-tone poetics,* where "structure" becomes a trace-tone in time and space. Here I will propose only that *alignment* relates only to verbal centers. The function of the term is to organize radically divergent vectors of the self in its various automatic propensities toward *belief* and the structural appropriations of that belief as integral expressive units. *(ED 32)*

In the Peircian phenomenology, the word-as-thing is in the center — is Secondness, is the actual — between the world of emergent being (things as things) and the world of representation in the mind (words as words). Emergent being, being, codified:
(things as things (words as things (Words as words)))
And going the other way art dissolving the barriers.
(Words as words (words as things (things as things)))
(∼ (∼ (∼))) < - - > (((∼) ∼) ∼)

The beginning of philosophical doubt

I knew intuitively that the mind itself was not the center of actuality, nor were, a *priori,* the "objects of perception." *(ED 33)*

The modern sense of where we are

We are no longer the center, but the vehicles of forces from within that recognize no centers as if the concept of Center were a synthesis of both material and psychic states. *(ED 34)*

Idealism's legacy from Kant, Locke, Berkeley...

Both Place and Form are assumed by the mind as modalities of a singular perception, and out of these modalities accrue a further fusion. Within the disjunctive assemblage the Automorph projects itself forward, as if unimpeded by the psychomorphic residue of the past, creating as by-products the perceptual data on which further integrations depend. Just as "sleep" originally constituted the horizon surrounding pre-logical disjunctive assemblage, so now "waking consciousness" surrounds the willful choices and semiconscious psychic coercions which define the poetic work as unique within a community of derivative human creations. The concrete actualities emerge initially as strange, premature facets of memory, so long retained within the unmanifested phase of particle or trace-tone awareness that it is only with a shock that they emerge, startled by their uniqueness, into the configurations we recognize as the world around us.

Of course the actualities themselves suffered no inattention: the medium of sleep, as well as the pre-sleep state, (the generative psychophysical reservoir out of which they emerged), sustained them within the attentiveness of their nature, long before they were thrust up from sheer potentiality into the conscious mind.

The kind of attentiveness there was more direct: since it did not know (partaking of their own indeterminacy) what resource or focus of being would be displayed as its own emergent aspect, it surrounds and embraces all possibilities, activating them equally as spatio/temporal occurrences.

The location of entities within the preconscious realm is the primary occasion of community out of which the semiconscious alignment of their natures occurs. Verbal units provide a clue. We shall look at them later. *(ED 35)*

Later in the chapter *Reflections on Poetry (Language and Predication)* Gray will delve into using language itself as the metaphor for the codification of emergent being.

The Poem as Mandala

In the essay titled *The Poem as Mandala (ED, 41)*, Gray pursues several analogies, perhaps I should say schemas. Besides the one in the title, he explores the analogy between the Physicist and the Poet, where he develops the parallels between phonemes and particles. He uses that to introduce the idea of field.

Analogy between particles in physics and phonemes in poetics

> If we take the signifying function of particles of meaning in conjunction, we immediately refer to a generative matrix or sustaining semiological medium not radically different from the antiquated concept of the pervasive yet "unanalyzable" *ether* central to classical mechanics. *(ED 41)*

Foreshadowing the move to a field poetics

> Physicists began to abandon the etheric theory of Newtonian mechanics and began to talk instead of "energy nodes" capable of quantum leaps which radically altered the energy potential of the system. *(ED 41)*

Gray then pursues the analogy between the received world view of a *classical* physicist and the classical or even Freudian criticism of the poem. He then points out the problem of not having a field poetic:

The Problem that not having a field theory presents.

> When we turn away from the "ordinary experiences" science relegates to itself, to such apparently different considerations as "What is a poem?", "How does it function?", and "In what spatial/temporal medium are we to follow the impulses it enacts in the present?", we initially find ourselves bringing with us a great collection of tools - just as pre-Einsteinian physicists brought with them conceptions of time and space as *absolutes.* Some of the tools we bring with us are Freudian fixations: we examine the text as an hermetic unit replete with subconscious mechanisms of referential *meaning,* much as a Freudian analyst considers his patient to be a self-enclosed system of processes (libido, id, ego, and super-ego) where the dynamism originates from within the system and external forces are, to the extent that they are not internalized, largely ignored. The psyche becomes a kind of container or *box* in which feelings and desires either approach or recede from harmonious integration. *(ED 42)*

In the following passage, Gray speaks to the developing situation in poetry (circa 1975) of the Language school. This is an interesting explanation of the predicament of a highly syntactical poetry that becomes enamored with its own armature.

Explanation of the thrust of the Language poetry

> Another analytic fallacy can be seen as Jungian, though here the hermeticity of regarding the poem as primal enactment of basic disturbances is minimized. The forces are more general and out of the generalization of tensions generalized images arise. The insistence on causative grounding conditions a poetic space where the individual elements cease to radiate toward a core where realization may be validated, as in the Freudian ethos, but rise instead toward the surface of the *text*. The text itself becomes a realization of "particles of meaning in conjunction." *(ED 43)*

Darrell Gray then goes on to develop the analogy between the Poem and the Mandala

Analogy between the aesthetics of mandala and poetics

> Beyond the Freudian and Jungian analyses of verbal integrations — analyses often equally appropriate to poetic as well as prosaic constructions — exists a methodology which locates the poem spatially (both on the page and in time) as a *mandala.*
>
> In a mandala the elements of simplification and elaboration enter consciousness on an equal level. First, there is established a uniform outline — a great tracery of activity one could delimit as the verbal activity of the poem. The "symbolism" doesn't ensue until we penetrate the inner, more convoluted layers, as if language were somehow looking at itself, a bit bemused at what it finds there. There we discover a concatenation of similar structures — sometimes complete or incompleted arcs around single words that continue the concatenation onward. *(ED 43)*

Gray invokes an analogy between the painted surface of the mandala and the surface of memory as he references a model of cognitive behavior.

The memory surface and the mandala

> A close study of Tantric mandalas reveals a harmonious confusion reconciled to a basic symmetry: the mind is at first stimulated by the complexity — the memory-surface (of de Bono in *The Mechanism of Mind)* — becomes agitated by a looping and re-looping of repressed or pre-conscious processes. The "looping phenomena" disturbs the memory surface until there arises into the consciousness a secondary *passive* surface. In the passive-surface phase of mandala meditation

the multiplicity of positions are integrated into the Whole. Linear relations which hitherto represented diversions in a two-dimensional space now suddenly radiate and form an omni-spatial matrix. The speed of the loops approaches a stillness, and in this phenomenon we see the function of the mandala most clearly: the denuding of *time,* and hence the velocity of relative points of their presentational immediacy. The poem considered as mandala acts similarly: it agitates, then pacifies, allowing through the integrated configuration of its elements the mind to return to and grasp the indeterminate and ineffable. *(ED 43)*

He uses a phrase the "coercion of integrities' and we see the context, from physics of "energy nodes" and the field theory. He is talking about the poem accessing the field — the field of signs, the field of metaphor, as the structure naturally focuses the categories of mind and the analogical explanations we give ourselves of the world. He then pulls it all together.

Signs, images, rhythms falling into the "right" place

A unified theory of signs depends on a unified theory of self, and it is most acutely therein that we find the poem as mandala: visual rhythms become transliterations of verbal ones. Although the source of the image may remain unknown to us, a necessary configuration develops from it, as if seeking the limits whereby it may express a verbal pregnancy: a gift from utter silence to the animated world wherein it has yet to be born. The birth of the image is thus twofold: first, it searches out its own confines, and second, having found them, adapts itself to those confines in such a way that even "nature" may not transgress them. A bird does not build its nest more adeptly, or a ray of light enter a prism without being directed more cogently to its end. *(ED 44)*

Look at this wonderfully abstract description of how the poem comes together. There is something quite joyous and funny about this.

The occasion of the poem

The selective occasion out of which the poem forms the mandala is thus one of "inverse pregnancy," in which informational delay and informational transmission are intrinsic. The binary nature of the system regulates the necessity of synapses by which the informational content is dispersed in formal patterns, or brought sharply into focus as nodes: image or sound configurations - transistors of "impeded concepts."

He then uses the concept of verbal pregnancy to delineate the difference between poetry and prose

The differences between prose and poetry

> For the poet, the language is non-different from the self — very similar to a chemist's saline solution into which the addition of a single molecule may produce "over-saturation" and precipitate a complex crystalline structure. Prose is concatenative in nature; poetry precipitative. *(ED 46)*

Note again the uses of previous themes in a much more specific context. The Valery dictum of language as chemistry, now being used on a chemical concoction.

He then uses the concept of verbal pregnance to talk about a poetic geometry

The poet visualizes the lines of force in his poem

> The poem as mandala resembles at first the integration of forces, and so far as the poet can visualize the lines of force in his poem he can likewise grasp the spatial and temporal distances between even the closest parts of speech. What may have originally seemed totally intuitive or mystically remote can be then seen as integrations and clarifications of a pattern — lexicography and semantics successively providing relevant structural formations. *(ED 46)*

How strongly and seriously we hold ideas changes. A metaphor is like a story, an aggregate of linkages and implicatives scattered over a beginning middle and end in time. The sophistication to realize that we conduct our lives through metaphors and stories is fairly recent. The troubles in Ireland are over wether the transubstantiation is metaphoric. The Catholics want to hold on to that part of the mind that holds metaphor to be real and gets into feelings and beliefs.

> Some of the analogies developed in this essay.
> Physics (source domain) — Poetry (target domain)
> particles — phonemes;
> field — tone fields (irony, understatement);
> velocity and position — nominal pregnance and verbal delay
> mass — the codification of signals into a formal display;
> coercivity — coercivity; impedance— impedance; node — node
> indeterminacy, inappropriate analytic tools, inaccuracy, ambiguity — inappropriate analytic tools inaccuracy or ambiguity, *spread* of meaning

Reflections on Poetry (Language and Predication)

In *Reflections on Poetry (Language and Predication)* Darrell Gray explores the interface at the edge of language. He explores the sentential logic of language, its organization of being into classes as a metaphor for the emergence of identity. We will also look ahead to his essay *Wittgenstein* because the two essays explore adjacent areas. Some key words here are "dispersion of actuality, " "facts of form," "terms of fact," "illusion of movement," "the sphere of perceptual distance," "gesture" as signage beyond the silence at the edge of language, "metalinguistic," "super-linguistical state."

The central analogy that Gray intends to explore here is this: "Association is to predication what the dream state is to the image." It speaks to the imortance of dreaming to poetry.

Gray will be mapping out the sphere poetry in that area beyond the sentential logic of language (sentential logic = boolean logic of classes or predicate calculus) to ask what is propositionality. He will be looking at: "predication as a function of propositionality." This will lead us into his later essay on Wittgenstein.

By now for me, one so inexperienced in the exposition of philosophy, I was getting the feeling that Darrell Gray was reeling out this story of the Actual as a kind of mythos, like the poet Blake talking about energy and the imagination and the archetypes as the aspects of Ureason. Or like Carlos Castaneda learning to live in the naugual and the tonal. But here instead of an old Yaqi brujo named don Juan, the guides were Heidegaar and Kant and Valery. All philosophers have sought to unplug from the unmitigated materialism of their time.

We will be seeking a metric of this propositional space, and how it relates to the perceptual distance. A visual analog of this would be seeing the two dimensional Venn diagrams of class inclusion extended to "spheres" in higher dimensional space of emergent being.

The broadest possible definition of poetry

Poetry is the schema of the nature of all possible predication. To predicate a schema is to know the configuration on which such a schema is built

Here the ghost of Wittgenstein raises his voluminous head, and here we face the central issue.

In poetry we stand apart from the predication, we let, through the flexibility of the schema, the unknown becomes the known, and, likewise, the known the unknown.

> I am not speaking here solely of the narrative or the lyric mode: I am referring to the schema of potential verbal distances — the poem as what happens to the perception and, what that resulting perception does to the perceptual distance. *(ED, 47)*

The flexibility of the schema suggests metaphoricity. Perceptual distance might be a measure of the *stretch* one has to make to ratiocinate a metaphor. This would designate whether a given metaphor was trivial — too close to be enlightening; or too far-fetched — so as to not relate on any discernible stretch of the imagination. Surrealism worked in this later area.

Next Gray connects the spheres of the possible and the predicating function to explore propositionality.

The sphere of predication within the sphere of propositionality

> Predication (as a function of propositionality) resides within the sphere of "possible predication," just as image formation resides within the sphere of associative detail. But with predication we have the important difference: the object of predication stands as an object for the predicating function.
>
> Association is to predication what the dream state is to the *image*. Valery says that we must "dance" — that mind/body movement in time is what the aesthetic experience is chiefly about. But the test is that we cannot always dance: sometimes we can only walk. The extensibilities of predication are such that we locate ourselves within the language in terms of what we can actually *do*. *(ED, 47)*

Here Gray is locating the observer within language. Feeling the power predication gives us in extending ourselves into the world. In the analogy (association:predicaton::dreamstate:image) we consider a mapping from predication to image. Just as the dream state is the container and generator of images, the associational facility of mind is the generator of predications. Predication is the means by which we distinguish qualities, compare classes in analysis and amplify perceptions to actionable signs.

In reference to Valery mentioning dance many aesthetics, in particular the Sanskrit poetic, talked about the Figure in the Poem. One speaks of the "body" of the text, follows where it is "heading." Sanskrit poetics was about theatre and performance linking Poetry and Dance. Transformational Grammar with its actor, action and goals paradigm, with its designation of the heading and dependencies in phrases, reifies the figure in the text. In this spirit of the dance Gray invokes the gesture as the edge of language. The silent unrefined gesture bringing toward or pushing away, indeed the mitigating of energy in the fulfillment of need, that is the social basis of psychology. Gesture is in taking things to the edge of the moment; it is how we are compelled to come out of ourselves, to go out into the higher spaces. The hope is to make this gesture in language and have someone follow it with you. The modern aesthetic of abstract expressionism, Action painting, Sam Francis, were of course a big influence on poetry. The New York school with its looseness and spontaneity, the Black Mountain school, Olson and projective verse, spontaneous be-bop were powerful gestural art forms.

Continuing with his *Reflections* we find Gray in the next paragraph aggrandizing the flat two-space of predicate logic into spheres of the imperium.

Quote on Mind moving

> So association must be linked with predication in a sphere that does not necessarily include the aesthetic response?
> Let us look again at what we call "aesthetics." When the mind moves, it does not move "as opposed to" some other static state. It simply moves... The mind's movement is, in this case, an involvement with and formalization of processes by which it might know itself.
> As conscious beings we must subsist on the images that time provides us. By "time" I mean that we are within the predicative sphere — that any known fact of form means and means only what it *says:* time delineates the *facts of form.*
> Poetry as predication unifies association and the facts of form. A predicate may be factual and not include the formal, just as a disposition may be actual and not be wholly factual. One may look at the ocean and not see the shoreline, may see the waves without seeing the rocks they beat upon, or focus merely on the gulls because they are what seizes the attention.
> A fact of form focuses on the movement of the fact. Poetry incorporates the form of that fact, just as the beach is a focus of whatever may happen on it. Poetry is a terrain, one might say, on which the facts of form play out their non-temporal lives. The temporal aspect of the fact dissolves into the being of the beach much as the terrain itself dissolves into the formal nature of the focus. *(ED 48)*

He posits the poet at the vortex of his own making:

The Vortex at the edge

> The vista does not contain the terrain of its own becoming in language as it does in objective awareness. We stand, as it were, at the vortex where what we knew is dissolving and what we are able to formulate has barely begun to appear. *(ED, 49)*

In the next passage Gray describes signification in need of a field extension. (This is just what Peirce gave it. The Interpretant ads a whole new dimension to semiosis.) Gray invokes Wittgenstein who was acutely aware of the problem.

Toward a reevaluation of signification

> ...we face a complete reevaluation of signification which threatens to reappropriate predication to the super-conscious real of Absolute Essences where we have neither "self certainty" or "intuition" to guide us. Here as Wittgenstein has said the terms of fact remain a product of the "capability of the signifier and signified achieving a purely logical identity." *(ED, 49)*

Peirce would certainly agree. If we look at the situation from the perspective of the Automaton, that code translating entity, it is —at one level — all code. At that level, where there are the thresholds of the nervous system, the signifier and the signified become logical elements in the concatenating machinery of predication, just elements in a syllogism. They are true *within* the system of logic.

We have seen an association between the Automorph and Maxwell's Demon of information. Here another isomorphism, the Automaton suggests itself. How the continuity of reality gets sequenced in the illusion of time is an old story: Zeno with his Tortoise and Hare studied it. Leibniz invented his Monad, the quantum of perception at the smallest window of resolution spokke to it. Gray begins looking below the surface of association and predication, describing propositional space with another analogy.

Propositional space as pre-meta-linguistical

> The transcendence of verbal states is here not in question: what *is* in question is the predicative efficacy inherent in poetic utterance which enables structures to simulate universal trans-verbal norms. On the surface this may seem one and the same. A universal state may be postulated, with terms of signification such that predication depends on integrations on a lower, pre-metalinguistic 'level. All such digressions from designation must assume minimal and determined meanings, much as simple propositions must reside,

> according to their delineations, within the realm of truth or falsehood.
>
> Furthermore, if we accept verbal transcendence as a possible mode of explanation we are faced with a closed system of predications such that the image (whether pre-conditioned or not) equalizes itself, and becomes a result of the dream-state of the logic that gave it birth.
>
> Language generates its opposite, and this is the source of all true meta-linguistics. The metaphysics of poetry is a stasis at the heart of that transformation where language sees itself as an openness within the non-propositional nature of its being, and moves outward to embrace the image of its own destruction.
>
> In this field composed of tensions between the past and the future, between predication and image, the poem moves.

Next Gray goes on to consider how we are transported out of ourselves in the poem.

How the poem transports one out of himself

> How then does one explain the "illusion" that we do actually enter such a sphere. For instance, one says of a particular poem "I felt transported – carried out of myself to a new world of perception."

One says this of the drug experience too. We are always trying to enter that sphere of feeling ourselves in the big time, in the presence of the great gift that we have received.

After clarifying his use of "illusion" as something produced in the mind like a dream or a hallucination and not an "unreality" he goes on to say:

The poem in Valery's crucible

> Now a poem is an event in time produced by the mind. This is true both as its inception and in the actuality of the reader's or listener's response. The terms of the event are particles of predication suspended in the sphere of perceptual distance. (ED 51)

The perceptual distance then, when in a sign system, is something we encounter often. Take a long trip on a street car and a train. You have to be on the lookout for signs, a map /diagram of the system. The perceptual distance is like what you imagine the unknown station to be like in the distance —the goal of your travels. You are constructing the links out of signs that you expect to be there. To find our way in a continuum of possibility through a discrete sequence of signs interpreted.

Accident and Creation / The Internal Mirrors

In his essay *The Internal Mirrors,* Gray discusses how the actual modes and modifications of Coercive Integrities culminate in the aesthetic creation. This he does after discussing the basis for what he calls Automorphology, "autistic generative phenomenology" in earlier essays. Two terms that he will use for methodologies in this effort are " hovering" and "focus" which he introduced in a previous essay *Accident and Creation*. So we will explore both essays here. This while "keeping in mind the subliminal assemblage of data prior to the "alignment process" of the Coercive Integrities, a term he first uses in the context of Olson and Projective verse. In *Accident and Creation* he starts off with a perspective that seems to be that of Leibniz's Monad.

Hovering and focus in the unfolding of matter

(ED 74, Accident and Creation)

> When we turn our attention to the realm of matter we detect a rhythm which seems to preclude the act of perception in several curious ways: particularity allows a distinction without diffusion, while the homogenous totality of sensory experience seems to hover within an ongoing multiplicity of occasion and temporality. I use the word "hover" to suggest the quality of being which enacts an internal dialectic when both terms of the dialectic are perpetually unmanifested, vacillating as it were, within a matrix of trans-substantial forgetfulness and memory. To say that matter "remembers" or "forgets" itself in this way is not to anthropomorphize it as it may at first appear. This error, which has plagued speculative thinking from the earliest stages of man's development, must be recognized if we are to progress to higher levels of focus. If we fail to do this the material dwellings (be they body-centered or world-centered in nature) will refuse access to their essences in even more startling ways than we have hitherto experienced, and we will once again find ourselves isolated within a hostile universe of conceptual polarities, as did the 18th and 19th century philosophers.
>
> It is the pure fact – the impingement of temporal resonance, inwardly animated – which illuminates through a series of finite disclosures, what we mean as a condition of a further, possible reality.

The essay then cleaves this matrix of matter into Accident and Creation. He introduces another methodology: "dissolution." The title of the last section of his book.

†*(Here 20 pages have been removed; complete essay in Sample area of Hitmotel web.)*

Dissolutions

The closing section of the book is *Dissolutions*. These are loose, aphoristic, penetrating, observations embodying the philosophy and inserted like a knife to go deeper into the world or like a lever to tilt it on its axis. The dissolution condition is a form of aesthetic.

The metaphor of Dissolution applies in three ways.

1) In the first instance, dissolution entails the "resolving or dissolving into parts or elements." The undoing or breaking down of a bond, tie, union, partnership. This sense describes what happens to a person who undertakes to overthrow the convention of consensus reality, that is Western naturalism, empiricism, idealism, reason. For this condition, dissolution is a form of dismantling and analyzing. Poetry is the method, experiment and practice of the discovery of this new science. This is the sense of it used in Donne's *The Dissolution*, as an alchemical augmentation and primordial fire. One of the main aspect of the modern avant garde is the dissolution of identity. Although this idea is not really all that avant garde; it is codified in most spiritual disciplines.

2) In the second instance, dissolution entails "dispersal into a medium." Gray extends the structuralist activity of dissolution which is to display the structure of a form spatialized in a matrix in which the diachronic elements, are suspended in the present, in the Actual.

3) The third sense of dissolution is the Philosophical Critique. This sense of dissolution is deconstruction, or the dismantling in the sense of reverse engineering of a philosophical system. Example: for Berkeley to deny the existence of primary qualities – the solidity and extension of things and of absolute space.

The philosophical work, the metaphysical poem (to some extend all serious writing and art) is a work of dissolution. It needs to be done, and redone in every generation to penetrate the world of mind.

Toward that end Darrell Gray accumulates in his book *Essays and Dissolutions* insights from neuronal anatomists using information theory, psychologist developing a hydrokinetic model of creativity and mind, poets seeking a deeper sense of the primary forces molding the world, spiritual ontologies and morphologies of the Vedanta, this brings us by way of philosophical discourse, past the activity of the structuralist perspective into a modern perennial philosophy.

He synthesizes contemporary thinkers with ancient ones to be able to carry out the understanding and liberation from the fallacies of metaphor and empirical reductionist reasoning. Actualism brings us to the dissolution of the line between art and life. He uses it to develop his super-senses of a higher dimensional world that is an extension of his psychic syntax. He writes a philosophic exploration of hazard and the creative will. He invents terminology for the Atman or the energetic creative milieux at the heart of matter.

A Dissolution *(ED 153)*

> What is this force that is living me? For as surely as I live, I cannot say that "I" am the active agent. Mind, body, dream, emotions, parade before me, but "I" do not "live them." I observe them being lived by something other than I — an automorphic center.

Further Attributions

My devoted and heartfelt thanks to all the artists who influenced and collaborated with me. Attributions for influences not formally stated in the text:

Doug Wilson — Frontis Page: Hawkeye; p 77: Side view of tongue placement; p 341: Collage bottom, Design for mural on 2019 Blake St.; p 342: Photo bottom, Headless horseman

Ruth Zaporah — improvisation partner of Bob Ernst, whose thorough codification of the exercises of Action Theatre are a generous support of that art

Floyd Merrell and other Peirce scholars for making a huge difference in understanding

George Lakoff for the liberating exploration of the cognitive structuring aspects of metaphor

Poets: Whitman, Eliot, Lord Buckley, Baraka, Wordsworth

Epilog

The warehouse theatre at 2019 Blake St. continued on for some 23 years under the directorship of Bob Ernst. Several personnel changes occurred. Its last celebration was in 1998. Through its doors came some actors who went on to become famous celebrities.

John O'Keefe became an award winning playwright and a national treasure, writing and producing dozens of plays and movies among them Shimmer, Vid (about the theatre at 2019 Blake), more.

Woopie Goldberg was a Hawkeye in the 80s. She went on to world wide fame as a comedian and Oscar winning actor.

George Coates went on to start Coates Performance Works and produced many popular grand operatic theatre spectacles.

Jim Nisbet went on to write many powerful thrillers that became famous in the noire culture. He writes poetry and reads regularly.

Jonathan Albert composes choral sound plays and teaches.

Doug Wilson continues painting and fine carpentry.

Peter Loschan returned to his native Germany.

Darrell Gray left us in 1986 through a tragic accident.

http://www.hitmotel.com

Free Poetry at HiT MoteL Press

I learn to walk again
Slow baby steps after a
serious skateboard accident.
Sequel to How I spent my
Christmas Break

Happy Trails to the Infinite
Fourteen Sonnets
The influence of form in
everyday life.

Diamond Head
Return to the
place of the
Honeymoon on a
family vacation.
Learn surfing,
and the secretes
of the sea.
Do to things
what light does
to them.

Selected Poems This is a selection of some
80 poems going back to the 70s up to the
present. The poems are selected from all the
books of Michael Lyons, including some
rare chapbooks.
The poetry is usually the personal, obser-
vations of the self in the world with others.
There are some sonnets. The poem are
loose spontaneous usually humorous.

Chap books and collection available **FREE**
in .pdf at www.hitmotel.com

HiT MoteL Press
www.hitmotel.com

These books by Michael Lyons can be ordered from any book seller or on-line. They are deeply discounted on Amazon, and Barnes& Nobles. Check www.hitmotel.com for selections and recordings.

Boho Books
The "Little House on the Prairie" Trilogy:
Cultivating the Texas Twister Hybrid, a portrait of the artist as a weed gardener (1998) ISBN 0-9655842-0-8 $20.00
The Secret of the Cicadas' Song, a peyote trip in poetry and prose (1998) ISBN 0-9655842-1-6 $20.00
Knight of a 1000 eyes, about Tai Chi, movement, Laban, and the I Ching (2002) ISBN 0-9655842-2-4 $25.00
others:
The Punctual Actual Weekly, about the life and times of a small mimeograph literary rag centered around artists living in a Berkeley warehouse and the Amphictionic Theatre (2007) ISBN 0-9655842-8-3
The Church of the Coincidental Metaphor, youthful adventures in Mexican radio

Novels: The "My Years of Apprenticeship at Love" Sextet:
Sex is the Anti-gravity of Metamorphosis, tales of romance and despair hitchhiking in North America. ISBN 0-9655842-9-1
The Indigenous Tribesmen of Neverland Bohemian life in Austin slacker enclaves. ISBN 0-9655842-7-5 $20.00
Dolores Park, Texan joins a California Tantric Buddhist commune (2001) ISBN 0-9655842-3-2 480 pages. $25.00
Seeing throught the Spell of Transference A cab driver's journal of psychotherapy. ISBN 0-9655842-4-0
A Blue Moon in August, about marriage and children late in life. (2005) ISBN 0-9655842-5-9
Thoughts on Vacation, a father is raised by his child and is enlightened by mortality. (2005) ISBN 0-9655842-6-7

Check into HiT MoteL Press at www.hitmotel.com for cover art, interactive Table of Contents, e-book sample chapters, recordings and other mindware.

http://www.hitmotel.com **HiT MoteL Press**

The "Little House on the Prairie" trilogy

The "My Years of Apprenticeship at Love" sextet

In progress

The Punctual Actual Weekly

Centered around a warehouse theatre in 1976 Berkeley and an ephemeral literary magazine called *The Punctual Actual Weekly* the story combines cultural history, biography and literary analysis in a thought-provoking memoir about the artist's struggle. It depicts the expansion of the poet's mind under the shaping influences of modern poetics in the pursuit of transcendence. In reprinting some of the pages of the magazine the entire spectrum of writing endeavors, including poetry, news writing, play writing, narrative, solo theatre, chanting based on an innovative sound language is evidenced. As well as a poets notebook in graphic novel format, and the catalog of an artist's show. This story of a Castaneda-like apprenticeship to the many word-shamans of modern literature, shows a mind fraught with personal challenges holding a precarious balance between acceptance and inundation and is often hilarious.

The book reads like the journey of the hero, encountering mentors, heralds, threshold guardians and shadow figures along the way. It returns a sense of self-realization by eruditely escorting us through a lost treasure, Darrell Gray's book *Essays and Dissolutions* a great treatise on poetry and Kantian treatment of Vedantic ontology and morphology. Lyons has done this parallelism with great works before: his book *Dolores Park* is a parallel to *The Tibetan Book of the Dead* ; his *Knight of a 1000 eyes,* a parallel and commentary to the *I Ching*.

The book achieves its mission of delineating what he calls the California Zen Aesthetic, or Flow. It captures that time of ebullience and positive joy in the 70s as seen through its theatre, poetry and art. For its insights into the history of modern poetry as well as its expansive exploration of the many sides of aesthetic movements, including structuralism, transformational grammar, imagism, semiotics, neuronal information theory, it will be a welcome addition to the library of poetry lovers and anyone interested in a more personal look at what goes into the development of expertise.

$30.00   Poetry/ Philosophy / Aesthetics / Literature

www.ingramcontent.com/pod-product-compliance
Lightning Source LLC
Chambersburg PA
CBHW050331230426
43663CB00010B/1823